The Yale Edition of the Works of St. Thomas More

SELECTED WORKS

Published by the St. Thomas More Project,
Yale University, under the auspices of
Gerard L. Carroll and Joseph B. Murray,
Trustees of the Michael P. Grace, II, Trust,
and with the support of the Editing Program
of the National Endowment
for the Humanities

Sig. B₅v of the Book of Hours More Annotated in the Tower
(Paris, Franciscus Regnault, 1530)

ST. THOMAS MORE

The Tower Works: Devotional Writings

edited by

GARRY E. HAUPT

New Haven and London, Yale University Press, 1980

*Set in Baskerville type.
Printed in the United States of America by
Vail-Ballou Press, Inc., Binghamton, N.Y.*

Library of Congress Cataloging in Publication Data

*More, Thomas, Sir, Saint, 1478–1535.
The Tower Works.*

*(The Yale edition of the works of St. Thomas More :
Selected works)
Bibliography: p.
Includes index.
CONTENTS: A treatise upon the Passion.—A treatise
to receive the blessed body.—The sadness of Christ.
[etc.]
1. Jesus Christ—Passion—Early works to 1800.
2. Lord's Supper—Catholic Church—Early works to 1800.
3. Meditations. 4. Prayers. I. Haupt, Garry E.
II. Title.
BT430.M66 1979 232.9'6 78-16995
ISBN 0-300-02265-4*

10   9   8   7   6   5   4   3   2   1

For George and Virginia

ACKNOWLEDGMENTS

The present volume is the fifth to appear in the modernized series of selected works of St. Thomas More, a series designed to make available to the general reader works which have already appeared or are about to appear in The Yale Edition of the Complete Works. Companion volumes published earlier are *Selected Letters,* ed. Elizabeth F. Rogers (1961), *Utopia,* ed. Edward Surtz (1964), *The History of King Richard III and Selections from the English and Latin Poems,* ed. Richard S. Sylvester (1976), *A Dialogue of Comfort,* ed. Frank Manley (1977). I wish to thank Mary Gay Daly for her excellent work in helping to prepare the modernized texts in this edition. Professor William Osborne, Chairman of the Department of English, Memphis State University, generously did all in his power to support and encourage my work, and the Office of Research Administration, Memphis State University, provided financial assistance. My friends Henry Hall Peyton III, Ramsey Fowler, and above all Naseeb Shaheen contributed significantly to this edition through their kindness during a critical period in its production. Professor Clarence Miller generously let me use his translation of the *De Tristitia Christi* as well as his notes in the Commentary to Volume 14 of The Yale Edition of the Complete Works (New Haven, 1976). Finally, my work has profited, as it so often has in the past, from the friendship and advice of the late Executive Editor of the St. Thomas More Project, R. S. Sylvester.

Memphis, Tennessee   Garry E. Haupt
1978

Garry Haupt's death on June 5, 1979, was a great loss to his friends at Yale and to the St. Thomas More Project. For the final stages of editing, this volume owes much to the skill and dedication of Stephen Foley, Richard Halpern, Joseph Loewenstein, Rosemarie McGerr, Ardelle Short, and James Warren.

Clarence H. Miller
Acting Executive Editor

CONTENTS

INTRODUCTION

The most profoundly moving literary achievements of Thomas More belong to a group of his writings called the Tower works, which include the *Dialogue of Comfort,* the letters written from the Tower, and the works in the present volume. Part of the appeal of the Tower works lies in the fact that they were written during a period of More's life that was characterized by unusual religious dedication and human courage. This is the period when he was incarcerated in the Tower of London and finally executed, or martyred, because he would not grant Henry VIII's supremacy over the English church (April 17, 1534–July 6, 1535). Despite convincing evidence that it was at least partially written before More's incarceration,[1] the *Treatise upon the Passion* is here considered part of the Tower works because it is thematically and spiritually linked to the others in this group, in which the Passion of Christ and More's attempt to imitate Christ are of major importance. The theme of the Passion in the *Treatise* strongly suggests that More's meditation on the Passion began in earnest before he entered the Tower, as well it might, for More resigned his chancellorship in May of 1532 and foresaw the dangers that lay ahead.[2]

The relevance of the Passion (including the agony in the gar-

1. *Treatise on the Passion,* etc., ed. Garry E. Haupt (New Haven, 1976), Vol. 13 in The Yale Edition of the Complete Works of St. Thomas More, pp. xxxvii–xli. The points made in the present Introduction are more fully developed in Vol. 13. of the Yale Edition.

2. See E. E. Reynolds, *The Field is Won* (London, 1968), pp. 257, 279–80; William Roper, *The Life of Sir Thomas More,* in *Two Early Tudor Lives,* ed. Richard S. Sylvester and Davis P. Harding (New Haven, 1962), pp. 227–28, 238 (cited hereafter as "Roper").

den) to More's own personal situation is apparent in one of his earliest letters from the Tower, written probably in May 1534 to his daughter, Margaret:

> A deadly grief unto me, and much more deadly than to hear of mine own death (for the fear thereof, I thank our Lord, the fear of hell, the hope of heaven and the passion of Christ daily more and more assuage) is that I perceive my good son your husband, and you my good daughter, and my good wife, and mine other good children and innocent friends, in great displeasure and danger of great harm thereby. . . . I can no further go, but put all in the hands of him, for fear of whose displeasure for the safeguard of my soul stirred by mine own conscience (without insectation or reproach laying to any other man's) I suffer and endure this trouble. Out of which I beseech him to bring me, when his will shall be, into his endless bliss of heaven, and in the meanwhile, give me grace and you both in all our agonies and troubles, devoutly to resort prostrate unto the remembrance of that bitter agony, which our Saviour suffered before his passion at the Mount.[3]

In a later letter, of May 2 or 3, 1535, More indicated to Margaret that the Passion was virtually at the center of his consciousness, recounting how he told the counsellors of the king that he would not meddle with the world, but "that my whole study should be upon the passion of Christ and mine own passage out of this world."[4]

There is profound religious feeling in the spectacle of the late More, in both his works and his private devotions, attempting to imitate Christ and meditate upon the agony in the garden and the crucifixion itself as he faced his own agony and eventual martyrdom. More's last prayer,[5] which, according to the 1557 edition of his English works, was written after his condemnation

3. E. F. Rogers, ed., *St. Thomas More: Selected Letters* (New Haven, 1961), p. 225. Cited hereafter as *SL.*
4. *SL,* p. 247   5. See below, pp. 305–09.

to death, almost summarizes his meditation on the Passion and can be used to survey briefly this great theme in the Tower works. In his last prayer More prays in his own fear and agony that he may have recourse to the fear and agony of Christ at the Mount of Olives, that he may have the grace to long for the holy sacraments, particularly the blessed body, that he may remember Christ's suffering with compassion at the eucharist, and that he may be made a member of Christ's mystical body, the Catholic Church. This prayer continues the themes of *A Dialogue of Comfort:* the agony in the garden and the crucifixion as sources of comfort in tribulation; the tensions between human frailty and spiritual courage revealed in the letters; the contemplation of the humanity of Christ's agony in the garden in *The Sadness of Christ;* the profound emphasis upon the real presence in the eucharist and upon the mystical body of Christ at the end of the *Treatise upon the Passion;* and the concern with the proper receiving of the eucharist in the *Blessed Body.*[6] More's stress in the *Treatise* and in the *Blessed Body* upon the real presence and Christ's mystical body is here fused with his devotion to the Passion—fused through a vision of Christ as both the great exemplar and as one who is really present in the eucharist and the church.

In addition to serving as a kind of coda for More's meditation upon the Passion in the Tower works, this last prayer also provides a clue to an important but sometimes neglected aspect of the Tower works. These works are significant in the way they allude to More's personal circumstances; and there is a legitimate spiritual grandeur in these expressions of a man approaching martyrdom. But in his last written prayer More transcends his own biography even after his condemnation to death. The last prayer, which reflects so many of More's preoccupations as

6. Louis L. Martz has convincingly demonstrated that the *Blessed Body* should be regarded as the concluding portion of the incomplete third lecture with which the *Treatise upon the Passion* breaks off. See Martz, "Thomas More: The Tower Works," *St. Thomas More: Action and Contemplation,* ed. R. S. Sylvester (New Haven, 1972), pp. 69–74.

he moved toward martyrdom, is liturgical in the sense that it is public and so constructed that anyone might meaningfully use it. It climaxes More's efforts to resolve the tension between the private and public elements in the Tower works in favor of the public and universal.

The theme of the Passion pervades *A Dialogue of Comfort*, echoing what must have been More's private meditations while he was in the Tower. Frank Manley has pointed out a number of personal references in this work.[7] But these personal elements are, as Martz suggests, transcended by the universal, for *A Dialogue of Comfort* touches upon all kinds of tribulation in contemplating "mankind's universal condition."[8] This universality also characterizes the *Treatise upon the Passion*, which, like *The Sadness of Christ*, is a work of biblical exegesis directed toward an outside audience. The *Treatise* begins with the fall of man and looks toward his redemption through the Passion of Christ. This historical panorama contributes to the work's universality.

However, part of the total impact of the *Treatise* and the other Tower works is due to the personal, biographical elements. The tension between private and public in the Tower works is resolved by a transcendence of the self through the universal. It is, therefore, important that the *Treatise* not only alludes to More's general preoccupation with the Passion toward the end of his life, but that some of its prayers convey faint biographical overtones. A number of the prayers offer aid in resisting temptation (important to a man who might be tempted to give in to Henry VIII), particularly through the power and example of Christ's Passion.[9] Another prayer is for spiritual comfort at the day of death, even in the presence of bodily pain[10] (More well knew that traitors were usually disembowelled alive). He also prays that he may set the "whole wretched world at nought," antici-

7. *A Dialogue of Comfort*, ed. L. L. Martz and F. Manley (New Haven., 1976), Vol. 12 in The Yale Edition of the Complete Works of St. Thomas More, pp. cxxxv–cxlvii. Cited hereafter as *CW 12*.

8. *CW 12*, lxvii.   9. See below, pp. 69, 79.

10. See below, p. 72.

pating a phrase in one of his "godly meditations" written in the Tower.[11] But perhaps the most explicitly autobiographical prayer in the *Treatise* is that which comes after More's exposition of the Jews' plotting of Christ's death, in which More prays he may never assent "to follow the sinful device of any wicked council."[12] Both the prayer and the incident seem to reverberate in harmony with More's own situation; but even so, there is in this prayer no direct line from the work to More's life—only from the life to the work. Although More did not write the *Treatise*—or at least not all of it—in the Tower, he doubtless wrote it, as I have already pointed out, at a time when he knew the worst might come. The significant reticence about himself in the prayers of the *Treatise* reflects his unending drive throughout the Tower works to transcend, while alluding to, his own personal peril.

In addition to the prayers there are many passages in the *Treatise* which appear to have special biographical relevance. For example, More writes that Christ withdrew to the city of Ephraim in order to teach His disciples to avoid persecution when they could, lest they fall through pride.[13] This theme is extensively developed in *The Sadness of Christ*, and it reflects More's musings on the spiritual dangers of deliberately seeking martyrdom. In the passage immediately preceding the above-mentioned prayer on a wicked council, More places a special emphasis on the irrelevance of rank and authority to a good council:

> so when men assemble them together to devise and counsel about mischief and wretchedness, the mo that are at it the worse is the council and the less to be regarded, be their personages in the sight of the world never so seemly and their authority never so great.[14]

We must remember that one of the temptations offered to More was the argument that many learned men had accepted the su-

---

11. See below, p. 86.   12. See below, p. 79.
13. See below, p. 75.   14. See below, p. 77.

premacy of Henry VIII over the English church; this argument provoked More at his trial to make an eloquent defense of his position by appealing to the authority of Catholic tradition: "And therefore am I not bound, my lord, to conform my conscience to the council of one realm against the general council of Christendom."[15] A related theme concerns the religious individualist who opposes the doctrine of the church by relying on his own private interpretation of scripture. Such men are soundly denounced in the *Treatise,* but the reference is as much to the whole Lutheran question as to the question of Henry VIII's supremacy over the church. As before, the personal element is muted and transcended by universal concerns.

The Sadness of Christ has erroneously been considered a continuation of the *Treatise* and part of an unfinished work on the Passion. Clarence Miller has argued convincingly that *The Sadness* is a nearly complete and self-contained work not on the crucifixion but on Christ's agony in the garden.[16]

The scale of the *Treatise* is much larger than that of *The Sadness,* which simply comments on consecutive texts from the gospel harmony of Jean Gerson. The *Treatise* follows a three-fold structure of gospel quotation, exposition, and prayer, complementing the meditative structure of reading, meditation, and prayer. This three-fold meditative structure, with an appeal to the affections in the concluding prayer, is responsible for a great deal of whatever depth of feeling is in the *Treatise.* There is much in the *Treatise,* however, that is somewhat arid in tone, encyclopedic, and unemotionally doctrinal. The encyclopedic tendency is particularly marked in the opening three points and the discussion of several "questions" in theology. A somewhat dry subtlety tends to pervade the abstract discussion of eucharistic doctrine at the conclusion, in which More indeed comes close to writing, for laymen, a theological treatise on the eucharist.

The Sadness has essentially the same public narrator or biblical

15. Roper, pp. 249–50.
16. *De Tristitia Christi,* ed. Clarence H. Miller (New Haven, 1976), Vol. 14 in The Yale Edition of the Complete Works of St. Thomas More, pp. 739–41. Cited hereafter as *CW 14.*

exegete as the *Treatise,* but *The Sadness* is more inward, more private in its effect. It has no three-fold structure but simply comments on biblical texts in sequence, avoiding the encyclopedic and doctrinal approaches. This simpler approach in *The Sadness* is accompanied by a greater emphasis on dramatic and psychological interpretation of the story as well as by a constant preoccupation with autobiographical themes. *The Sadness* is rooted in the concrete and the personal.

From an autobiographical perspective the main theme of *The Sadness* is martyrdom, a theme which is developed with an emotional depth and understanding exceeding anything in the *Treatise.* This is one reason why from a literary point of view *The Sadness* is the greater work. More returns almost compulsively, again and again, to the theme of martyrdom. Repetition is, of course, one of More's characteristic traits, but in this case it appears to be a dramatic projection of his own highly personal concern with the example offered to martyrs by Christ's mental anguish in the Garden of Gethsemane. One senses a psychological pressure to return to and dwell on the subject. The theme is first introduced[17] with the assumed questions of those who would marvel that Christ, being God, could suffer in the garden. The immediate answer, which is crucial to More's conception of Christ in *The Sadness,* is that in the garden Christ was acting in His human nature. Such is More's realism—his grasp of the actual—that he exclaims, it is stupid not to fear torment; we are not asked to do such violence to human nature. Although some martyrs went joyously to martyrdom, many of them feared as did Paul and Christ. Fear in itself is not to be condemned, and may be an additional source of merit if it is overcome. Christ's example may also warn us of the dangers of desiring a sudden ascent to martyrdom. Like T. S. Eliot's Becket, More is well aware of the dangers of spiritual pride in a martyrdom which is deliberately sought.[18] The personal note is perhaps also evident

17. See below, pp. 195–96.
18. Clarence Miller has suggested that even More's attempt to save his own life by hiding behind the law was part of an effort to avoid the spiritual pride of a deliberately sought martyr's death. See *CW 14, 775.*

in More's belief that anyone who is faced with the choice of sustaining punishment or denying God was undoubtedly led into that difficulty by God.

More returns to the theme[19] as he suggests that one of the reasons Christ wished to suffer such agony was to comfort the weaker members of His church, who might be driven to desperation by a fear of their own fear. The impression that More ultimately is talking about himself, his own human anguish, his own intimate and realistic perception that man's nature is always a part of him on this earth, is confirmed by one of the most moving speeches in *The Sadness,* that in which Christ urges the fainthearted to be comforted and not to fear, and in a moving irony asks that they be content with Him alone.[20]

More warns of the dangers inherent in seeking martyrdom, in trusting too much in oneself, as Peter did. In the subsequent discussion of the theme,[21] the only really new consideration is the argument that Christ's suffering was greater than that of any martyr, indeed that it was greater than any suffering that ever existed—not because of the physical torments of the crucifixion itself, but because of the mental anguish of Christ's anticipation of His torment, an anguish so great that He sweat blood. More's own greatest battle was not with physical suffering, but with fear and, perhaps, the fear that fear would cause him to yield through desperation. For this reason he returns once again in this section to the martyrs who apparently felt no fear and joyously offered themselves to death, arguing that those who felt fear before death deserve at least as much reward. He again cautions about the perils of approaching martyrdom too confidently. The second half of this section is a highly repetitious exploration of the whole problem, the very repetition suggesting More's personal involvement. The problem is raised again toward the conclusion of *The Sadness,* where on the basis of the flight of the apostles after the seizure of Christ More argues on

19. See below, p. 203.   20. See below, pp. 203–04.
21. See below, pp. 227–31.

the one hand against trusting too much in our own strength, and on the other against flying from danger if God requires us to stand.[22]

There can be no doubt that the balanced, realistic, and psychologically acute attitude revealed in these discussions of martyrdom reflects More's preoccupations as well as his actions. Chambers has written, "More's resistance was passive."[23] He did not foment rebellion, kept his own counsel, and was willing to consent to the succession of Anne Boleyn's child, although not to the supremacy of the king over the church—all of this accords with More's view that one should not seek the martyr's crown, but if it is imposed it must be accepted as the will of God.

The autobiographical feel of the theme of martyrdom in *The Sadness* is perhaps present in another major Tower work, *A Dialogue of Comfort,* particularly in the important chapters 17, 21, and 27 of Book III. Chapter 17 discusses the fear of bodily pain with particular attention to the fear that one may fall. But, as in *The Sadness,* Christ's agony in the garden is used as an example of how one may fear but nevertheless must submit his will to that of the Father. In chapter 21 Vincent generalizes that all men, for the most part through the fear of shameful and painful death, may lose the fervor of their faith and fall. In chapter 27, the last in the dialogue, the whole issue is summarized in one pungent sentence: "but to fear while the pain is coming, there is all our let [hindrance]."[24] In the same chapter the fear of fear is linked to the fear that one may commit the sin of pride if one seeks martyrdom.

The personal immediacy of More's preoccupation with fear and martyrdom in both *The Sadness* and *A Dialogue of Comfort* is amply illustrated in his letters, where he comments both on the boldness of offering oneself to death and on the fear that one may fall and deny the faith. That More's fears about falling were

22. See below, pp. 291–93.
23. R. W. Chambers, *Thomas More* (London, 1935), p. 294.
24. *A Dialogue of Comfort,* ed. Frank Manley (New Haven, 1977), p. 325.

not without justification is suggested by his letter to a priest, Master Leder: "And I trust both that they will use no violent forcible ways, and also that if they would, God would of his grace and the rather a great deal through good folks' prayers give me strength to stand."[25]

Another autobiographical aspect of *The Sadness* is that it focuses sharply on the mental anguish of Christ in the garden as opposed to the physical torment of the crucifixion. For More, the anticipation of agony is more agonizing than the final agony itself. Although the last chapter of *A Dialogue of Comfort* begins with a description of the physical torments of Christ during His crucifixion, a little later More turns to the consolation of the agony in the garden. The same pattern is present at the end of the passage from a letter by More quoted at the beginning of this Introduction, and the pattern reaches its climax in More's last prayer. If More had continued *The Sadness,* would his description, in the orthodox devotional manner, of Christ's physical suffering have been as rich, as psychologically moving, as his discussion of Christ's mental anguish? The conclusion of *A Dialogue of Comfort,* which does describe Christ's physical suffering, suggests that the answer is no. Because More's imagination is most fully alive when he discusses mental suffering, we may infer that he experienced it intensely himself and that he faced his own agony in the garden when he was writing.

The inwardness of feeling which in *The Sadness* derives from More's acute, personal exploration of the problems of martyrdom, arises also from a feeling for the dramatic and the psychological in More's presentation of biblical texts. Note, for example, More's dramatic timing as he portrays the sudden and bitter onrush of sorrow before Christ exclaims: "My soul is sad unto death."[26] More's awareness of the sharp sting concealed in a few words of Christ to Peter leads into a dramatic paraphrase of considerable effect because of its heavy repetition.[27] More's explana-

25. *SL,* p. 243.·   26. See below, p. 195.
27. See below, pp. 213–14.

tion of why the throng revealed to Christ whom they were looking for is also psychological and dramatic: they were so stunned
by meeting Him that they blabbed out the main purpose of their
undertaking to someone whose identity they did not know.[28]
Again in the psychological vein, More explains that when the
apostles heard the prophecies of Christ's seizure by the throng,
they took the matter sluggishly, but now that it was happening
before their very eyes they were torn by violent and conflicting
emotions: anxiety for Christ, fear for their own lives, and shame
for not keeping their promise to die for Him.[29] Another example of More's sense of the dramatic in *The Sadness* is Christ's
long speech to His persecutors, a speech in which He is speaking
as God, not as the man who suffered in the garden.[30] The
speech, exploiting the irony of the powerlessness of Christ's enemies who seemingly have power over Him, amounts to a rhetori-
cal triumph of Christ over His enemies, a magnificent statement
of divine power which provides dramatic and moral satisfaction
to the reader.

Many readers might like a more overtly personal More in the
Tower works, one who expresses an obviously personal *cri du
coeur*. Ours is an age of self-revelation and self-expression, with
literary interest stronger in the personal drama than in great im-
personal issues. But if the Tower works were more personal and
autobiographical, much of More's stature would be lost. Somewhat paradoxically More is all the greater as a saint and a man
because he restrained the personal elements in the Tower works.
Their ultimate drama lies in the transcendence of the personal
through a stress upon an audience outside the self and, above
all, upon universal Christian themes and experience.

28. See below, p. 263.   29. See below, pp. 269–70.
30. See below, pp. 282–86.

A NOTE ON THE TEXTS

The texts of *A Treatise upon the Passion* and the *Instructions and Prayers* are based on those given in Volume 13 of The Yale Edition of the Complete Works (New Haven, 1976). Spelling and punctuation have been modernized, adjustments in paragraphing have been made, and glosses have been provided for words which have changed meaning or become archaic since the early sixteenth century. When archaic words occur frequently in the text, glosses are given twice near the beginning of each treatise, but not thereafter. A Glossary of these words is provided for the convenience of the reader. Biblical and patristic references are interwoven with the glosses.

The text of *The Sadness of Christ* is the translation by Clarence Miller of More's Latin *De Tristitia Christi*. It originally appeared in Volume 14 of The Yale Edition of the Complete Works (New Haven, 1976). Some minor changes in paragraphing have been made in the translation, and biblical and classical references have been provided in the notes.

BIBLIOGRAPHY

The following list of books is designed to serve as a guide for further reading and to supplement the information supplied in the Introduction and footnotes.

I. TEXTS

The following volumes have already appeared in The Yale Edition of the Complete Works of St. Thomas More (New Haven and London, 1961–). Volumes 13 and 14 of the Yale Edition are the two major sources of information for the detailed study of the works in this volume.

Vol. 2, *The History of King Richard III*, ed. R. S. Sylvester, 1963; third printing, 1975.

Vol. 3, Part I, *Translations of Lucian*, ed. C. R. Thompson, 1974; second printing, 1979.

Vol. 4, *Utopia*, ed. E. Surtz and J. H. Hexter, 1965; fourth printing, 1979.

Vol. 5, *Responsio ad Lutherum*, ed. J. M. Headley, 1969.

Vol. 8, *The Confutation of Tyndale's Answer*, ed. L. A. Schuster, R. C. Marius, J. P. Lusardi, and R. J. Schoeck, 1973.

Vol. 9, *The Apology*, ed. J. B. Trapp, 1979.

Vol. 12, *A Dialogue of Comfort against Tribulation*, ed. L. L. Martz and F. Manley, 1976.

Vol. 13, *Treatise on the Passion*, etc., ed. G. E. Haupt, 1976.

Vol. 14, *De Tristitia Christi*, ed. C. H. Miller, 1976.

A companion volume to the Edition is:

Thomas More's Prayer Book, ed. L. L. Martz and R. S. Sylvester, 1969; second printing, 1976.

In the Selected Works of St. Thomas More series, the following modern-spelling texts are available in both clothbound and paperbound editions:

E. F. Rogers, ed., *St. Thomas More: Selected Letters*, 1961.

E. Surtz, ed., *Utopia*, 1964.

R. S. Sylvester, ed., *The History of King Richard III and Selections from the English and Latin Poems*, 1976.

F. Manley, ed., *A Dialogue of Comfort against Tribulation*, 1977.

The standard edition of More's correspondence is E. F. Rogers, ed., *The Correspondence of Sir Thomas More* (Princeton, 1947). An expanded and revised edition of this volume will be published as Volume 15 of the Yale Edition, ed. Schulte Herbrüggen.

II. BIOGRAPHIES

A. Sixteenth and Seventeenth Centuries

William Roper, *The Lyfe of Sir Thomas Moore, knighte* (1557), ed. E. V. Hitchcock, London, 1935, Early English Text Society. Roper's *Life*, together with Cavendish's *Life of Wolsey*, is conveniently available in paperback in *Two Early Tudor Lives*, ed. R. S. Sylvester and D. P. Harding, New Haven, 1962.

Nicholas Harpsfield, *The Life and Death of Sir Thomas Moore, knight* (1557), ed. E. V. Hitchcock and R. W. Chambers, London, 1932. Early English Text Society.

Thomas Stapleton, as Part III of his *Tres Thomae, the Life and Illustrious Martyrdom of Sir Thomas More* (1588), trans. P. E. Hallett, 1928, rev. ed. by E. E. Reynolds, London, 1966.

Ro. Ba., *The Lyfe of Syr Thomas More* (1599), ed. E. V. Hitchcock, P. E. Hallett, and A. W. Reed, London, 1950, Early English Text Society. (The author is not identified.)

Cresacre More, *The Life and Death of Sir Thomas More* (1626–31). The last of the family biographies, written by More's great-grandson. A modern edition is being prepared by Michael Anderegg.

B. Modern Biographies

T. E. Bridgett, *Life and Writings of Blessed Thomas More,* London, 1891, 3d. ed. 1904.

R. W. Chambers, *Thomas More,* London, 1935.

E. E. Reynolds, *The Field is Won,* London, 1968.

G. Marc'hadour, *Thomas More ou la sage folie,* Paris, 1971

R. S. Sylvester, ed., *St. Thomas More: Action and Contemplation* (essays by R. J. Schoeck, G. Elton, L. L. Martz, and G. Marc'hadour), New Haven, 1972.

III. STUDIES AND COMPLEMENTARY MATERIALS

The most important studies of the works in the present volume are in Volumes 13 and 14 of The Yale Edition of the Complete Works of St. Thomas More (see above, I), and the best complementary material is in the late correspondence of More and those portions of his biographies (see above, II) devoted to his incarceration in the Tower and martyrdom. A few other items are:

Curran, Michael, "St. Thomas More's *Treatise upon the Passion,*" unpublished doctoral dissertation, University College, Dublin, 1956.

Hallett, P. E., ed., *St. Thomas More's History of the Passion,* tr. Mary Basset, London, 1941.

Marc'hadour, G., *Thomas More et la Bible,* Paris, 1969, esp. pp. 327–60.

Martz, L. L., "Thomas More: The Tower Works," in *St. Thomas More: Action and Contemplation,* ed. R. S. Sylvester, New Haven, 1972.

———. "Thomas More: the Sacramental Life," *Thought,* 72 (1977), 300–18.

Sylvester, R. S., and Marc'hadour, G., eds., *Essential Articles for the Study of Thomas More,* Hamden, Conn., 1977.

A TREATISE UPON
THE PASSION

A treatise upon the passion of Christ (unfinished) made in the year of our Lord 1534 by Sir Thomas More, Knight, while he was prisoner in the Tower of London, to which he made this title following:

A treatise historical, containing the bitter passion of *our Savior Christ, after the course and order of the four evangelists,* with an exposition upon their words, taken for the more part out of the sayings of sundry good old holy doctors,[1] and beginning at the first assembly of the bishops, the priests, and the seniors[2] of the people about the contriving of Christ's death, written in the 26th chapter of Saint Matthew, the 14th of Saint Mark, and in the 22nd of St. Luke. And it endeth in the committing of His blessed body into His sepulchre, with the frustrate[3] provision of the Jews about the keeping thereof with soldiers appointed thereto, written in the 27th of Saint Matthew, the 15th of Saint Mark, the 23rd of Saint Luke, and the 19th of Saint John.

1. early church fathers.　　2. elders.　　3. ineffectual.

First an introduction unto the story.

Non habemus hic civitatem manentem, sed futuram inquirimus.[4] "We have not here a dwelling city, but we seek the city that is to come."

If it be (good Christian reader) true, as out of doubt it is even very true, that (as Saint Paul in the afore–rehearsed words saith) we have not here any city to dwell in, but we be seeking for the city that we shall dwell in hereafter, then seemeth me[5] that many men are very far overseen,[6] such men I mean as I am (alack) myself, that so much time and study beset[7] about their night's lodging here in passing by the way, and so little remember to labor and provide[8] that they may have some house commodious for their ease, and well favoredly trimmed[9] to their pleasure, in that place whither once go we shall, and when we come once there, dwell there we shall and inhabit there forever.

Sir Thomas More wrote no more of this introduction.

The first point: the fall of angels.

The glorious blessed Trinity, the Father, the Son and the Holy Ghost, three distinct and divers equal and like mighty persons, and all three nevertheless one undivisible and undistinct infinite almighty God, being from before all time eternally stablished in the infinite perfection of their incomprehensible and undecayable glory, did when it pleased themself, not of any necessity nor for increase of any commodity[1] that their full and perfit and not increasable bliss could receive thereby, but only of their mere liberal goodness, create of nothing the noble high beautiful nature of angels to make some creatures partners of the creator's goodness. And albeit that in that excellent company of

4. Heb. 13 : 14.   5. *seemeth me:* I think.
6. imprudently mistaken.   7. bestow.   8. get ready.
9. *well favoredly trimmed:* handsomely adorned.   1. benefit.

angels all were not of like perfection, but ordinately[2] divided into divers orders and degrees, the higher in excellence of nature far surmounting the lower, yet did the lowest far pass[3] and excell the natural state that mankind afterward had in his[4] creation.

But yet had not the angels forthwith in their creation given unto them the perfit bliss, heaven, nor were forthwith endued with the very[5] fruition and plain beholding of the glorious Trinity, but were left in the hand of their own free will and liberty, either with help of God's grace, by turning to God with laud[6] and thank for that they had already of His gift to be received by grace unto that glory, or else, willingly declining from grace and turning themself from God, as graceless caitiffs[7] frowardly[8] to fall into wretchedness. For if they had once already had the very sight of God at that time, in such wise as the glorious company of angels and saved souls blessedly have it now, the heavenly beholding thereof must needs have been so delectable and so joyful unto them, and so should have pierced and fulfilled them thoroughly with sweetness, that it should not have left any place in them for any contrarious appetite or affection[9] to enter. But now, standing[10] thus in the liberty of themself, with those excellent beauteous gifts of their nature, and being by grace moved to turn unto God and love Him and give Him condign[11] thanks for the same, great multitude followed that instinct of grace, and so did, and were of God therefore exalted into the clear sight of the Godhead and by grace confirmed and established in the full surety of joyful perfit bliss and everlasting glory.

Lucifer on the tother[1] side, an angel of excellent brightness, wilfully letting slip the grace and aid of God, wherewith he was stirred to look upward unto his maker, began in such wise[2] to look downward upon himself and so far forth[3] to delight and

---

2. in ordered sequence. 3. surpass. 4. its. 5. actual.
6. praise. 7. villains. 8. perversely. 9. inclination.
10. remaining. 11. deserved. 1. other.
2. *in such wise:* in such a way. 3. *so far forth:* to such an extent.

dote in the regarding and beholding of his own beauty, that albeit he well wist[4] he had a maker infinitely far above him, yet thought he himself meet to be His match. And as wise as he was of nature, yet pride made him so frantic[5] that he boasted that he would be God's fellow[6] in deed, saying unto himself: *In caelum conscendam super astra dei. Exaltabo solium meum et sedebo in monte testamenti in lateribus aquilonis. Ascendam super altitudinem nubium: similis ero altissimo.*[7] (I will ascend into the heaven above the stars of God. I will exalt my seat and will sit in the hill of the testament[8] in the sides of the north. I will ascend above the height of the clouds and I will be like unto the highest.) But as he used this blasphemous presumption in his mind against the great majesty of God, he was suddenly cast out and thrown down with an infinite number of the like traitorous angels, as the prophet Isay toucheth[9] him in these words: *Quomodo cecidisti de caelo Lucifer, qui mane oriebaris? Corruisti in terram.*[10] (How art thou fallen out of the heaven, Lucifer, that sprangest in the morning? Thou art fallen into the earth.) And afterward he saith: *Veruntamen ad infernum detraheris in profundum laci.*[1] (Howbeit thou shalt be drawn down into hell into the depth of the lake.) These words with other[2] the prophet Isay rehearseth in the fourteenth chapter in resembling[3] the fall of Nabuchodonosor unto the ruin of Lucifer.

And as well of[4] his fall as the fall of his fellows may well be verified the words of Saint John in his Apocalypse, where he saith in the twelfth chapter: *Et factum est praelium magnum in caelo. Michael et angeli ejus praeliabantur cum dracone, et draco pugnabat et angeli ejus, et non valuerunt, neque locus inventus est eorum amplius in caelo. Et projectus est draco ille magnus, serpens antiquus qui vocatur diabolus, et Satanas qui seducit universum orbem. Et projectus est in terram, et angeli ejus cum eo missi sunt.*[5] (There was a

4. knew.   5. insane.   6. equal.   7. Isa. 14 : 13–14.
8. covenant.   9. treats of.   10. Isa. 14 : 12.
1. Isa. 14 : 15.   2. others.   3. comparing.   4. by.
5. Rev. 12 : 7–9.

great battle in heaven. Michael and his angels fought with the dragon. And the dragon and his angels fought and were not able, nor their place was no more found in heaven. And out was thrown that great dragon, the old serpent which is called the devil, and Satan which seduceth and deceiveth the whole world, and he is thrown down into the earth, and his angels be cast down with him.)

Thus the inflexible justice of almighty God cast out of heaven Lucifer and all his wicked proud spirits and deprived them from His grace forever, and thereby from all hope and comfort of recovery of any manner attaining to the celestial glory, but forever condemned to pain. Howbeit not to the uttermost part of their pain at the first, nor all to pain alike. But as their offenses were not all alike, but some part of them by reason of their more noble nature and greater gifts of God received, their unkindness so much the more, and their sin so much the more grievous, and in divers angels also divers degrees of malice, in some the more, in some the less, so did the righteousness of God temper and proportion their punishments, driving the great devil down into the deep dark den of hell, into the very bottom and center of the earth, and other hove[6] about into the air and over part of the earth and the sea, which with continual recourse and counsel had with their chief prince and ruler Lucifer, that reigneth as king over all the children of pride, do (and shall do till the day of doom) persecute, attempt,[7] deceive, trouble, vex and punish such as they can catch into their claws of the silly[8] sinful kind[9] of man. And then at the final judgment, they shall all (as they to their further discomfort be surely showed already) leese[10] all their authority and rule over man, and enter with evil men into the self-same infernal fire that was first and principally prepared for themself, and therein shall they, with the sinful souls that have left God and followed them, in torments intolerable burn in hell forever.

6. heaved others.   7. tempt.   8. weak.   9. race.
10. lose.

Let us here now, good readers, before we proceed further consider well this matter, and ponder well this fearful point, what horrible peril there is in the pestilent sin of pride, what abominable sin it is in the sight of God when any creature falleth into the delight and liking of itself, as the thing whereupon continued, inevitably faileth not to follow, first the neglecting, and after the contemning, and finally, with disobedience and rebellion, the very full[1] forsaking of God.

If God was so wroth with pride that He spared not to drive down into hell for pride the noble high excellent angels of heaven, what state[2] can there be so great in this wretched world that hath not high cause to tremble and quake every joint in his body as soon as he feeleth an high proud thought enter once into his heart, remembering the terrible commination[3] and threat of God in holy scripture: *Potentes potenter tormenta patientur.*[4] (The mighty men shall mightily suffer torments.) And then if it be so sore a thing and so far unsitting[5] in the sight of God to see the sin of pride in the person of a great estate, that hath yet many occasions of inclination thereunto, how much more abominable is that peevish[6] pride in a lewd, unthrifty javel,[7] that hath a purse as penniless as any poor peddler and hath yet an heart as high as many a mighty prince. And if it be odious in the sight of God that a woman beautiful indeed abuse the pride of her beauty to the vainglory of herself, how delectable is that dainty damsel to the devil, that standeth in her own light and taketh herself for fair, weening[8] herself well liked for her broad forehead while the young man that beholdeth her marketh more her crooked nose. And if it be a thing detestable for any creature to rise in pride upon the respect and regard of personage, beauty, strength, wit, or learning, or other such manner[9] thing as by nature and grace are properly their own, how much more foolish abusion[10] is there in that pride by which

---

1. complete.   2. person of rank.
3. threat of divine punishment.   4. Sap. 6 : 7.   5. unfitting.
6. foolish.   7. *lewd . . . javel:* low-class, prodigal rascal.
8. thinking.   9. kind of.   10. corruption.

we worldly folk look up on height[11] and solemnly set by[1] ourself, with deep disdain of other far better men, only for very
vain worldly trifles that properly be not our own? How proud be
men of gold and silver, no part of ourself, but of the earth, and
of nature no better than is the poor copper or tin, nor to man's
use so profitable as is the poor metal that maketh us the
ploughshare, and horseshoon,[2] and horse nails. How proud be
many men of these glistering stones, of which the very brightest,
though he[3] cost thee twenty pounds, shall never shine half so
bright nor show thee half so much light as shall a poor halfpenny candle. How proud is many a man over his neighbor because the wool of his gown is finer. And yet as fine as it is, a poor
sheep wore it on her back before it came upon his, and all the
while she wore it, were her wool never so fine, yet was she pardie[4]
but a sheep. And why should he be now better than she by that
wool, that, though it be his, is yet not so verily his as it was verily
hers?

But now how many men are there proud of that that is not
theirs at all? Is there no man proud of keeping another man's
gate? another man's horse? another man's hound or hawk?
What a bragging maketh a bearward[5] with his silver-buttoned
baldric[6] for pride of another man's bear. Howbeit what speak
we of other men's and our own? I can see nothing (the thing
well weighed) that any man may well call his own. But as men
may call him a fool that beareth himself proud because he jet-
teth[7] about in a borrowed gown, so may we be well called very[8]
fools all if we bear us proud of anything that we have here. For
nothing have we here of our own, not so much as our own bodies, but have borrowed it all of God, and yield it we must again,
and send our silly[9] soul out naked no man can tell how soon.
"What hast thou," saith Saint Paul, "that thou hast not received?
And if thou have received it, whereof gloriest thou, as though

---

11. *up on height:* on high.   1. *set by:* esteem.   2. horseshoes.
3. it.   4. indeed.   5. keeper of a bear.
6. belt worn over one shoulder.   7. struts.   8. true.
9. defenseless.

thou haddest not received it?"[10] All that ever we have, of God we have received: riches, royalty, lordship, beauty, strength, learning, wit, body, soul and all. And almost all these things hath He but lent us. For all these must we depart from every whit again, except our soul alone. And yet that must we give God again also, or else shall we keep it still[1] with such sorrow as we were better leese[2] it. And for the misuse thereof and of our bodies therewith, and of all the remnant of that borrowed ware whereof we be now so proud, we shall yield a full strait accompt[3] and come to an heavy reckoning, and many a thousand, body and soul together, burn in hell eternally, for the peevish[4] pride of that borrowed ware so gloriously boasted[5] before in the transitory time and short, soon passed life of this fond wretched world. For surely this sin of pride, as it is the first of all sins, begun among the angels in heaven, so is it the head and root of all other sins and of them all most pestilent.

But it is not my purpose to declare[6] here, by the manifold branches thereof, all the kinds of mischief that proceedeth upon it (for that would occupy more time than were meet for this present matter) but only will I counsel every man and woman to beware even of the very least spice[7] thereof, which seemeth to be the bare delight and liking of ourself for anything that either is in us or outwardly belonging to us. Let us every man lie well in await[8] of ourself, and let us mark well when the devil first casteth any proud vain thought into our mind, and let us forthwith make a cross on our breast and bless it out by and by[9] and cast it at his head again. For if we gladly take in one such guest of his, he shall not fail to bring in two of his[10] fellows soon after, and every one worse than other.[11] This point expresseth well the Spirit of God by the mouth of the prophet, where he noteth the

10. 1 Cor. 4 : 7.   1. always.   2. lose.
3. *strait accompt:* strict account.   4. foolish.
5. *gloriously boasted:* vaingloriously boasted of.   6. explain.
7. trace.   8. *lie . . . await:* remain very watchful.
9. *by and by:* immediately.   10. *i.e.,* the guest's.
11. Cf. Matt. 12 : 45.

perilous progress of proud folk, in the person of whom he saith
in this wise: *Dixerunt linguam nostram magnificabimus, labia nostra a
nobis sunt, quis noster dominus est?*[1] (They have said, "We will
magnify our tongues, our lips be our own, who is our Lord?")
First they begin, lo, but as it were with a vain delight and pride
of their eloquent speech, and say they will set it out goodly to the
show,[2] wherein yet seemeth little harm save a fond, foolish vanity if they went no farther. But the devil, that bringeth them to
that point first, intendeth not to suffer them rest and remain
there, but shortly he maketh them think and say farther: *Labia
nostra a nobis sunt* ("Our lips be our own, we have them of
ourself"). At what point are they now, lo? Do they not now the
thing that God hath lent them take for their own, and will not be
aknown[3] that it is His? And thus become they thieves unto God.
And yet, lo, the devil will not leave them thus neither, but carrieth them forth farther unto the very worst point of all. For
when they say once that their lips be their own and of themself,
then against the truth that they have their lips lent them of our
Lord, their proud hearts arise and they ask, *Quis noster dominus
est?* ("Who is our Lord?"), and so deny that they have any Lord at
all. And thus, lo, beginning but with a vain pride of their own
praise, they become secondly thieves unto God, and finally from
thieves they fall to be plain rebellious traitors, and refuse to take
God for their God, and fall into the detestable pride that Lucifer
fell to himself. Let us therefore (as I said, good Christian readers) beware of this horrible vice, and resist well the very first
motions thereof; and the first suggestions[4] of the devil, as the
young infants of Babylon, let us all to frush[5] and break in pieces
against the stone[6] that is our sure strong Savior Christ, with consideration of His great humility, by which He (being as verily
God as man) humbled Himself for our sake (to redeem us out of

---

1. Ps. 11 : 5 (*Authorized Version,* 12 : 4; cited hereafter as *AV*).
2. *goodly . . . show:* well for display.   3. *be aknown:* acknowledge.
4. temptations.   5. *all to frush:* smash completely to pieces.
6. Ps. 136 : 9 (*AV*, 137 : 9).

the proud devil's dominion) unto the vile death of the cross,
which is the matter of His bitter passion, whereof I have taken in
hand to treat, and have for the first point toward it told you the
sore[7] fall of the proud angels, whereby in part the occasion of
our damnation, and consequently for our redemption the occasion of Christ's passion grew.

A prayer.

O glorious blessed Trinity, whose justice hath damned unto
perpetual pain many proud rebellious angels, whom Thy
goodness had created to be partners of Thine eternal glory, for
Thy tender mercy plant in mine heart such meekness that I so
may by Thy grace follow the motion[8] of my good angel, and so
resist the proud suggestions[9] of those spiteful spirits that fell, as
I may through the merits of Thy bitter passion be partner of
Thy bliss with those holy spirits that stood and, now confirmed
by Thy grace, in glory shall stand forever.

The second point: the creation and fall of mankind.

The glorious majesty of almighty God, after the forerehearsed
ruin and fall of angels, not willing to suffer the malice of His
proud envious enemies make such a minishment[1] in His
glorious court of heaven, determined of His great goodness to
create a new kind of creature, wherewith He would make up
and fulfill[2] with glorious blessed people the number of all those
evil angels that were thorough their high malicious pride thrown
out of wealth[3] into wretchedness.

This new kind,[4] then, that He would for this purpose create,
the deep wisdom of God determined marvelously to mingle[5]
and temper.[6] For sith[7] it should be able (with help of His

---

7. grievous.   8. prompting.   9. temptations.
1. diminution.   2. fill to the full.   3. well-being.   4. race.
5. make of more than one element.   6. mix.   7. since.

grace) to attain unto such high heavenly glory, He would have it spiritual and immortal. And yet, to refrain[8] it from the proud heart that Lucifer had and his fellows in their spiritual and immortal substance, God determined that this new kind of creature should also be bodily gross and mortal. And thus, after this visible world made,[9] and air, earth, and sea furnished with fowl and fish, and beasts, grass, herbs, trees, and fruit, He made the body of man of the slime of the earth, and created of nothing the spiritual substance of the soul after the image and similitude of Himself, in that He endued it with the three great gifts, memory, understanding, and will, in a certain manner of resemblance of the glorious blessed Trinity, the Father, the Son, and the Holy Ghost.

This kind of man created God of a marvelous convenience[1] also with all other manner of creatures. For He made it have a being, as hath the dead stone, a life, as hath the insensible tree, a sensible feeling, as hath the unreasonable beast, a reasonable understanding, as hath the celestial angel.

Thus our forefather Adam being created of the earth, and our mother Eve formed and framed out of the rib of his side (as in the first and the second chapter of Genesis is declared), albeit that they were ordained unto the high pleasant palace of heaven, yet lest over-sudden enhancing so high might make such pride spring in their hearts as might be the cause of their driving[2] down again, the great goodness of God measured their state and wealth,[3] setting them not on high in heaven, but beneath in the pleasant garden or orchard of earthly paradise. And for the farther safeguard of their persons from pride, He gave them precepts and commandments, whereby they should remember and consider themself to be but servants. And therefore He both bode[4] them there to be occupied and work in the keeping of that pleasant garden, and also forbode them the eat-

8. restrain.   9. *i.e.*, had been made.
1. *of . . . convenience:* with a marvelous fitness.   2. being driven.
3. well-being.   4. instructed.

ing of the fruit of the tree of knowledge. And yet unto their farther knowledging[5] of subjection and repressing of all occasion
of pride, He set upon the breaking of His behest the threat of a
very sore pain, that is to wit, that whensoever they did eat of the
forboden tree they should die, that is to wit, that whereas they
had now their bodies such as though they might die by their own
default,[6] yet such as without their default should never die,
there should, after that His commandment were by them broken, enter into their bodies and into the bodies of all their posterity an inevitable necessity of dying. Thus had God of His high
goodness set them in the possession of a right wealthy[7] state,
and in the expectation of yet a far passing[8] better, of which they
could never fail without their own default. And to keep them
from falling into the fault, He was ready to assist them with His
grace, and against proud disobedience that might make them fly
from His grace He graciously fenced and hedged in their hearts
with fear.

Now stood our father Adam and our mother Eve lords of all
the whole earth, had[9] full dominion over all the beasts of the
same, out of[10] dread of death or any bodily hurt. And authority
they should have had over all their own offspring, with which
they were with the blessing of God commanded to increase and
multiply and replenish the world. Their palace was the most
pleasant place of paradise. Their apparel was the vesture of innocency, more glorious than cloth of gold. Their nakedness as
far from dishonesty and all cause of shame as their bodies were
far from all filthy tokens of sin. Their sensual parts com-
formable unto reason. Against their souls no rebellion in their
obedient bodies, which for a season[1] should have endured there
without age, weariness, or pain, without spot or wem[2] or any
decay of nature, preserved continually by the wholesome fruits
and help of God's hand, and all their children forever after the

5. acknowledgment.   6. fault, misdeed.   7. prosperous.
8. surpassing.   9. *i.e.,* and had.   10. *out of:* free from.
1. *for a season:* for some time.   2. stain.

same rate.³ And each at sundry times when God's pleasure were, should have had their bodies changed suddenly into a glorious form, and without death depart out of the earth, carried up with the soul into the bliss of heaven, there to reign in joy and bliss eternally with God, fulfilling⁴ the places from which the proud angels fell. This was, lo, the state in which our first father stood, a state full of heavenly hope of eternal joy to come, and a state for the meanwhile full of present wealth.

But, oh, woe worth⁵ wicked envy, the daughter of pestilent pride. For the proud hateful enemy of God and traitorous wretch, the devil, beholding this new creature of mankind set in so wealthy state, and either conjecturing by his natural understanding, or (to the increase of his grief for his proud, envious stomach⁶) having it revealed unto him that of this kind should be restored the ruin that was happed⁷ in heaven by the fall of himself and his fellows, conceived so great heart-burning again the kind of man therefore, that he rather would wish his own damnation doubled, so that⁸ he might destroy them, than suffer God honored in them, and them so to proceed and prosper that their gross mingled nature, so base in respect of his, should ascend up to that height of heaven that himself was fallen fro.

The devil then, devising with himself upon some mischievous mean⁹ by which he might bring mankind unto destruction, called to mind the mean by which he had before wretchedly destroyed himself. And as he saw his own damnation grown by the occasion of pride, so wist¹ he well that if he might by some wily suggestion bring pride into the kind of man and make the first fathers disobey God's commandment, then would God of His justice keep His promise in their punishment and take from the posterity the gift that He promised their forefather for them, if the condition were broken upon which He gave it.

Upon this, this old serpent, the devil, being as the scripture

3. *after . . . rate:* in the same manner.   4. filling.
5. *woe worth:* cursed be.   6. disposition.
7. *was happed:* occurred.   8. *so that:* provided that.
9. *mischievous mean:* wicked method.   1. knew.

saith, "wilier than all the beasts of the earth,"[2] would not begin
at the man, whom he perceived to be wiser and more hard to
beguile, but first began at the woman, as the kind in wisdom
more weak, more light[3] of belief, and more eath[4] to be beguiled,
whom if he might make on his side, then should he and she
together be twain against one. And the wily wretch perceived
well also the tender mind that the man had to his make,[5] and
thereby guessed (as it there happed[6] and elsewhere happeth oft)
that to bring man to woe the woman may do more than with all
his craft the devil can do himself. This wily serpent therefore,
the devil, devising to entice this woman to this deadly deed, took
his time[7] for his wretched wooing when her husband was not
with her. And then gan he[8] fall familiar[9] with her and inquisitive
of such things as pertained to her husband and her and nothing[1]
at all to himself. For there he asked her this question: "Wherefore did God," quoth he, "command you that ye should not eat
of every tree of paradise?" Or as it rather seemeth by the Greek
phrase usual in many places of scripture, he asked her thus:
"Why did God command you that you should eat of no tree in
paradise?" And that his question was such appeareth by the
manner of her answer.

Howbeit, if she had showed herself unwilling to fall familiar
with him and had said again,[2] "What is that for you," or had answered him and said, "My husband shall answer you," all his
wretched wooing had been at end and he confounded and gone.
But while she was content to be talkative with a stranger and wax
a proper[3] entertainer (which property some gentlewomen
ween[4] were a goodly praise), mark well what followed thereon.
She answered the serpent and said: "Of the fruit of the trees
that are in paradise we eat. But of the fruit of the tree that is in
the mids of paradise, God hath commanded us that we shall not
eat and that we should not touch it, lest we may hap to die."[5]

2. Gen. 3 : 1.   3. unsteady.   4. easy.   5. mate.
6. occurred.   7. *took his time:* chose the right time.
8. *gan he:* he began to.   9. *fall familiar:* become intimate.
1. in no way.   2. in reply.   3. perfect.   4. suppose.
5. Gen. 3 : 2–3.

Mark here, that in these words the contagious conversation of this wicked serpent, with his questioning and her ear-giving thereto, wrought not as it seemeth, not outwardly only with her eye and her ear, but inwardly also with some subtle suggestion in her heart. For by this answer of hers it appeareth that forthwith upon his questioning she began to stagger and half to doubt of the truth and steadfastness of God's word. For whereas God had precisely promised that if they did eat of the fruit of that tree they should die, she, by the inward leaning to the devil's instigation and not cleaving to the grace of God, by this her answer turned it into a doubt, saying: *Ne forte moriamur* ("Lest peradventure we die"). By reason of which doubting, and thereby but half dreading, she made half the way herself for the devil to walk farther with her. For thereupon he letted[6] not boldly to blaspheme God before her and say: "Nay ye shall not die. But God doth know that whatsoever day you shall eat of that tree, your eyen shall be opened and you shall be as gods, knowing both good and evil."[7] And upon these words, she seeing that it seemed a good tree to eat of, and fair to the eye, and delectable to behold, she by and by[8] plucked off the fruit thereof and ate it, and gave it to her husband, and he ate it too.

O wretched wicked serpent, how much of thy deadly poison hast thou put into the silly soul of this woeful woman at once? For here had he made her believe that of his own devilish conditions[9] God had had twain, that is to wit, falsehead[10] and envy. For he made her think that God had told them a lie, in that He said that whensoever they ate thereof they should die, and also that God were envious and could not for envy suffer it that they should have so high a thing as the knowledge of good and evil.

Then strake[1] he into her heart the poison of proud curious appetite and inordinate desire to know the thing which for her weal[2] God had forboden her to know. For God would of His goodness she should have known but good. But she by the devil's enticement would needs know evil too. And when her

---

6. forbore.   7. Gen. 3 : 4–6.   8. *by and by:* immediately.
9. attributes.   10. falsehood.   1. struck.   2. welfare.

curious mind had made her once set her fair hands unto the feeling of that foul pitch, she could never rub the filth from her fingers after. What should I speak of the other less[3] evils that he allured and allected[4] her with, as the pleasure of the eye in the beholding of that fruit, with lickerous[5] desire of the delicious taste?—sins not small in themself, but small in respect of the far passing greater, when he made her desire and long by reason of high knowledge to be like a goddess, and for that cause proudly to disobey God and eat of the forboden fruit. And she being thus infected and so sore envenomed with so many poison spots, infected her husband forthwith. For at her enticement, and not so much for credence giving to[6] the serpent's words as to content his wife (whose request he could not find in his heart to contrary), he kept her company in her lewdness[7] and letted[8] not to eat with her. But the wallow sweet[9] pleasure of that fruit soon turned to displeasure and pain. For scant[1] was the fruit passed down both their throats, when it so began to wamble[2] in their stomachs that they wished it out again and in his belly that counselled them to eat it. For anon[3] was there such a marvelous change spread thorough both their bodies, that whereas when they put it in their mouth they were such as it was a great pleasure each of them to behold other and be beholden of the other, as soon as they both had eaten it they felt such filthy sensual motions of concupiscence rise and rebel against reason in their flesh, that their hearts abhorred to be beholden and seen, either of any other or themself either, and for shame of their nakedness covered their flesh with fig leaves.

Now is there no doubt but that their wicked enemy the serpent (which, as appeareth by the Bible, abode still by them till the sentence given by God upon their all three punishment[4]) in his mischievous[5] manner highly rejoiced to see his devilish de-

3. lesser.   4. enticed.   5. greedy.
6. *for . . . to:* because he credited.   7. wickedness.
8. hesitated.   9. *wallow sweet:* cloyingly sweet.   1. scarcely.
2. roll about (in nausea).   3. at once.
4. *their . . . punishment:* the punishment of all three.   5. wicked.

vice brought unto such pass,[6] and had a great game[7] to behold them come forth so comely, apparelled so richly in their royal robes of fig leaves.

O what a confusion was this unto them, to see their feigned friend, their very deadly enemy the devil, first by their own folly so harmfully deceive them and then so spitefully sit and laugh them to scorn. But they had no long leisure left them to take heed to that ere that great confusion was overwhelmed with a greater. For suddenly, lo, they heard our Lord coming, and therewith for shame they fell in a fear and fled and hid themself from the face of God in the mids of a tree. And our Lord, as though He saw them not, called for Adam and said: "Adam, where art thou?" And he answered: "Lord, I heard Thy voice and was afeard[8] to come before Thee because I was naked, and therefore I hid me." "Who showed thee," quoth our Lord, "that thou were naked, but because thou hast eaten of the tree of which I commanded thee thou shouldest not?"[9]

Then took Adam a way far awry fro[1] forgiveness. For he confessed not his fault, but began to excuse himself and lay the fault from him to his wife and in a manner unto God too. "The woman," quoth he, "that Thou gavest me for my companion, she gave it me, and so I ate it." Then said our Lord God unto the woman: "Why didest thou so?" And she in like wise never knowledged[2] her fault nor asked forgiveness, but excused her by the serpent and said: "The serpent deceived me, and so I ate it."[3]

Then gave God the sentence of punishment upon all three, using like order in declaring of His doom[4] as they did in the doing of their sin. For first He began at the serpent, the first malicious contriver of all this mischief. And unto him He said: "Because thou hast done this, accursed be thou among all the living things and beasts of the earth. Upon thy breast shalt thou creep, and earth shalt thou eat all the days of thy life. Enmity

6. completion.   7. delight.   8. afraid.   9. Gen. 3 : 9–11.
1. *awry fro:* opposed to.   2. confessed.   3. Gen. 3 : 12–13.
4. judgment.

will I put between thee and the woman, and between thy seed
and hers, and she shall frush[5] thine head in pieces, and thou shalt
lie in await[6] to sting her heel."[7] Then gave He the woman her
judgment and said unto her: "I shall multiply thy miseries and
thy conceptions, and in sorrow shalt thou bring forth thy children, and thou shalt be under the power of the man, and he
shall be lord over thee." Then finally said He to Adam: "Because
thou hast given ear unto thy wife's words and hast eaten of the
tree of which I forbode thee to eat, accursed be the earth in thy
work. With labor shalt thou eat of the earth all the days of thy
life. It shall burgeon thorns and briars, and thou shalt eat the
herbs of the earth. In the sweat of thy face shalt thou eat thy
bread, till thou return again into the earth out of which thou
were taken. For dust art thou, and into dust shalt thou return."[8]
Then our Lord made them coats of skins, and clothed them
therein, and said: "Lo, Adam is like one of us now, knowing
both good and evil."[9] And God with that angry scorn, to keep
him from the tree of everlasting life, put them both forthwith
out of that pleasant paradise into the wretched earth.

Long were it here, and not of necessity pertaining to this
present point, that is to wit the fall of our forefather, to note and
declare such things as in the discourse of this matter men may
note and mark upon this part of the scripture. As for ensample,[10] that in these words of God with which He scorned
Adam, saying, *Ecce Adam factus est sicut unus ex nobis* ("Lo, Adam
is now made as one of us"), may be well marked that, like as by
all words of the whole text appeareth plain that there is but one
God, so is there in that God mo[1] persons than one. For else
could He not conveniently[2] say, "Lo, Adam is now as one of us,"
that is to wit, a god as we be, but He would have said, "Lo, Adam
is now as I am."

Those words also seem well to declare that though Adam were

5. crush.   6. ambush.   7. Gen. 3 : 14–15.
8. Gen. 3 : 16–19.   9. Gen. 3 : 22.   10. example.
1. more.   2. suitably.

not so fully deceived by the persuasion of the serpent as Eve was
(for which Saint Paul saith, "The man was not seduced but the
woman,"[3] whereupon Saint Austin[4] at good length declareth
certain difference between them[5]), yet was Adam by the mean[6]
of his wife somewhat seduced and brought into a foolish hope to
be thorough the eating of that fruit, by the knowledge of good
and evil, made like a god. For God, speaking to Eve no word of
that foolish proud affection, taunted and checked Adam therewith specially by name, saying: *Ecce Adam quasi unus ex nobis factus est, sciens bonum et malum.* (Lo, Adam is now made as one of us,
knowing both good and evil.) But this was not by the serpent's
persuasion, whom Adam would not have regarded but shortly
shake[7] him off. But the seducing of Adam was by that that[8] the
serpent's shrewd[9] words came to his ear out of his wife's mouth,
whom he would suffer to speak. And therefore our Lord, in
declaring his punishment unto him, laid for the cause: *Quia au-
disti vocem uxoris tuae, maledicta terra in opere tuo etc.*[1] (Because
thou hast given ear to the words of thy wife, accursed be the
earth in thy work, and so forth.) And because that the woman's
preaching and babbling to her husband did so much harm in the
beginning and would, if it were suffered to proceed, do alway
more and more, therefore Saint Paul commandeth that a woman
shall not take upon her to teach her husband, but that her husband should teach her and that she should learn of him *in
silentio* (that is, in silence), that is to wit, she should sit and hear
him and hold herself her tongue.[2] For Saint Paul well foresaw
that if the wife may be suffered to speak too, she will have so
many words herself that her husband shall have never one.

There may be marked also in the foresaid discourse the marvelous mischievous nature of envy. For the devil so well knew

---

3. 1 Tim. 2 : 14.   4. Augustine.
5. Cf. St. Augustine's *De civitate Dei*, XIV, 11, and *De Genesi ad litteram*
(*Patrologia Cursus Completus: Series Latina,* ed. J. P. Migne [Paris,
1844–1903], *34*, 453–54; cited hereafter as *PL*).
6. means.   7. shaken.   8. *by that that:* because.
9. malicious.   1. Gen. 3 : 17.   2. 1 Tim. 2 : 11–12.

the justice of God, and by his own destruction so sore[3] had as-
sayed it, that he doubted not but that his malicious deceit should
not pass unpunished. And yet was he rather content to take
harm himself than suffer another take good. And such a devilish
delight he took in beholding their harm and shame that he
voided[4] not at God's coming, but abode to see the sentence of
their damnation till he took his own with him too.

In this discourse is to be considered also that when God pun-
isheth the sinner by and by, He showeth him thereby more favor
than when He deferreth it longer. And oftentimes when He
delayeth it, He doth it not of favor but of indignation and anger.
For if He had here punished Eve as soon as herself had broken
His commandment, both had Adam been warned by it and their
offspring by her sin alone, as holy doctors[5] declare, had not lost
original justice nor fallen in damnation of death. But for as
much as, though she was created to be Adam's fellow, she was
yet of less perfection and more frail and more eath[6] to fall than
he, albeit he had as then no dominion given him over her, yet
his reason might show him that to give her good counsel he
should have kept her company, which if he had done, the serpent had not deceived her. Therefore sith[7] he did not, but by
wandering another way from her he suffered her to miscarry
and be infected, God suffered the contagion of the selfsame in-
fection to stretch unto himself too and thereof to grow his destruction.

And this may be a warning to every man in this world to do
the diligence[8] that he possibly can to keep every other man from
hurt. For as the holy scripture saith: *Et mandavit illis unicuique de
proximo suo.*[9] (God hath given every man cure[10] and charge of
his neighbor.) And harm creepeth from one to another by mo
means than men be ware[1] of. And he that care not though his
neighbor's house fall afire may hap[2] to leese his own. Howbeit,

3. grievously.   4. departed.   5. church fathers.   6 easy.
7. since.   8. *do the diligence:* do the utmost.
9. Ecclus. 17 : 12.   10. care.   1. aware.   2. chance.

as this lesson generally pertaineth to every man for the natural love and Christian charity that every Christian man is bounden to bear other, yet pertaineth it most specially to those that have over other men that special charge given unto them, that our Lord therefore by the mouth of Ezekiel terribly threatneth them in this wise: *Si dicente me ad impium, morte morieris, non annunciaveris ei, neque locutus fueris uti avertatur a via sua impia et vivat, ipse impius in impietate sua morietur, sanguinem autem ejus de manu tua requiram.*[3] (If when I say to the wicked man thou shalt die, thou do not show it him, nor do not speak unto him that he may turn from his wicked way and live, both shall that wicked man die in his wickedness and yet the blood of him shall I require of thine hands.) This is a fearful word, lo, to those that have the cure[4] over other folk and a necessity to take good heed to their flock, to guide them well, call upon them and give them warning of such ways as they may perish in. For else shall the sheep not perish and be punished only, but the scab[5] of the flock shall catch and consume shepherd and all for his negligence.

This is here another thing specially to be marked, that like as the kind of man was not corrupted with original sin nor lost the state of innocency by the fault of Eve alone, which was but the feebler and inferior part, till Adam that was the stronger and superior part made himself partner to the same sin also, so is there no man accounted afore[6] God for an offender in any deadly actual sin[7] by any manner[8] motion[9] or suggestion of the devil unto the sensual part, as long as the will after[1] the judgment of reason resisteth and refuseth to consent. But when reason giveth over to sensuality, whereby the man whole and entire falleth into the consent either to do a deadly sin or to delight in the devising and thinking upon any such sinful act for the pleasure that he

3. Ezek. 3 : 18.   4. care.   5. skin disease.   6. before.
7. *actual sin:* sin derived from one's acts, as opposed to inherited original sin.
8. kind of.   9. prompting.   1. in accordance with.

taketh in that thought, all were it[2] so that he thought therewith he would not do the deed, yet were the full consent to the pleasure of that only[3] thought, full and whole deadly sin. Howbeit a sudden surreptitious delight cast by the devil into the sensual part is no sin at all, but may be matter of merit, except the will, with reason giving over thereto, either consent to delight therein or else is so negligent in looking to sensuality that he letteth her over-long alone therein, and listeth[4] not to do his diligence[5] in driving that sinful suggestion from her. For surely such manner negligence is afore the face of God accounted for a consent and so for a deadly sin.

It is also specially to be marked that the stubborn manner of Adam and Eve, not praying God of forgiveness but excusing their sin, was in manner more displeasure to God than was their sin itself.

This is also notably to be marked, that as tenderly as Adam loved Eve, rather content to displease God than her, yet when he saw that sorrow should come thereon, he would fain[6] have laid it from himself unto her. And thus will it fare by these fleshly wretched lovers here: when they come in hell together, they shall curse each other full fast.[7] Howbeit, letting pass as impertinent to my matter many things that might be marked mo, let us not forget to mark this one point well, which is the sum of all the second point, that is to wit, let us consider deeply from what weal[8] into what wretchedness, by the folly of our forefathers, mankind is woefully fallen thorough the false wily suggestion of our mortal enemy the devil. On which thing when I bethink me, me thinketh[9] I may well say the words of Saint John in the Apocalypse, with which he bewaileth this wretched world by reason of that the devil fell out of heaven thereinto: *Vae terrae et mari, quia descendit diabolus ad vos, habens iram magnam, sciens quia modicum tempus habet.*[10] (Woe to the earth and to the sea, for the

---

2. *all . . . it:* even though it were.   3. mere.   4. chooses.
5. *do his diligence:* do his utmost.   6. gladly.
7. *full fast:* very vigorously.   8. well-being.
9. *me thinketh:* it seems to me.   10. Rev. 12 : 12.

devil is come down to you, having great anger, knowing that he hath but a little time.) This woe well found our forefathers when the devil, full of ire for his own fall and envy that they should succeed him, labored to bring them to the place of his final damnation, from which he saw well he had but a little time left, that is to wit the time of this present world, which is transitory and soon shall pass and is a time in all together[1] very short, from the first creation to the final change thereof at the day of doom, if all that time be compared with his everlasting fire that followeth. He found them innocents joyful and merry, much in the favor of God, and oft rejoicing[2] His visitation and company, the man and his wife each delighting in other, finding nothing to mislike in themself, lords of all the world, all beasts obedient unto them, their work without weariness, their meat[3] pleasant at hand, no necessity to die, nor any bodily hurt, high pleasure in hope of heaven, and all their children after them.

All this hath this false serpent bereft them by his deceitful train,[4] poisoning them with his own pride, that threw himself out of heaven. For as himself would have been[5] God's fellow, so made he them ween[6] they should. But while they went[7] to be gods by the knowledge of good and evil both, they lost, alas, the good that they had and gat[8] but evil alone. They lost their innocency and became sinful. God's favor they lost and fell in His displeasure; His visitation they rejoiced not but were afeard to come near Him, each of them ashamed to behold the other or themself either. All beasts were at war with them, and each of them with themself, their own bodies in rebellion and battle against their souls, thrust out of pleasant paradise into the wretched earth, their living gotten with sore sweat, their children born with pain. Then hunger, thirst, heat, cold, sickness sundry and sore. Sure sorry looking, for[9] the unsure time of death, and dread after all this of the fearful fire of hell, with like pain and wretchedness to all their offspring forever.

1. *in all together:* in its entirety.   2. feeling joy on account of.
3. food.   4. snare.   5. *would have been:* wished to be.
6. think.   7. thought.   8. got.   9. because of.

This is, lo, good readers, the wretched change that our forefathers made with falling into pride at the devil's false suggestion. In honor they were and would not see it. Honor they sought and thereby fell to shame. They would have waxed gods and were turned into beasts, as the scripture saith: *Homo cum in honore esset non intellexit, comparatus est iumentis insipientibus, et similis factus est illis* [10] (When man was in honor, he perceived it not, but he was compared unto the foolish beasts, and to them was he made like), and yet brought indeed into far worse condition. For many beasts live with less labor and less pain too than man, and none of them go to hell. In danger whereof all the kind of man stood by the occasion of their fall if the goodness of God had not by His grace holp [1] with His merciful hand. And unto heaven had no man gone had not our blessed Savior redeemed man and paid his ransom by His bitter painful passion, whereof the occasion was this wretched fall of man. And thus finish I the second point that I said I would show you before I come to the woeful history of Christ's bitter passion.

A prayer.

Almighty God, that of Thine infinite goodness didest create our first parents in the state of innocency, with present wealth [2] and hope of heaven to come, till thorough the devil's train [3] their folly fell by sin to wretchedness, for Thy tender pity of that passion that was paid for their and our redemption, assist me so with Thy gracious help, that unto the subtle suggestions of the serpent I never so incline the ears of mine heart, but that my reason may resist them and master my sensuality and refrain [4] me from them.

The third point: the determination of the Trinity for the restoration of mankind.

When the devil has thus guilefully betrapped [5] and thus falsely betrayed our first father and mother by their own oversight and

10. Ps. 48 : 13, 21 (*AV*, 49 : 12, 20).   1. helped.   2. prosperity.
3. deceit.   4. restrain.   5. entrapped.

folly, and thereby brought into miserable estate[6] and damnable themself with all their posterity, neither would the mighty majesty of God endure and suffer His malicious proud enemy the devil to rejoice the withdrawing of the kind of man from doing Him honor, nor the marvelous mercy of God abide and sustain to see the frail kind of man eternally destroyed by the deceit and circumvention[7] of the false wily devil. For though His justice was content forever to leese all thankful service (for thankless they serve Him still) of those malicious angels, that without other motion than their own malice wilfully turned from Him, and that His mercy no cause had to counterplead[8] His justice, in abridging the eternity of the proud spirits' pain, that of obdurate heart would never be sorry for their sin, yet in beholding the wretched decayed kind of man brought into sin not all of himself but by the subtle suggestion of his false envious enemy, and that would after wax meek and repent and pray for pardon, the sharp justice of God and His tender mercy entered into counsel together. And by the deep wisdom of God was the mean found that man should so be restored as they should both twain be satisfied, that is to wit, both man by justice for his sin somewhat punished and yet upon repentance by mean of mercy should his fault be paid for, and from all eternal bondage man redeemed and saved and, in spite of the devil, enhanced to more honor than ever he was entitled to before he took the fall.

To devise this way, lo, was a wonderful thing, far passing the capacity of all the angels in heaven. For sith the amends must needs be made and, in maintenance of the true justice of God, the ransom must needs be paid for the kind of man, that was by sin addicted[9] and adjudged to the devil, as his perpetual thrall never to come in heaven, whosoever should pay this ransom must and was most convenient[10] to be such as would and were able and ought[1] it. Now ought there this ransom no creature but man, and therefore sith by him that ought it of reason it should

6. condition.   7. outwitting by craft.   8. plead in opposition to.
9. delivered over formally by sentence of a judge.   10. suitable.
1. owed.

most conveniently be paid, man must he be that should of duty pay it. But now was there no one man able to pay the ransom for the whole kind of man. For sith all the whole kind had lost heaven and were all in one damnation, condemned all to bodily death already, any of them all, though he should willingly suffer death in recompense of the sin, it could nothing serve his fellows, nor yet himself neither, for he paid but his debt of death for his own part, in which debt and much more himself was condemned already.

Now as for angels, neither can we know that any would then do so much for man, man being fallen by sin fro[2] God's favor, nor any of them all was able, being but a creature, to satisfy for the deadly trespass done unto the creator. And yet was it over[3] this far fro good convenience[4] that any angel should have be suffered to do it. For the redemption of man after his fall was a greater benefit unto him than was his creation. For as our mother holy church singeth in the paschal service: *Quid enim nasci profuit, nisi redimi profuisset?*[5] (What availeth it man to be born were not the profit of his redemption?) And therefore if angel had, by payment man's ransom and recompense made for his trespass, redeemed him, then would man have thought himself more in a manner beholden to angel than to God. And the occasion[6] thereof had been a very foul disorder.

Thus was as I say, therefore, the device of a mean convenient for man's redemption the thing that far passed the wisdom of all the wise angels of heaven. But the deep and infinite high wisdom of almighty God devised the marvelous merciful just mean Himself, that is to wit, that by the cruel painful death of that innocent person that should be both God and man the recompense should be made unto God for man. For that person both, being God, should be of that nature that was able to do it and, being man, should be of that nature that was bounden[7] to do it.

2. from.   3. besides.   4. suitability.
5. From the Easter office, specifically the prefatory prayer used on Holy Saturday at the blessing of the paschal candle.
6. result.   7. obliged.

And the devil (unware[8] that he were) unrighteously procuring that righteous man's death should righteously leese the power upon man that God had for man's unrighteousness righteously given unto him before.

This excellent mean of man's redemption the deep wisdom of God devised; and in time convenient the second Person (the Son of God, the wisdom of the Father, and the Father's express absolute image and brightness of His Father's glory), being sent by His Father and Himself and the Holy Ghost down here into the earth (and nevertheless abiding still above in heaven), and in the blessed womb of the pure Virgin Mary taking into unity of person the poor nature of man (by the obumbration[9] of the Holy Ghost, of the pure blood of her body, without man's seed or fleshly delectation,[10] and therefore without original sin conceived and without help of midwife or pain of travail born), living here in pain and labor, fasting, watch,[11] preaching and prayer, and finally, for the truth of His doctrine, by the procurement[1] of the devil, the treason of Judas, the malice of the Jews, and cruel hands of the paynims,[2] thorough the painful bitter passion and death of His innocent manhead[3] (not bounden or subject unto death, neither by nature nor sin, but by death for man's sake willingly suffered), that excellent mean, I say, of man's redemption so by Himself devised, Himself most graciously fulfilled; and by the pleasant acceptable sacrifice of Himself obediently offered on the cross up to the Father, He pacified the wrath and indignation of God against man, and by His glorious resurrection and marvelous ascension, sitting in the nature of man upon the Father's right hand, hath reduced[4] mankind (in such as will take the benefit) to more joy, more wealth, and far more honor too than ever the fall of our first father lost us.

Now albeit (as I suppose) few men have less lust[5] to move

8. unaware.   9. overshadowing.   10. pleasure.   11. vigils.
1. contrivance.   2. pagans.   3. human nature.
4. restored.   5. desire.

great questions and put manner of[6] dispicions[7] in unlearned laymen's mouths than I, which rather would wish every man to labor for good affections[8] than to long for the knowledge of less necessary learning or delight in debating of sundry superfluous problems, yet of some such demands[9] as I now see many men of much less than mean learning have oft right hot in hand,[10] I shall not let[1] one or twain myself here a little to touch.[2]

A question.

First be they commonly willing to search this thing: wherefore mankind should, mo than[3] Adam and Eve themself, need any redemption at all. For how could it (say they) stand with the justice of God that for the fault of only Adam and Eve all that ever came of them should fall into such miserable fault? This question and many such other like, when they be of a curious bold presumption demanded, be not to be harkened unto and answered, but with the words of the blessed apostle Paul rather to be rejected and rebuked: *O homo tu quis es qui respondeas deo? Numquid dicit figmentum ei qui se finxit, quid me fecisti sic?* [4] (O man, what are thou to take upon thee to dispute with God? Is there any workman's work that asketh the workman, "Wherefore hast thou made me thus?") And must almighty God then of His work wrought in man give a reckoning to man that is but His handwork? Howbeit, on the tother[5] side, where such questions are not demanded of frowardness,[6] of a vain pride, nor of blasphemous purpose, it is not only no displeasure to God but is also a good occupation of the mind in that a man delighteth to think upon heavenly things rather than upon earthly. And many an holy man hath, of no vain curious mind but of very pure devotion, beset[7] much study upon the foresaid question. And of those holy men hath divers had divers opinions. One sort have

---

6. *manner of:* various kinds of.   7. disputations.
8. inclinations.   9. questions.
10. *have . . . hand;* are very eager about.   1. forbear.
2. treat of.   3. *mo than:* over and above.   4. Rom. 9 : 20.
5. other.   6. perversity.   7. bestowed.

thought that by the fall of Adam the whole kind of man not only lost original justice,[8] and became subject unto the necessity of temporal death, and therewith lost also the joyful bliss of heaven, but over[9] that by the filth of original sin (with which every man born into this world by natural propagation is infected in the vicious sinful stock, in that[10] we were all in, of Adam, as the fruit is in the tree, or the ear of corn in the grain that it came of) was also damned unto perpetual pain and sensible[1] torment in hell, although it were a child that died in the cradle, which to the original sin taken of his parents (of which the prophet saith: "Lo, in wickedness was I conceived, and my mother conceived me in sin"[2]) never added actual sin[3] of his own. And from this eternal damnation of sensible pain in the fire of hell, they thought that never any of the kind of man should be preserved but by the merits of the passion of Christ and faith in Him comen[4] or to come—faith, I say, actual or habitual,[5] and in infants by the faith of their parents and the faithful church (with certain sacraments or sacrifices duly referred to God, after[6] the sundry laws and ceremonies of sundry divers times, wherewith these infants have habitual faith infused).

And as touching the faith of Christ, that He should once come by whom they should be saved, revelation was given to Adam, Noah, Abraham, and all the old fathers and by them to the people of every generation before the law written;[7] and at[8] the law written, revelation given to Moyses, and by him to the people; and after to all the prophets, and by them to the people of Jews of every generation, unto the coming of our Savior Christ Himself. Now as for such folk, either now or then, as among the paynims[9] lived well according to nature, so that they lacked

8. righteousness.   9. besides.   10. *i.e.,* which.

1. perceptible by the senses.   2. Ps. 50 : 7 (*AV,* 51 : 5).

3. *actual sin:* sin derived from one's acts, as opposed to inherited original sin.

4. having come.

5. *actual or habitual:* exhibited in deeds or inherent in the character.

6. in accordance with.   7. *i.e.,* was written.

8. *i.e.,* at the time when.   9. pagans.

nothing to keep them from the perpetual fire of hell but the
faith of Christ, some holy doctors have thought that God of His
merciful goodness by one mean or other failed not to give them
the faith, as He that is of so merciful goodness that He will fail
no man in thing necessary without the man's own fault.

But then other doctors that were in this point of opinion with
them, that original sin damned every man to sensible pain of
hell without the faith of Christ, were not in that point agreed
with them, that unto all such paynims as in any place lived naturally well and kept themself from idolatry, God sent the faith of
Christ to keep them from hell, as not suffering any man to be
perpetually damned to the sensible pain of fire without his own
actual fault, sith they themself denied not but that the infants of
paynims and of the christened both that deceased without baptism were damned unto perpetual sensible pain in hell, and yet
had they none actual sin of their own but only the sin original.

Now whereas this thing might haply [10] seem hard in the hearts
of some such as direct their eye to the merciful nature of God
and cannot also perceive by any rule of justice taught unto man,
either by reason or scripture, how this thing could agree with
the merciful justice of God, these good men answer that hell is
the place for sinful folk and that pain is due to sin and that those
children and all be sinful in original sin. For all are sinful that
are thorough filthy concupiscence brought by propagation out of
that sinful stock of our first sinful father, for in that stock were
we all and were infect with sin in the same in such a certain manner as all the sour crabs [11] that ever come of the crab tree do take
their sourness of the kernel whereof the tree grew. And if a
poor potter may, without reproach and uncontrolled,[1] make (as
Saint Paul saith) of one self[2] piece of clay two vessels, the tone[3]
to serve in honest use, the tother in vile and filthy,[4] where the
clay whereof he maketh the vile vessel was nothing[5] faulty but
good, who should be so bold and so blasphemous as to think that

10. perchance.   11. crabapples.   1. unrestrained.
2. same.   3. one.   4. Rom. 9 : 21.   5. in no way.

God doth wrong to make and use all those vessels for vile (that is to wit, all the kind of man) whereof the clay that they all came of (that is to wit, their first father and mother) were ere they came of them waxen[6] by their sin both twain very vile and nought.[7]

Besides this (say these good holy doctors) the scripture declareth us that God thus doth in deed. For Saint Paul calleth all the offspring of Adam by nature the children of wrath, saying: *Eramus natura filii irae.*[8] ("We were," saith he, "by nature the children of wrath.") And that we became such by the corruption of our nature in our first father, Adam, he showeth well where he saith: *Per unum hominem peccatum in hunc mundum introivit, et per peccatum mors, et ita in omnes homines mors pertransiit, in quo omnes peccaverunt.*[9] (By one man sin entered into the world, and by sin death, and so passed death thorough into all men, thorough that one man in whom all men have sinned.)

And after he saith: *Sicut enim unius delicto mors regnavit per unum, multo magis abundantiam gratiae et donationis et justiciae accipientes in vita regnabunt per unum Jesum Christum. Igitur sicut per unius delictum in omnes homines in condemnationem, sic et per unius justiciam in omnes homines in justificationem vitae. Sicut enim per unius hominis inobedientiam peccatores constituti sunt multi, ita et per unius obedientiam justi constituentur multi. Lex autem subintravit, ut abundaret delictum. Ubi autem abundavit delictum, superabundavit et gratia. Ut sicut regnavit peccatum in mortem, ita et gratia regnet per justitiam in vitam eternam, per Jesum Christum Dominum nostrum.*[1] (Likewise as by the sin of one man death hath entered by one, much more men, receiving the abundance of grace and of the gift and of justice, shall reign in life by one Jesus Christ. Therefore likewise as by the sin of one man it went into all men unto condemnation, so by the justice of one man also it goeth into all men unto justification[2] of life. For likewise as by the disobedience of one man many be constitute[3] and made sinners, so shall also by the obedience of one many men be constitute and made righteous.

6. become.   7. wicked.   8. Eph. 2 : 3.   9. Rom. 5 : 12.
1. Rom. 5 : 17–21.   2. being made righteous.   3. established.

The law truly hath entered,[4] that sin should abound. But where sin hath abounded, there hath grace also more abounded, that likewise as sin hath reigned unto death, so grace should also reign by justice unto everlasting life thorough Jesus Christ our Lord.)

By these words of wrath, of sin, of condemnation, of death grown by the sin and disobedience of Adam into all his offspring, that is to wit, into all the kind of man by natural propagation engendered and begotten of him, and by the contrary words of justice, of obedience in Christ, and of justification and righteousness in man thorough grace growing into everlasting life, it well appeareth (say some doctors) that Saint Paul meant that the death grown to all mankind contracted by original sin from Adam should be the death of everlasting pain. From which Saint Paul well, by all the process[5] of the same words, declareth that no man can be saved but by our Savior Christ. Which thing Saint Peter showeth yet more expressly where he saith: *Non aliud nomen est sub caelo datum hominibus, in quo oporteat nos salvos fieri.*[6] (There is none other name under heaven given to men in which we must be saved.) And that no man shall be saved without faith Saint Paul declareth where he saith: *Sine fide impossibile est placere deo,*[7] that is to wit, either actual or habitual,[8] infounded[9] in the sacrament of baptism, or otherwise if God be so pleased, whose power is at liberty, not so bounden[10] to His holy sacraments but that He may beside them give His grace where He list. But with His sacraments He hath by His promise bound Himself to do, and without them He doth unto few men, and with contempt of them to no man. And for this cause say those holy doctors infants be received to baptism to keep them from the peril of eternal damnation and perpetual pain in the fire of hell. And of this

4. *i.e.,* the Mosaic law came into being.
5. *all the process:* the whole tenor.   6. Acts 4 : 12.   7. Heb. 11 : 6.
8. *actual or habitual:* exhibited in deeds or inherent in the character.
9. infused.   10. bound.

opinion was holy Saint Austin,[1] as in sundry plain places of his works well appeareth.[2]

Now sith it is so (say they) that by the scripture this point so plainly appeareth, what should we dispute the righteousness thereof, as though that man might attain to see the bottom of God's righteousness? How many things be there very well done and righteously by men which yet seem unto children to be no right at all. And infinitely farther asunder be the wisdom of God and the wisdom of the wisest man than is the wisdom of the wisest man above the wisdom of the most foolish child. The prophet in the person of God saith: *Non enim cogitationes meae cogitationes vestrae, neque viae meae viae vestrae, quia sicut exaltantur caeli a terra, sic exaltatae sunt viae meae a viis vestris, et cogitationes meae, a cogitationibus vestris.*[3] (My thoughts be not like your thoughts, nor my ways be not like your ways, for as high as heaven is above earth, so high are my ways above your ways, and my thoughts above your thoughts.) And therefore saith Saint Paul: *O altitudo divitiarum sapientiae et scientiae dei, quam incomprehensibilia sunt judicia ejus, et investigabiles viae ejus? quis enim cognovit sensum domini? aut quis consiliarius ejus fuit?*[4] (O the altitude or height of the riches of the wisdom and cunning[5] of God. How incomprehensible or unable to attain unto be His judgments? And how investigable[6] be His ways?—that is to wit, how unable to be sought and found out. Who hath known the mind of our Lord or who hath been of His counsel?) God hath no rule of justice to be ruled by but is Himself the rule by whose will all justice must be measured and shapen.[7] And therefore He can do none unjustice.[8] And when we be discharged once of this gross, corruptible body, that aggrieveth and beareth down the soul and oppresseth the mind that many things thinketh upon, then shall

1. Augustine.
2. See esp. Augustine's *De peccatorum meritis et remissione et de baptismo parvulorum (PL 44, 109–200).*
3. Isa. 55 : 8–9.   4. Rom. 11 : 33–34.   5. knowledge.
6. unsearchable.   7. formed.   8. injustice.

such folk as shall be saved behold and see in the glorious God-head the very clear solutions of such inexplicable problems.

With such things as this, and many mo that were too long to rehearse here, have those good fathers answered this matter, those I say that have thought that by the sin of Adam every man old and young, though he deceased with none other sin than original only, was in like wise and in like reason[9] damned to perpetual sensible[10] pain in the fire of hell, as by the bondage of the father all his offspring is in this world bounden unto perpetual thralldom. Howbeit, to tell you the whole truth, holy Saint Austin, which was (among other[11]) of this mind and opinion, for all the reasons with which he answered other men therein concerning the justice of God in the damnation of infants unto perpetual sensible pain for that only sin original that they contracted by the natural propagation of the first condemned father, with all those reasons, I say, with which he contented other men, he could never yet satisfy and content himself. For in a certain epistle which he writeth unto Saint Hierome[1] he debateth this matter at length, very substantially and with great erudition. And in that epistle he confesseth the defense and maintenance of that opinion for so hard that, as he there toucheth, some great cunning[2] men for the defense thereof have been driven to the devising of a very great perilous error. For they, to maintain the justice of God in that point, said that the souls which every man have put in their bodies by succession of time were all created at once before the seventh day in which God rested. And of those words, that God in the seventh day rested, they took a foundation for that error, forgetting the words of our Savior: *Pater meus usque modo operatur, et ego operor*[3] (My Father worketh still yet, and I work still also), but in the seventh day God rested from the creating of any new kind of creature. Then said they that the souls offended God before they came into the bodies

9. *in like reason:* for the same reason.
10. perceptible by the senses.
11. others.   1. St. Jerome, *Epistola* 166 (*PL 33*, 720–33).
2. learned.   3. John 5 : 17.

and that they were put into the bodies, some to be purged in them, and some to be damned with them, so that the infants that die with original sin have the bodies worthy damnation because they naturally proceed out of the damned stock with lack of original justice,[4] and the soul was worthy to come into that body, by the society whereof it should be bounden unto eternal pain. The soul they said was worthy for that other sin with which it had offended God before it came into the body. This fantasy[5] were some fain[6] to find,[7] for maintenance of God's justice, of those that held the foresaid way in the damnation of infants unto sensible pain in hell.

But this erroneous opinion, as reason is, Saint Austin rejected and confuteth. Howbeit, that yet notwithstanding, he confesseth himself to find such difficulty in the maintaining of God's justice to stand with his own opinion of condemning infants to sensible pain in hell, that himself seemeth to doubt whether God create alway[8] every soul of new,[9] or else that as well the soul as the body be produced and propagate[10] of the father and the mother as well as the body. For if they so were, he thought that then the answer were more easy if the whole person of the man were taken by natural propagation of the substance of our first father and mother, being subject unto that damnation. And therefore he desireth Saint Hierome to consider well that point and search whether it might stand with the scripture or not. And if it might, he thought it meet that Saint Hierome should take that way too. And if not, himself would not hold it neither. Howbeit, if that way would not be maintained, he then desired Saint Hierome to write unto him by what reason he thought that the justice of God might be maintained in the damning of infants unto sensible pain in hell. For he said that himself could not see how it could stand with justice that God should create a new soul that never offended and put it without any desert of itself into that body, by whose company it should contract forthwith such

4. righteousness.   5. capricious speculation.   6. glad.
7. contrive.   8. always.   9. *of new:* anew.   10. propagated.

an infelicity that, the body dying and the soul departing there-fro[11] unchristened before it come to discretion, it should be damned to perpetual torment. And then layeth he forth there certain reasons with which himself was wont to answer other men in that point for the time, for lack of better. But there he requireth Saint Hierome to devise him better. For he plainly con-fesseth that those answers which himself was wont to make other folk in the matter never satisfied nor contented himself. Would God there remained the answer of Saint Hierome again. But whether ever he made any or not, we none find.

And thus have I, good readers, showed you the mind of some good holy doctors which were of the opinion that original sin, without actual adjoined thereto, damned the kind of man natu-rally descended from Adam unto perpetual sensible pain in the fire of hell. Now shall ye farther[12] understand that there are other which have another manner mind therein, whereupon there ensueth nothing so great difficulty concerning the righ-teousness of God.

Their mind in the matter is this, that God in the creation of man gave to him two states: one, competent[13] and convenient for his mortal nature; another, of special grace, a farther state of special prerogative,[1] that is to wit, the possibility of immortality put in his own hand and of the obtaining of eternal bliss in heaven, of which two things there was neither nother[2] naturally pertaining to him. If God had given him only the first, that is to wit, only natural, his soul yet should have been immortal, for God created the nature such. But unto the bliss of heaven, the fruition of the Godhead, He did not create it to attain by nature, nor as it seemeth angel neither, but by a special gift and prerogative of His grace. The body, being made of the earth and mixed with other elements, was of nature dissoluble and mortal, as the bodies of other beasts be. Howbeit, if God had given Adam no farther gift than competent unto his nature, he

11. from it.   12. further.   13. proper.
1. divinely given privilege.   2. *neither nother:* neither of the two.

had yet had a good state far above all beasts, and yet a state far under the state that he stood in by God's farther gift. For first, if man had had but his natural state, albeit he should have had (as some men think) the rebellion of his sensuality against his reason, yet had he had (while he lived) the use of the reasonable soul, and should have had knowledge of God, and cause to love Him, honor Him, and serve Him, and had been bounden to master his sensuality and resist the devil, and by the doing of the contrary should have deserved hell, and by doing his duty to God should have deserved to have after this life not the fruition of the Godhead (that is the bliss of heaven) but a life good, quiet and restful, with spiritual delight in such knowledge of God and His wonderful works as reason at the least, without revelation, might attain unto. Which should have been a pleasure far above the pleasure that ever any man had by only natural means in this world sith this world first began, and such as (I suppose) whosoever might attain it would not change that state with the state of the greatest king that ever reigned on earth.

And yet, though they call this the natural state of man, they mean not (I think) thereby that man was or should have been able to have lived well after his nature and have attained the end of that state by his own only[3] natural power, without special aid and help of God, sith there is no creature nother[4] high nor low, but as it could not without God be created, no more can it without God be conserved. And man, if he never had had but his natural state, he should have been in danger to do sin more than he was with the state of innocency that God gave him farther, and yet in that state he sinned. And therefore, if not only we, which now by mo means than one have our naturals[5] vitiated, but also Adam, that had more than his naturals in paradise whole and in good plight, had need yet of God's grace to help him there to stand, it must needs be (as I said) that he must have needed the help of God's grace to maintain him if he had had his only natural state. And if any man marvel that God made all

3. solely.   4. neither.   5. natural gifts.

His creatures such as they should alway[6] need aid of His grace,
let him know that God did it of His double goodness: first, to
keep them from pride, by causing them perceive their feebleness
and to call upon Him; and secondly, to do His creatures honor
and comfort. For the creature (that wise is) can never think himself in so noble condition, nor should take so great pleasure or
so much rejoice that he were made able to do a thing well
enough himself, as to remember and consider that he hath the
most excellent majesty of God his creator and maker ever more
attendant Himself at his elbow to help him.

If any man will herein take a contrary part and affirm that
man in the state of innocency, and the angels that fell, were able
of themself to have standen[7] in their former state and, by natural liberty of their will without peculiar help of God, to have
chosen the better and to have refused the worse; and that their
strength therein then, and our feebleness in this state corrupted
now, have their differences by reason of their nature then whole
and unhurt and ours now sore impaired and wounded; and that
the cause why we cannot now without help of grace choose the
good, but willingly apply the freedom of our will to the choice of
the evil, is the corruption of our nature grown by the sin of
Adam; and that therefore (before that sin) Adam was (before
that fall) able to choose the good of his own natural power, and
angel yet more able than he, before the fall of Lucifer; and
thereupon list[8] to conclude that neither angel nor man in the
state of their first creation needed unto the resisting of sin none
other help of God but only their natural power—to him that this
list to reason, mine answer will I temper[9] thus: that they were of
nature stronger and better able naturally than we, that will I
gladly grant. But that they were so able to resist sin of their own
nature then, that they needed for their assistance none help of
God at all, that can I full hardly consent.[10] Howbeit, if any man
affirm stiffly[11] yes, I will keep no schools[1] upon the matter nor

6. always.   7. remained.   8. wishes.   9. devise.
10. *full hardly consent:* scarcely agree with.   11. stubbornly.
1. *keep no schools:* engage in no academic disputations.

almost in nothing else, but leave off and be content with that that I trust he will grant me, that is to wit, that they were never so able to withstand sin by their own natural power but that, at the least wise yet, with God's help (which was ready when they would ask it) they should have been able the better.

Thus have I somewhat showed you of what mind some men be concerning the only[2] natural state given by God unto Adam. And now shall I farther[3] somewhat show you, what mind they be of, concerning that state which he had by the reason of the other gifts given him conditionally, by special prerogative, above his natural state, which things he lost by the condition broken.

They say that, above the natural condition and state of his body, God gave him this gift, that his body should never have died. He gave him this gift also, that his sensual parts should never have rebelled against his reason. He gave him also therewith, that he should never have had dolor or pain in body nor heaviness[4] or sorrow of mind but all thing necessary without weariness or grief. He had farther given him, above his nature, this excellent high gift very far surmounting all the remnant, that is to wit, undeceivable[5] hope and ability both body and soul through grace to come to glory, the bliss (I say) of heaven, the joyful fruition of the glorious Trinity forever. All these gifts God gave him above his naturals, and not for himself only, but for him and for all his posterity. But all these supernatural gifts He gave him with the knot[6] of this condition, that is to wit, that if he brake[7] His commandment, then should he leese them all. And that was understanden[8] by the promise of death, and not only the necessity of temporal death, the dissolution of the soul and the body (by which the man doth indeed but half die, sith his far better part, that is to say the soul, by that death dieth not at all) but, by the loss of heaven, the whole entire man hath a very sore death in that he is separate[9] and departed[10] from the fruition of the very fountain of life, almighty glorious God.

2. merely.   3. further.   4. grief.   5. certain.
6. obligation.   7. broke.   8. signified.   9. *i.e.,* separated.
10. severed.

Now say there, as I told you, therefore some good men that
Adam by his sin lost from himself and all his posterity all those
gifts that God gave him above his nature. And therein could his
posterity have no wrong nor any cause to complain upon God
but upon Adam only. For they were all given unto us but upon
condition hanging on his hand,[1] which condition when he brake,
those gifts could by no reason belong or be due unto us. But yet
remained there high cause for us to thank God for the remnant.
For the gifts only pertaining to the natural state of man (which I
showed you before), those gave not God unto the kind of man
upon condition to be lost by the sin of Adam, nor no man to be
perpetually damned by sensible feeling of the fire of hell for
original sin contracted without his witting,[2] but only for actual
sin freely committed by his own vicious will. And then if the
truth thus be, this matter may partly be resembled unto some
great good prince, which, giving to a poor man for him and his
heirs of his body forever lands to the yearly valure[3] of one
hundred pound, frank and free *simpliciter*[4] and without any condition, would give him farther other lands to the yearly valure of
ten thousand pound with the honor of a dukedom also to him
and his said heirs forever, restrained nevertheless with this condition, that, if he commit any treason against this prince's majesty, this duchy with all those lands of the yearly ten thousand
pound should be forfeited and lost from him and his said heirs
perpetually, and that yet the other lands should still remain in
the blood, and that every man of them, if he do either treason or
other great crime against the king, should stand unto his personal peril of death or other pains, according to justice for his
personal fault, without the loss of the land from the stock[5] for
the fault of any their ancestor. If now this man committed treason and lost this duchy from his heirs by his deed and yet left

1. *hanging . . . hand:* depending upon his action.   2. knowing.
3. value.
4. *frank . . . simpliciter:* held without obligation of rent or service, un-
conditionally.
5. descendants.

them this hundred pound lands of the king's gift beside, there were (ye wot[6] well) none of his heirs that ever could have cause to blame the king for the loss of the duchy but had yet greater cause to thank him for their living of the yearly hundred pound, which they still enjoy of his liberal gift, more by every groat[7] than ever the good king ought[8] them.

Lo, thus say they that likewise God took from the posterity of Adam the royal duchy, that is to wit, the joys of heaven with the commodities[9] of those other gifts above man's nature, which He gave Adam for himself, and then upon condition, which condition Adam brake. But yet He left them still the good honest living of the yearly hundred pound, that is to wit, the commodities of man's competent[1] state natural, which I have before partly showed you, which state also man hath without his desert received, of the only mere liberal goodness of God, and which commodities by affliction of perpetual pain felt in fire God never taketh from any man for the original sin contracted from his forefather without actual deadly sin of himself. Now to that that[2] the whole kind of man are called in scripture the children of wrath by nature[3] and put under condemnation and death by the sin of Adam, and such other words like, they answer that those words are and well may be meant of the loss and condemnation of mankind in the loss of the inheritance of heaven and of those other gifts that God had conditionally given it, above the competent state of man's nature, for[4] the wrath of the condition broken by the sin of Adam, as it were a great condemnation to leese a duchy with ten thousand pound and retain only a mean[5] man's living of one hundred pound.

And they farther declare that there are two manner of pains, that is to wit, *poena damni et poena sensus* (pain of loss and pain of feeling), as a man may be pained by loss of money or loss of his hand. Pain of loss may be also by two means, either by the lees-

6. know.   7. coin worth four pence.   8. owed.
9. benefits.   1. suitable.   2. *that that:* the fact that.
3. Eph. 2 : 3.   4. because of.   5. inferior.

ing[6] of a thing that he hath in possession, or by duty should
have come unto him, or by the leesing of a thing that should
have come unto him, and yet of no duty but of the mere liberal-
ity of some other man, which for displeasure given changeth his
will and withdraweth it. Now say they that, for actual deadly sin,
every man that impenitent dieth therein is damned both to the
pain of loss and to the pain of feeling, that is to wit, to the pain
of the loss of the joys of heaven, the fruition of the glorious sight
of the Godhead forever, and to the perpetual sensible pain of
feeling the fire of hell perpetual.

But for only original sin they say that no man is damned unto
the pain of feeling, but only unto the pain of the said loss alone.
And whereas the same pain of loss of the fruition of the Godhead is yet, unto those Christian people that are damned for actual deadly sin, a greater grief than is their intolerable feeling of
the hot fire of hell, because they were by regeneration of their
baptism made inheritors of heaven and have lost it by their own
fault, yet unto those that die unchristened with none other sin
than original, the pain of that loss is not grievous, because it was
the thing which, though it might have comen[7] to them, yet were
they never entitled thereto indeed, nor were not by their own
fault the cause of their own loss. And thus say some as I show
you, concerning all folk old and young that, never being christened nor nothing hearing of Christ, carry no deadly sin with
them out of this world but sin original only. And as for infants
dying unbaptized, albeit that in many of these things that I have
rehearsed by the way, many men will peradventure think otherwise, yet in the effect and substance of the point whereunto all
the matter draweth, that is to wit, that those infants be damned
only to the pain of loss of heaven, and not unto the pain of feeling by any sensible pain in the fire of hell, to this point I think
the most part of all Christendom both learned and unlearned
agree.

Now as for such as die unchristened at man's state and never

6. losing.   7. come.

heard of Christ, some say one and some say another, as I have showed you before. And some say that without the faith of Christ, if they come to discretion, they must beside original sin die of necessity in actual sin and be damned to sensible pain. For they say that all the deeds that ever they do be sin. Which saying me seemeth[8] hard, but I will not dispute it here. Howbeit, well I wot[9] that some texts of scripture that they lay[10] therefore nothing prove for their purpose. Yet shall I not leave unshowed you one comfortable[1] saying that Master Nicholas de Lyra[2] toucheth upon those words of Saint Paul in the eleventh chapter of his epistle to the Hebrews: *Sine fide autem impossibile est Deo placere quenquam. Credere enim oportet accedentem ad Deum, quia est, et inquirentibus se remunerator sit.*[3] ("Without faith," saith Saint Paul, "it is impossible any man to please God. For every man that cometh unto God must believe that God is, and that He is the rewarder of them that seek Him.") Upon these words saith Master Lyre that, although the people of the Jews to whom the law was given were bounden to the belief of more than this, and the learned men of the Jews to the belief of more than the common people, and we Christian people and those that are the priests and learned among us be rateably[4] bounden to the belief of mo things than were the Jews, or they that were learned among them, yet unto the paynims and gentiles, to whom the law was not given, nor never had heard of Christ, it was sufficient for their salvation to believe those two points only which Saint Paul here rehearseth, that is to wit, that there is one God and that He will reward them that seek Him. And those two points be such as every man many attain by natural reason, holpen[5] forth with such grace as God keepeth fro[6] no man but from him that by his own default either will not receive it or deserveth to have it withdrawn.

8. *me seemeth:* seems to me.   9. know.   10. present, allege.
1. consoling.
2. De Lyra's *Postillae* (1322–30), printed with other biblical glosses in the glossed Bibles of More's period.
3. Heb. 11 : 6.   4. proportionately.   5. helped.   6. from.

So that, if this be true that Master Lyre saith, then is there no man of discretion among the gentiles or paynims unsaved without his own default, and so no color of quarrel against the justice of God in this matter. And it is to be considered that Master Lyre there saith that in the belief of those two points is implied the belief of Christ, which is the mean of our salvation, in that that[7] he which believeth that God will reward them that seek Him hath therein implied that God hath a respect unto man's salvation and provideth a mean thereunto, and so believeth he that there is a mean of man's salvation and reward, though he know not that the mean is Christ. And there though he believe not on Christ by the name of Christ, yet believeth he and hopeth for the mean of salvation, which is indeed Christ. And that belief sufficeth (saith Master Lyre) for his salvation, though he think not on Christ, of whom he never heard.

Thus have I showed you, concerning the necessity of man's redemption, and the manner of man's fall, and the things that he lost thereby, and the justice of God used therein, and as well His justice as His mercy tempered[8] together in the marvelous mean of man's redemption, sundry divers things. And concerning Adam's gifts and his losses for his posterity, I have showed you sundry things of divers other men's opinions, in which I will bind myself to the defense of neither part. But this thing am I very sure of, that by the fall of Adam every man and child that by natural propagation came of him had so verily lost and forfeited the bliss of heaven that never should nor never shall any of them all attain again thereto without the mean of our mediator and savior, Jesus Christ, the merits of whose bitter passion hath redeemed us and thereto made us inheritable[1] again, as many of us (I mean) as by His faith, without contempt of His sacraments, use ourself[2] in such wise[3] as by our own sin we do not willfully and finally fall again fro the benefit. And thus upon this first question, without any bold affirmations or opinion that

7. *in that that:* insomuch as.   8. mingled.
1. capable of inheriting.   2. *use ourself:* behave ourselves.
3. *in such wise:* in such a way.

I will hold or maintain, I have somewhat showed you divers things that divers doctors say.

Another question.

Then are there many men in hand[4] with another question, and therein demand[5] they this: while our Savior Christ (say they) bestowed upon the redemption of man all the blessed blood of His body to the very following of the water after, and that not only being an innocent sinless man and a good, but also being beside that very God too, by reason whereof the least drop of His blessed blood might have sufficed to recompense and satisfy for the sin of seven whole worlds, wherefore be not all men, by the virtue[6] of His such painful death, either taken up into heaven, glorified in body and beautified in soul, forthwith as soon as they be born, or else at the least wise restored to the state that Adam by his sin lost them before in Paradise? That is to wit, that their bodies might be preserved from death, and the reasonable soul fro rebellion of the sensual body, and have but the devil alone left him to strive withal,[7] and man discharged of all pain and vexation, and live here in such pleasant plight as we should have lived if Adam had not sinned, and (by serving God in such wise) then in such time or times after as God should think convenient all men to be translated[8] out of earth into the joys of heaven.

In this question are there mo things than one. But for the first, we must mark and consider well that Christ willingly would, by the ordinance of the whole Trinity, suffer more pain for our redemption than was of necessity requisite. Howbeit, though He so did without necessity, yet did He it not without a great good cause. For the pleasure of God was that, by the hideous torment and willingly taken pain of that holy blessed and almighty person, man should two things consider: one, how much we be bounden and beholden to Him that would endure

4. *in hand:* occupied.   5. ask.   6. efficacy.   7. with.
8. transported.

and sustain such horrible affliction for our sake; the tother, that we should thereby consider the burden and weight of sin and well remember in ourself, sith that innocent almighty person willingly suffered so sore bitter pain for the sin of other, how much we very sinful wretches should of reason be well content, every man to suffer for our own. For unto sufferance for our sin, how loath and irksome[1] would we be of ourself,[2] when we be so scantly[3] stirred yet thereto, for all that wonderful sample?[4] And whereas our hard hearts are so dispiteous[5] that many for all the consideration of Christ's bitter passion and most painful death cannot yet with compassion relent into tears and weep, if He had paid our ransom but with one drop of His blessed blood pricked out with a pin, what doubt is there but that thereat then many a wretch would laugh?

Now as for bringing every man unto heaven forthwith upon his birth without any more ado, why God would not the effect of His passion to weigh to[6] such purpose, there are mo causes than one. First that thing had been impertinent[7] to the nature of redemption, the nature whereof were at the farthest[8] but to restore men to the liberty and freedom of their former state. But man in the state of innocency living in Paradise should not have been in that case[9] to have been forthwith translated into heaven, but should first have served God in Paradise, and somewhat have done therefore,[10] and in all that while have standen still[1] upon the winning or losing of heaven after his abearing.[2] For if he had abiden[3] in Paradise untempted many years mo than he did and had afterward before his translation,[4] upon the suggestion of the old serpent the devil and of the young serpent the woman, eaten of the fruit as he did, he had in any time of his life had the selfsame fall. And peradventure any of his sons, if

1. weary.   2. *of ourself:* on our own.   3. barely.
4. example.   5. pitiless.   6. *weigh to:* be sufficient for.
7. irrelevant.   8. most.   9. *in that case:* in such a state as.
10. for it (heaven).   1. *standen still:* relied always.
2. *after his abearing:* according to his conduct.   3. dwelt.
4. *before his translation:* before he was taken (up to heaven).

he had happed[5] any to beget before his fall, might, for himself and the posterity coming after of his own body, have lost by the like fall the self-same state. And therefore I say that to bring man to heaven by and by upon his birth was nothing belonging to the nature of redemption, which nature is to restore him only to the freedom[6] of his first estate,[7] which was not (as I show you) man to go forthwith to heaven.

But then why be we not at the least wise restored unto the same state, the state of innocency that Adam had in Paradise with all the commodities thereunto pertaining? To this I answer you, Christ when He redeemed us, how much pain soever Himself took thereabout, was yet at His own liberty to temper the fruit that we should take thereby. And therefore if we took thereby much less fruit than we do, there could no man in reason find any fault therein. Howbeit, as there is no doubt but that God could by the passion of Christ have redeemed and restored us, not only to the conditional title of inheriting heaven at length, but also to the immediate attaining of heaven forthwith upon our birth or to the state of innocency in Paradise first for the meanwhile, if He had would,[8] so doubt I nothing also but likewise as He restored us not straightways to heaven because His high wisdom wist it was not for God convenient, so restored He us not to the state of innocency because His high wisdom well wist it was for ourself not best. To be stablished[9] in the possession of eternal wealth, without any manner pain taken or anything done toward the deserving thereof, was and is so proper to God alone (the three persons of the glorious Trinity, the creator) that God would never communicate[1] that thing with any other person being but a creature, neither man in earth nor yet angel in heaven. And therefore man to look for that point as the effect of his redemption were full unreasonable and far over-proud a request.

Now man to be restored to the state of innocency, God saw

5. happened.   6. privilege.   7. condition.   8. so desired.
9. set firmly.   1. share.

that for man it was not best. For as the scripture saith: *Homo cum in honore esset, non intellexit.*[2] (When man was in honor, his understanding failed him, he could not know himself.) And therefore to the keeping of him from sin, and specially fro pride the root of all sin, a more base estate was better. And better was it also for him to have two enemies, that is to wit, the devil and his own sensuality both, than for to lack the tone.[3] For the having of both is a cause of double fear, and therefore of double diligence, to set his reason to keep sure watch to resist them, and for double help to call double so much upon almighty God for grace. And then with his so doing, he is more able and more sure now to subdue them both, than with less looking for[4] God's help he was before the tone,[5] and hath yet also thereby for his double victory against his double enemies the occasion of double reward.

Besides this, if God should by His passion have restored them that came to His faith both in the old law and in the new unto the state of innocency, so that the children circumcised or christened should never have died till they were comen to discretion and had done some deadly sin, and that then their nature should change and by the sacrament of penance yet be restored again, then should it (as holy Saint Austin saith[6]) have been a great occasion to make folk come to the faith and sacraments for the commodities of this present life, whereas God will have heaven so sore desired and sought for that He will have the desirers thereof set by[7] the pleasures of this world not only nothing at all but also seek for the contrary and suffer displeasure and pain.

Moreover, if it so should have been, every person's secret sinful state should by the sudden open change of his nature have been, to his open shame, detected and disclosed in the sight of

2. Ps. 48 : 13, 21 (*AV*, 49 : 12, 20).   3. one.
4. *looking for:* expectation of.
5. *he . . . tone; i.e.,* he was able before (the fall) to subdue the one (the devil).
6. *De civitate Dei,* XIII, 4.   7. esteem.

all the people. And over this, if it should thus have been, then must there have been so many common open miracles continually that man should in manner [8] have been drawn to the faith by force, and by that mean have lost more than half the merit, which God would in no wise of His great goodness suffer. And yet besides this, God, that well wist what thing the bliss of heaven is, saw that it was not convenient to give so great a gift to every slothful javel [9] that nothing did set thereby. And he well showeth himself to set nothing by it that can find in his heart to do nothing for it. Finally, God wist that it was nothing meet, the servant to stand in better condition than his master, as our Lord saith Himself in the gospel. And therefore would He not suffer that, while He came to His own kingdom not without travail and pain, His servants should be slothful, and sit and pick their nails, and be carried up to heaven at their ease, but biddeth every man that will be His disciple or servant take up his cross upon his back, and therewith come forth and follow Him. And for this cause, lo, though the painful passion of Christ, paid for all mankind, was of the nature of the thing much more than sufficient for the sins of us all, though we nothing did but sin all our whole life, yet God, not willing to fill heaven with hell hounds, limited of His own wisdom and goodness after what rate and stint [1] the commodity thereof should be employed upon us, and ordinarily devised that the merits of His pain taken for us should make our labor and pain taken for ourself meritorious, which else, had we taken for our sin never so much and done never so many good deeds toward the attaining of heaven, could not have merited us a rush. And this, I say, ordinarily. For by special privilege His liberal hand is yet nevertheless at liberty to give remission of sin, and to give grace and glory, where and whensoever he list.

And thus have I somewhat touched the answer unto this question: wherefore the painful passion of Christ restored not man again unto the former state of innocency that Adam before had in Paradise.

8. *in manner:* as it were.   9. rascal.   1. measure.

Now albeit that sundry other questions both may be moved
and are, which might be induced[2] and entreated[3] here, yet (lest
I should therewith make this work too tedious and the introduction longer than the principal process[4] of the passion) we shall
be content with these few as those that most properly pertain
unto the matter of the redemption; and, beseeching almighty
God of His great grace that, all curious appetite of vain problems put apart, we may with meekness give our hearts to the
very fruitful learning of those necessary things that we be bound
to know, we shall haste us to the matter of the blessed passion itself.

The prayer.

O holy blessed Savior Jesus Christ, which willingly didst determine to die for man's sake, mollify mine hard heart and supple[5]
it so by grace that through tender compassion of Thy bitter passion I may be partner of Thine holy redemption.

Whereas I have here before showed you three points, that is
to wit, the ruin of angel, the fall of man, and the determination
of the Trinity for man's redemption by mean of Christ's passion,
as three things that were causes going before, whereupon His
bitter passion followed, I doubt not but that such as are learned
will like also that, ere I begin with the lamentable story of the
passion self,[6] I should first show farther some other points, that
is to wit, by what means this determination of the Trinity was
notified[7] unto man. And also the other causes of Christ's death
and passion, as the malice of the Jews, the treason of Judas, and
the obedient will of His own holy manhead.[8] And verily these
points might well and conveniently have been declared[9] before,
and in the treating of these three other points, somewhat have I
made mention of all these points too. But I have not thought it

2. adduced.   3. considered.   4. narrative.
5. make compliant.   6. itself.   7. announced.
8. human nature.   9. explained.

like[10] requisite to declare them before so full as those other, because the words of the gospel self give us more occasion to declare these points in the process of the passion self than those other three points which I have as a preamble touched more at large[1] before.

A warning to the reader.

Here I will give the reader warning that I will rehearse the words of the evangelists in this process of the passion in Latin word by word after my copy as I find it in the work of that worshipful father, Master John Gerson, which work he entitled *Monotessaron*[2] (that is to wit, "one of all four") as I have declared you before in my preface, because I will not in any word willingly mangle or mutilate that honorable man's work, but so rehearse it that learned[3] which shall read it here may have the selfsame commodity thereby that they may have by the reading of the same among his own other works, as in considering such doubts as he sometime moveth concerning the context[4] of the story, and in searching (if their pleasure be) every word in his[5] own proper place, where it was gathered and taken out of the four evangelists, and for their own learning list confer[6] the place and use their own judgment in the allowing[7] or in the controlling[8] of any part of his context, in the gathering and compiling of his present work.

But yet will I not fully follow the same fashion in the rehearsing of the same thing in English. For if I should, there neither could any such fruit grow thereof, and also the context of the story should in the eye of the English reader (and yet much more in the ear of the English hearer) seem very far unsavory by

10. equally.   1. *at large:* at length.
2. Here and in *The Sadness of Christ,* More takes the gospel texts he expounds from the *Monotessaron,* a gospel harmony by John Gerson (1363–1429), a French churchman and spiritual writer.
3. learned persons.   4. coherent structure.
5. its.   6. compare.   7. approving.
8. calling into question.

reason of the often interposition of the initial letters signifying
the names of the four evangelists, and some one sentence[9] with
so little change so often repeated, and in some place the context
so diversely entricked[1] in his collection,[2] that himself with a note
in the margin declareth himself to doubt and stand unsure
whether in that place he join and link well in one the sundry
words of the evangelists or no. And therefore in the rehearsing
of his context in English, nothing will I put in of mine own, but
out will I not let[3] to leave any such thing as I shall think to be
unto the English reader no furtherance but an hindrance to the
clear progress of this holy story, which we shall with help of God
in this wise now begin.

The first chapter.

The context of Master Gerson, whereof first the rubric, *De festo azimorum appropinquante. M. 26, R. 14, L. 22, Jo. 13*.[4]

"Of the feast of the unleavened loaves approaching."[5]

"There approached near the holy day of the unleavened
loaves, which feast is called pascha.[6] For the pascha and the

9. meaning.   1. entangled.   2. arrangement.
3. hesitate.
4. The letters—abbreviations for Matthew (M.), Mark (R.), Luke (L.),
and John (Jo. or J.)—are used by Gerson to label the sources of words,
phrases, and sentences in his gospel harmony. In the *Treatise,* More
quotes Gerson's Latin only here (and perhaps in one other place). Contrary to what More himself wrote (pp. 53–54, above), he (or some editor)
inserted these identifying letters into the English translations. Gerson's
Latin and the letters in the English translations have been omitted in this
edition.
5. Gerson takes his account from Matthew 26 : 1–5, 14–16; Mark
14 : 1–2, 10–11; Luke 22 : 1–6; and John 13 : 1.
6. Passover.

unleavened loaves was two days after. And so was it that, when Jesus had ended all these sermons, He said unto His disciples: 'You know that after two days shall be the pascha, and the Son of Man shall be delivered[7] to be crucified.' Then gathered there together the princes of the priests, and the ancients[8] of the people into the palace of the prince of the priests which[9] is called Caiphas, and took counsel together. And they sought the ways, both the chief priests and the scribes, how they might with some wile take Him and put Him to death. For they were afeard[10] of the people. They said therefore: 'Not on the holy day, lest there arise some seditious ruffle[1] among the people.' But there entered Sathanas into Judas, whose surname is Scariot, one of the twelve. Then went he to the princes of the priests and to the chief priests to betray Him to them. And he had communication with the princes of the priests and with the rulers, in what manner he should betray Him to them. And he said unto them, 'What will ye give me and[2] I shall deliver Him to you,' who, when they heard him, were well apaid,[3] and promised and covenanted with him to give him money, and appointed to give him thirty groats.[4] And he made the promise. And from that time forth he sought opportunity that he might commodiously[5] betray Him out of the presence of the people. Before the holy day of the pascha, Jesus, knowing that His hour came on to go out of this world unto His Father, whereas He had loved those that were His, unto the end He loved them."

A prayer.

Good Lord, give us Thy grace, not to read or hear this gospel of Thy bitter passion with our eyen and our ears in manner of a pastime, but that it may with compassion so sink into our hearts, that it may stretch to[6] the everlasting profit of our souls.

---

7. handed over (to destruction).   8. elders.   9. who.
10. afraid.   1. tumult.   2. if.   3. pleased.
4. coins worth four pence each.   5. opportunely.
6. *stretch to:* serve for.

The first lecture.

"There approached near the holy day of the unleavened bread, which is called pascha.[7] For the pascha and the unleavened loaves was two days after."

These words, good Christian readers, be the words of Saint Matthew, Saint Luke, and Saint Mark, three of the four evangelists, which, by the mention-making of the pascha and the unleavened bread, give us here in the beginning occasion to speak of the point which I before touched, that is to wit, in what wise the merciful, just, and high devised means of man's redemption, the deep secret mystery of the blessed Trinity (which, till God revealed it unto them, none angel in heaven knew or could think upon) was of God's comfortable[8] goodness signified and declared to man. For which ye shall understand that, albeit our first parents Adam and Eve were disobedient, and thereby brake God's commandment, and were also stubborn in the beginning (whereby they rather excused their default, and each of them put it from himself to some other, than meekly confessed their fault and asked for pardon and mercy) for which demean,[9] beside the sentence of death conditionally pronounced (before mentioned in the second chapter of Genesis, that whatsoever day Adam did eat of the tree of knowledge he should die), God, as is recited in the third chapter, declared after[10] certain other punishments that either of them should have for them and their offspring too (the tone with sore travail about the getting of his daily living, the other with sore travail in bringing forth of her children, and either of them some other thing beside, as you have in the second point heard rehearsed before), yet never find we that of God's mercy they fell into despair, as we find of Caim and of Judas.

And therefore after their not desperate[1] but fruitful repen-

7. Passover.   8. consoling.   9. conduct.   10. afterward.
1. despairing.

tance, taken upon[2] God's inward motion, and thereby calling to
God for remission and mercy (with taking great wreak[3] willingly
themself upon themself, as well with inward heaviness[4] and sorrow as outward labor and pain for their heinous offenses committed against God by the bold breaking of His high commandment), the great goodness of God giving them knowledge of the
mean of their salvation and of that Mediator by whose death
they and their offspring should be redeemed again to bliss, did,
in the faith of the said Mediator, remit and forgive them the
eternality of the pain due unto their offense, reserving their actual enhancing[5] into heaven until the great mystery of Christ's
passion should be performed, and thereby the ransom paid, in
such time as the high foresight and providence of God had from
the beginning, before the world wrought,[6] laid up out of sight in
the deep treasure of His unsearchable knowledge, little and little
at sundry seasons to be signified and insinuate[7] conveniently[8] to
man before.

And therefore this great secret mystery did God reveal in
divers wise, that is to wit, partly with inward inspiration, partly
with outward means, as well by words as other outward tokens.
The first mention that we find made thereof is the third chapter
of Genesis, where God unto the serpent said among other things
thus: *Inimicitias ponam inter te et mulierem, et semen tuum et semen
illius. Ipsum conteret caput tuum, et tu insidiaberis calcaneo illius.*[9] ("I
shall put enmity," said our Lord to the serpent, "between thee
and the woman, and between the seed of thee and the seed of
her. That seed shall tread[1] and all to frush[2] thine head, and
thou shalt lie in await[3] for his heel.") In these words was there a
secret insinuation[4] and (as men might say) a watchword[5] given
of Christ, which should be the seed of the woman (and the only

2. *taken upon:* derived from.   3. punishment.   4. grief.
5. raising.   6. *i.e.,* had been wrought.
7. imparted to the mind subtly.   8. suitably.   9. Gen. 3 : 15.
1. trample.   2. *all to frush:* smash completely to pieces.
3. ambush.   4. covert suggestion.   5. premonitory sign.

seed of only woman without man), which seed should all to
tread[6] and frush[7] in pieces the devil's head and his power upon
man, and that all that ever the devil should do again against
Christ should not be able to reach His head (that is to wit His
Godhead), but only to fumble about His foot (that is to wit His
manhead), and yet rather lie in await to hurt it than able to hurt
it indeed. For all that ever the devil (when with long lying in
await therefore, he could nothing prevail by himself) caused by
his wily train the Jews and the Gentiles to do against His holy
manhead, was yet, the thing well weighed and considered, not
able to do it hurt, but (as the prophet saith): *Sagittae parvulorum
factae sunt plagae eorum.*[8] (The wounds that they gave him were
like as they had been made with the arrows that are shot out of a
little boy's bow.) For all the wounds that they gave Him in His
body could not so take hold, but that within three days after, all
His flesh was rid of all manner pain, and in far better health and
incomparable[9] better condition after forever than it was five
days before.

And here, good reader, marvel not though I rehearse you the
text of Genesis otherwise here than I did in the second point
before. For whereas I there rehearsed it after the Latin translation, whereof the sentence[1] may stand very well, yet seemeth
this letter[2] after the Hebrew text to serve more meet and more
proper for the matter, in that by the Latin text the treading
down of the devil seemeth applied unto our blessed Lady (which
she did indeed by mean of her holy seed, our Savior), but by the
Hebrew text it is, as you see, referred (as more meet is) unto her
holy son Himself.

But now when this mystery of man's redemption was thus
there prophesied by God, I doubt it not but that of this watchword[3] the devil gathered somewhat and ever gnawed after
upon that bone from that time to the coming of Christ, as a matter of his grief and torment. But yet will I not warrant that he

6. *all to tread:* trample completely to pieces.   7. crush.
8. Ps. 63 : 8 (*AV*, 64 : 7).   9. incomparably.   1. meaning.
2. text.   3. premonitory notice.

very well understood it. And Adam (would I ween) at the first hearing understood that word yet much less. For though God suffered the serpent, whom He threatened therewith to his grief and displeasure, somewhat to guess thereat, yet while man was at that time nothing yet reconciled, but in his heinous offense stubbornly stood at his defense and his sorrow shortly after thereupon declared unto him, it seemeth me[4] not likely that God gave him the knowledge of his pardon before the full knowledge of his punishment or the knowledging[5] and repentance of his fault. Howbeit upon his repentance after, I nothing doubt but that God gave him farther understanding what was by those words meant. Besides this, He signified this mystery to them by the sacrifice. For by the killing and offering up unto God the innocent beast in sacrifice was betokened the death of our innocent Savior and offering up of His body by the hot fervent pain of the cross.

And thus by divers ways was there revelation given of this great mystery unto other of the old fathers (as Noah, Abraham, Isaac, and Israel and Joseph) by sundry divers tokens too long here to rehearse, before the law given[6] in writing. Then was there in the law written express warning given by Moyses unto the children of Israel in desert,[7] when he wrote unto them in the eighteenth chapter of the Deuteronomy: *Prophetam de gente tua et de fratribus tuis sicut me, suscitabit tibi Dominus Deus tuus, ipsum audies.*[8] (A prophet of thine own people and of thy brethren, like unto me, shall thy Lord God raise up unto thee, and that prophet shalt thou hear.) Here in these words Moyses gave them warning of Christ, that He should be a very man coming lineally of one of their own tribes, and that He should be a bringer of a new law to them, as himself was, and that they should therein, upon the pain of the vengeance of God (as after followeth in the text), be bounden when He should come to hear and obey Him. Now to bring them a new law, as Moyses did, God never sent none

4. *seemeth me:* seems to me.   5. acknowledgment.
6. *i.e.,* was given.   7. *in desert:* in the wilderness.
8. Deut. 18 : 15.

after but only Christ. And therefore Him were they, by those
words of their old lawyer[9] Moses, commanded for to hear and
obey in those words, *Ipsum audies* (Him shalt thou hear).

And therefore sith they so were commanded of God by the
mouth of Moyses, though there had been before Christ's coming
no word spoken of His Godhead, yet when Himself so plainly
declared it unto them, they were, I say, by the said commandment of God given them by Moyses, bounden to give therein full
faith and credence to Him. Howbeit, that Christ was the very
Son of God, and Himself very God, beside the figures[1] and
prophecies of the old law very plain and plenteous, the Father of
heaven Himself, present with the Holy Ghost at Christ's baptism,
testified and recognized Him for His very Son, saying: *Hic est
filius meus dilectus, in quo mihi complacui.*[2] (This is my well beloved
Son, in whom hath been my delight.) Besides this, of His birth,
of the place and the time of His doctrine and His miracles, and
the malice conceived against Him by the Jews, and the false
treason of His familiar[3] enemy, of His passion, His death, His
resurrection, and His glorious ascension was warning given by
sundry wise, as well by the words of the holy prophets as by
tokens and figures[4] of things done among the chosen people
(both before the law written[5] and after) and by things also commanded to be done among the children of Israel in their sacraments, rites, ceremonies, and sacrifices, commanded them (I say)
by God (by the mouth of Moyses) in the law given them by writing. For as saith Saint Paul: *Omnia in figura contingebant illis.*[6] (All
thing came to them in figures.)

But forasmuch as I wot well no wise man would look that I
should in this place rehearse all those things, which would make
a long book alone, I will therefore (letting all the remnant pass)
only with a word or two show you what feast the evangelists here
speak of, in these words of theirs which I have rehearsed you,
that is to wit, the feast of pascha and of the unleavened bread.

9. lawgiver.   1. types.   2. Matt. 3 : 17.
3. *i.e.*, of his own household.   4. types.   5. *i.e.*, was written.
6. 1 Cor. 10 : 11.

That the children of Israel were in servitude and thralldom in Egypt under the proud prince Pharaoh; and that God conducted them thence in strong and mighty hand and made that high stubborn king, maugre his teeth,[7] fain[8] to let them go; and that when he farther followed them of his heart-burning malice through the Red Sea, the same way where God had sent His own people through safe, this fierce furious king with all his whole main[9] mighty army was—with the waves of the water (which water, while the children of Israel passed thorough, stood up like high walls of crystal on both sides, leaving a great broad space of dry ground all the mids[1]) suddenly relented[2] and fallen and flowing shortly together again—involved[3] and tossed up, overthrown and tumbled down, overwhelmed and wretchedly drowned: all this process (I say) shall I nothing need to speak of, as things so commonly known that, for the atrocity[4] of the story and the wonderful work of God therein, almost every child hath heard.

And every man almost is (I trust) instructed also that, though these things be no feigned tales told for parables, but were things verily done indeed, yet did they by the provident ordinance of God serve also to signify certain great secret mysteries concerning the redemption of man. As for ensample,[5] the thralldom of the children of Israel under King Pharaoh and the Egyptians signifieth the bondage of mankind under the prince of this dark world, the devil and his evil spirits. Their delivery[6] thence under the leading of Moyses betokeneth the delivery of man from the devil and his evil angels under our captain Christ. The safe passage of the children of Israel through the Red Sea, and all the power of Pharaoh drowned in the same, signifieth mankind passing out of the devil's danger[7] through the water of baptism, the sacrament taking his force of the red blood of Christ that He shed in His bitter passion, and all the devil's

7. *maugre his teeth:* in spite of everything he could do.   8. willing.
9. strong.   1. *all the mids:* in the middle.   2. broken loose.
3. enveloped.   4. savage enormity.   5. example.
6. deliverance.   7. power.

power, usurped upon[8] us before and laboring to keep us still, drowned and destroyed in the water of baptism and the red blood of Christ's passion. And by all the course after of the people conveyed from the Red Sea, by the desert[9] toward the land of behest,[1] and their waywardness and many punishments, with manifold mercy showed again by the space of forty year together ere any of them came there, is there signified and figured[2] the long, painful wandering of men in the wild wilderness of this wretched world ere we can get hence to heaven and the frowardness[3] of ourself that so sore[4] keepeth us from it that, with great help of God's grace, in respect of the multitude that by their evil desert eternally perish in this worldly desert, very few (I fear), and with much work, attain unto it.

But for the perceiving of these words of the gospel, "There approached near the feastful[5] day of the unleavened loaves, which feast is called pascha,"[6] ye shall understand that the Jews among all their feasts and holy days through the year had one feast the most solemn that was called "pascha" and "the feast of the unleavened bread" which God specially commanded them to celebrate yearly forever, as appeareth at length in the twelfth chapter of Exodi.[7] For, after that the proud, stiff-necked Pharaoh, being by Moyses in the name of God commanded to suffer the children of Israel to depart out of his land into desert with all their wives and their children and all their cattle,[8] would in no wise suffer it, but albeit that by the force and constraint of sundry sore strokes and plagues (wherewith God wonderfully smote him) he granted their delivery[9] for the time that he stood in dread (the rod of God laying the lashes upon him), yet, after the rod scant[10] removed, ever more his stubborn pride sprang into his hard heart and made him forbid their passage again and hold them in thralldom still, our Lord at the last commanded

8. *usurped upon:* appropriated wrongfully from.   9. wilderness.
1. *land of behest:* promised land.   2. symbolized.   3. perversity.
4. grievously.   5. festal.   6. Luke 22 : 1.
7. Exod. 12 : 14 and 17.   8. possessions.   9. deliverance.
10. scarcely.

Moyses that the tenth day of that month they should take every
household a lamb without spot, and the fourteenth day of the
same month, in the evening, offer it and eat it up all together,
head and guts and all, so that they should leave nothing thereof,
but if anything were left they should burn it up. And of this
lamb should they nothing eat raw nor sod,[1] but only roasted at
the fire. And they should eat it with wild lettuce and unleavened
bread, and should have no leaven, neither that night nor in
seven days following, within their house upon pain of death.
And they should eat it having their gowns gird[2] or tucked up
about the reins[3] of their back, and their shoon[4] upon their feet,
and their walking staves in their hands, and so eat it in haste, as
folk that had made them ready to be going and therefore might
not tarry because they were upon their passage.

And then God showed them of two passages: the tone of
theirs, the tother of His. For He showed them that the twenty-
first day of the same month, which should be at the end of the
said seven days of the unleavened bread, they should all pass
and depart out of Egypt over the Red Sea. And He showed
them that in the night of the said fourteenth day, in which they
should offer in sacrifice and eat the unspotted lamb, Himself
would make a passage through Egypt and by His angel kill in
that one night all the first begotten of the Egyptians, as well men
as cattle in every house, from the first begotten son of Pharaoh
that sat in his seat, to the first begotten son of the poorest and
most simple slave that lay in prison. And He commanded them
that with a bundle of hyssop they should besprinkle the posts
and the hance[5] of their doors with the blood of the lamb, which
blood should be the mark unto him that should strike these first
begottens that should that night be slain, so that upon the sight
of that mark the striker should pass by their houses so marked
and not enter thereinto to do there any harm; but He warned
them that there should that night none of them come out of
their doors.

1. boiled.   2. girdled.   3. loins.   4. shoes.   5. lintel.

And likewise as God had promised, so performed He that great sore slaughter and vengeance thorough all Egypt in that one night, so that thereupon Pharaoh with all the Egyptians were so sore daunted that both Pharaoh and all his people not only licensed[6] but also required and prayed the children of Israel to get them out of Egypt into the desert about their sacrifice, and, in all that they might, they also hasted them forward, and not only let them carry and convey out with them all their own but lent them also so great substance of theirs that the Hebrews, as the scripture saith, in their going with that plentuous borrowing, "spoiled the Egyptians,"[7] and that by the special commandment of God—either in recompense of the wrongful oppression that the Egyptians had done them before, or because that, sith *Domini est terra et plenitudo ejus, orbis terrarum, et universi qui habitant in eo*[8] (The earth belongeth to our Lord, and all thing that is therein, the whole roundel[9] of the world and all the people that dwell therein), God might well with reason take what He would from whom He would, and give it where He would, and make their possession lawful.

But now was this feast of the unleavened bread yearly kept holy the space of the said seven days by the special commandment of God, and called *dies azymorum* in the Greek tongue, that is to say, "the days of the unleavened bread." And the first day of them was the great solemn day. And that first day began alway the night before in the evening in the feast of pascha, wherein was immolate[1] and offered in sacrifice the unspotted lamb. For, as I have showed you, that lamb were they commanded to eat with unleavened bread, and so forth from that time to continue the unleavened bread seven days after. This feast, therefore, of the sacrifice of the unspotted lamb is that feast that is called pascha, whereof the evangelists here speak. And they call it also the feast of the unleavened bread, because that feast began the same night in which the lamb was sacrificed.

6. allowed.   7. Exod. 12 : 36.   8. Ps. 23 : 1 (*AV*, 24 : 1).
9. sphere.   1. sacrificed.

This feast which was in the Greek called *pascha,* and which name the Latins have taken of the Greeks and continued, was in the Hebrew tongue called *phase* and (as Saint Hierome saith[2]) *pascha* too. It was called *phase* for that *phase* in the Hebrew signifieth "passing" or "going" and the feast was (as I have showed you) ordained in remembrance of God's passing through Egypt in doing the vengeance upon the Egyptians by the slaughter of all their first begottens to compel them to suffer the Hebrews pass out of their thralldom. It is also called *pascha,* for that that (as Saint Jerome saith) *pascha* in the Hebrew signifieth "immolation," and therefore for the immolation of the lamb that feast hath in Hebrew that name. The Greeks, as I have told you, have taken the name *pascha*—and that peradventure the rather for that that the same Hebrew word signifieth also in their tongue another thing, very consonant and convenient for the season and the matter. For *pascha* in the Greek tongue signifieth "passion." And because that in that night of His maundy,[3] in which He immolated the lamb, He began His bitter passion—the immolation of the very unspotted Lamb, His own blessed body, which immolation and passion He finished on the morrow— therefore they took and used the name of *pascha,* wherein the Latin church followeth them.

Thus have I somewhat showed you, good Christian readers, the first point that I spake of rising of the text, that is to wit, in what wise the determination of the Trinity for man's redemption was notified[4] unto man, that is to say, by the inspiration and prophecies in words and writing, and by figures contained as well in other things done among the chosen people as in their rites, sacraments, ceremonies, and sacrifices. I have also showed you somewhat concerning this feast of the unleavened loaves and the pascha. But, as I said before, all these things which then were verily done foresignified in Christ and His church things

2. More could have based this and the following reference to Jerome on the *Glossa ordinaria,* one of the common biblical glosses found in Bibles in More's period.
3. last supper.　　4. announced.

after to be done. For that innocent lamb without spot was a figure betokening our Savior Christ, the very innocent Lamb of whom Saint John the Baptist witnessed: *Ecce agnus Dei qui tollit peccata mundi*[5] (Lo the Lamb of God which taketh away the sins of the world), by whose immolation and sacrifice on the cross, and by His holy body received into ours as that lamb was into theirs, His faithful folk should be delivered out of thralldom of the devil's dominion. And therefore may we to the fruit[6] of our souls consider, in the foresaid figure, by these Egyptians that in Egypt (which signifieth by interpretation "darkness") do labor to keep in captivity the children of Israel—the people which God calleth from their thralldom into the liberty of His service—we may (I say) understand by the proud King Pharaoh and his chief captains, the great high proud prince, the Soldan[7] of Babylon, the devil. And as two the[8] special bashaws of that proud souterly[9] soldan, may we well consider the world and the flesh. And the whole people of the Egyptians under them may well betoken the devilish people, and the worldly people, and the fleshly people that follow them and willingly be governed by them.

For verily all these labor to draw into their service and to make their thrall servants, bondmen, and slaves all those whom the goodness of God calleth out of the dark, devilish, worldly, and fleshy subjection into the lightsome[10] liberty of His celestial service. For surely the devil himself, nor the world, nor a man's own flesh do not so much by their own strength to the bringing of good folk into their bondage as they do by the mean and help of the devilish, worldly, and fleshly people, by occasions of pride, envy, wrath, and covetise,[1] gluttony, sloth, and lechery (to which one vice of lechery, for an ensample, how oft hath an old, wily, wretched bawd brought and betrayed a good simple maid, whom else neither the lust of her own flesh, nor the rewards of all the world, nor the labor of all the devils in hell should never have drawn thereto). By the first begotten children of the Egyp-

5. John 1 : 29.　　　6. advantage.　　　7. sultan.
8. *two the: i.e.,* the two.　　9. vulgar.　　　10. easy.
1. covetousness.

tians we may well understand the first motions of sin, as the subtle inward suggestions of the devil, and the inward incitation[2] of the flesh, and the outward occasions and provocations of the world and evil people, by all which manner of motions good, well-disposed folk be many sundry wise solicited unto sin. And surely killed must there be these first begotten children, not only of the Egyptian people (that is to wit, the first motions unto such vices as have their springing of the soul) but also the first begotten of their beasts too (that is to wit, the first motions unto such vices as specially spring of the sensual beastly body), or else it will be very hard for the children of Israel, the well-disposed people, to escape well out of bondage of these Egyptians.

But now to destroy those first begotten children of the Egyptians the children of Israel are of themself not sufficient,[3] but it must needs be the work of God for them. And yet will God that themself shall do somewhat too. For He will that they shall make and receive this sacrifice of the paschal lamb, and then, if they do worthily the tone for Him, He will do the tother for them. And therefore He will that we shall receive the holy paschal lamb, His own blessed body, both bodily in the blessed sacrament and spiritually—with faith, hope, and charity—receive it worthily,[4] and in such wise also virtually[5] when we receive it not sacramentally. But He will we shall eat it with no leaven bread, that is to wit, with no sour taste of malice or sin, but with the sweet unleavened loaves of sincere love and verity. We must also, with a bundle of the low-growing herb of hyssop that signifieth humility, mark the posts and the hance[6] of the door of our house with the blood of the lamb, that is to wit, have remembrance of His bitter passion and His blessed blood shed therein. And likewise as with a bundle of hyssop, the bitter eisell[7] and gall was given Him to drink in the painful thirst of His passion, which He so humbly suffered, we should with a bundle of humility (as it were with a painter's pencil[8]) dipped in the red

2. stimulation.   3. able.   4. with a fitting disposition.
5. with spiritual effect, even though the eucharist is not taken bodily.
6. lintel.   7. vinegar.   8. paintbrush.

blood of Christ, mark ourself on every side and in the hance of our forehead with the letter of *Tau*,[9] the sign of Christ's holy cross.

And then will God Himself with His holy angels pass by, and kill and destroy for us those first begotten of the Egyptians, from the first begotten child of the king that sitteth in his seat (that is to wit of pride, which is of all sin the prince) unto the first begotten child of the poorest prisoned slave that is covetise,[1] lo, the very caitiff knave. For he is yet of all wretched vices the most base, by setting[2] and binding his affection neither unto God, nor man, nor woman, nor unto himself neither, but only made in the pleasure of possessing a great heap of round metal plates, which while he liveth he loveth better than himself and cannot find in his heart to break his heap to help himself. And when he goeth, he carrieth none hence with him, but is while he liveth in like wise rich (as the prophet saith) as a poor man is in a dream, which, when he waketh, hath never a penny of all the treasure that he was so glad of in his sleep.[3] And covetise is a very prisoner, for he cannot get away. Pride will away with shame, envy with his enemies' misery, wrath with fair entreating, sloth with hunger and pain, lechery with sickness, gluttony with the belly too full. But covetise can nothing get away—for the more full the more greedy, and the elder the more niggard, and the richer the more needy.

And while God killeth those Egyptians, that mark of Christ's bloody cross upon the posts of our house shall defend us, and be the mark by which we shall be marked from harm, as were the twelve thousand marked with the same sign of the letter *Tau*, mentioned in the seventh chapter of the Apocalypse Saint John.[4] But yet we must remember that in that perilous time we may not walk out abroad, but keep ourself close (God biddeth us) within

9. The name of the letter T in the Greek, Hebrew, and ancient Semitic alphabets. It has the form of a St. Anthony's cross.
1. covetousness.   2. bestowing.   3. Ps. 75 : 6 (*AV*, 76 : 5).
4. Rev. 7 : 2–4. The letter "tau" is not mentioned in this passage but is in a related passage, Ezek. 9 : 4.

our so marked house from all evil outward occasions. We must also have our garments girt, and our walking staff in our hand, and eat apace for token of haste, in consideration of Christ's passage to kill the Egyptians for us by His own bitter passion, and in remembrance also that we may not tarry here long about our meat, nor take leisure as we list at our meal, but with our gear[5] girt and tucked up (for letting[6] us by the way), and our shoon[7] upon our feet (for filing of[8] our affections with the dirt of sin), and with our walking staff in our hand (the remembrance of Christ's cross, to stay us with and beat from us venomous worms), get us forward apace upon our way out of the Egyptians' danger.[9]

A prayer.

Good Lord, which, upon the sacrifice of the paschal lamb, didst so clearly destroy the first begotten children of the Egyptians that Pharaoh was thereby forced to let the children of Israel depart out of his bondage, I beseech Thee, give me the grace in such faithful wise to receive the very sweet paschal lamb, the very blessed body of our sweet Savior, Thy Son, that, the first suggestions of sin by Thy power killed in mine heart, I may safe depart out of the danger of the most cruel Pharaoh, the devil.

The second lecture.

"So was it that, when Jesus had ended all these sermons, He said unto His disciples: 'You know that after two days the pascha shall be, and the Son of Man shall be delivered[10] to be crucified.'"

In these words we may, good Christian people, well perceive the goodness and the prescience of our holy Savior Christ—His prescience in that He foreknew the time of His parting by death

5. clothing.   6. *for letting:* as a precaution against hindering.
7. shoes.   8. *for filing of:* as a precaution against defiling.
9. power.   10. handed over (to destruction).

out of this world unto His Father in heaven. And how could He
but foreknow it, sith He was not only man but God also, that
foreknoweth all thing and not His own passion only, whereof He
gave His disciples warning in this wise: "Two days hereafter not
only shall the paschal feast be, which thing you know well, but
also, which thing you think not on, the Son of Man shall be delivered to be crucified." Christ was by mo than one delivered to
be crucified. His Father delivered Him for pity upon mankind.
Judas delivered Him for covetise, the priests and the scribes for
envy, the people for ignorance and folly. The devil delivered
Him for fear, lest he might leese mankind by His doctrine, and
then lost he mankind after indeed more fully by His death than
before by His doctrine.

His high provident goodness appeareth well in these words: *Et
factum est cum consummasset Jesus sermones hos omnes, dixit discipulis
suis.*[11] (When Jesus had ended all these sermons, then He gave
His disciples warning of His death coming so near at hand.)
What sermons these were appeareth well in the context of the
gospels before, that is to wit, His doctrine (that He taught them
as well in the temple as elsewhere) and the revelations of the
things to come (as of the destruction of Jerusalem and the day of
doom), which things of doctrine and revelations He had
preached unto them sundry days before that time. For sith the
cause of His coming into the earth was to bring man into
heaven, and sith He had also His life and His death in His own
hand so that no man could, before Himself would, force or compel Him to die, He would not take the time for His death till He
had first finished and ended those words and those things of
heavenly doctrine that He had determined to do; and that done,
as the thing finished that He had to do first, then sped He Him
apace toward His death.

And here is it good to consider that, as our Savior wist when
He should die (because He should not nor could not till He
would) and yet did nevertheless diligence in those things that He

11. Matt. 26 : 1.

had to do before His death (albeit He might have deferred His death unto what time Him list[1] and have done in the meantime everything at ease and leisure), how much need have we—poor wretches that shall die ere we would, and cannot tell the time when, but peradventure this present day—what need have we, I say, to make haste about those things that we must needs do, so that we may have nothing left undone when we be suddenly sent for and must needs go. For when death cometh, the dreadful, mighty messenger of God, there can no king command him, there can none authority strain[2] him, there can no riches hire him to tarry past his appointed time one moment of an hour. Therefore let us consider well in time what words we be bounden to speak and what deeds we be bounden to do, and say them and do them apace, and leave unsaid and undone all superfluous things (and much more all damnable things), witting[3] well that we have no void[4] time allowed us thereunto.

For as our Lord saith, "the day of our Lord shall steal on us like a thief,"[5] and "we wot not when He will come, whether in the morning, or in the midday, or in the evening, or at the midnight."[6] And therefore have we need, as our Savior saith, "to watch well that the thief break not in at the walls upon us, ere we be ware,[7] when we be asleep in deadly sin."[8] For then he robbeth us of all together[9] and maketh us poor miserable wretches forever. Let us then evermore make ourself so ready for death, nothing left undone, that where our Savior said, after all His sermons ended, that after two days He should be delivered to be crucified, we may by help of His grace say to ourself and our friends every day, I have done all my business[10] that I am come into this world for. For I shall, I wot ne'er how soon, but peradventure this day, be delivered by God unto the cross of painful death. From which if I die nought,[1] I depart from death to the

---

1. *Him list:* He chose.   2. control.   3. knowing.   4. idle.
5. 1 Thess. 5 : 2. See also 2 Pet. 3 : 10 and Rev. 3 : 3.
6. Mark 13 : 35–36.   7. aware.
8. This passage perhaps alludes to Matt. 24 : 43 and Luke 12 : 39.
9. *all together:* everything.   10. duty.   1. wicked.

devil, as did the blasphemous thief that heng on his cross beside
Christ. And if I die well, as I trust in God to do, I may with His
mercy straight depart into paradise, as did the penitent thief
that heng on His other side. And God give us all the grace so to
do all our business in time that we spend not our time in vanities, or worse than vanities, while we be in health, and drive off[2]
the things of substance that we should do till we lie in our death
bed, where we shall have so many things to do at once, and everything so unready, that every finger shall be a thumb and we
shall fumble it up[3] in haste so unhandsomely[4] that we may hap,[5]
but if[6] God help the better, to leave more than half undone.

A prayer.

Good Lord, give me the grace so to spend my life that when
the day of my death shall come, though I feel pain in my body, I
may feel comfort in soul and, with faithful hope of Thy mercy,
in due love toward Thee and charity toward the world, I may
through Thy grace part hence into Thy glory.

The third lecture.

"Then gathered there together the princes of the priests and
the ancients[7] into the palace of the prince of the priests, which is
called Caiphas, and took counsel together. And they sought the
ways, both the chief priests and the scribes, how they might with
some wile take Him and put Him to death. For they were afeard
of the people. They said therefore: 'Not on the holy day, lest
there arise some seditious ruffle[8] among the people.' "

Upon these words, good Christian reader, riseth there occasion to speak of another point that I touched also before, that
is to wit, the other cause of Christ's death, rising upon the malice of the Jews. For in these words is touched (as you see) their
malicious assembly in devising and compassing[9] His death.

2. *drive off:* put off.   3. *fumble it up:* do it clumsily.
4. unskillfully.   5. chance.   6. *but if:* unless.   7. elders.
8. tumult.   9. contriving.

Howbeit, before this council assembled here (which was the day before His maundy, that is to wit, the Wednesday before His passion, and the morrow after the afore-remembered[1] warning of His passion given unto His disciples), there was another council gathered together among them for the selfsame purpose, whereof mention is made in the eleventh chapter of Saint John. For whereas our Savior Christ had oftentimes reproved the priests, the scribes, and the pharisees for their pride and their hypocrisy, their avarice and their evil constitutions[2] (made unto the commodity of themself in derogation of the law and commandment of God), with which monitions[3] their part had been to have amended their manners[4] and to have given Him thank for His good doctrine, they on the tother side took so far the contrary way that for His goodness they so maliciously hated Him that, albeit they perceived well by the prophecies fulfilled in His birth and His living and His doctrine—with the manifold marvelous miracles which He continually wrought—that He was Christ, yet so mighty was (I say) their malice that they labored to destroy Him. But specially after that He had raised Lazar from death to life, the thing so well and openly known, and the wonder so far spread and so much in every man's mouth, and the man well known once for four days dead and buried, and so many men seeing him alive again, and eating and drinking and talking with him (for which the people fell so thick unto Christ that the priests, the scribes, and the pharisees were afeard to leese their authority), they waxed so wood[5] therewith, that they thereupon devised both to have slain Lazar and also to destroy Christ. For without His death they thought it in vain to slay Lazar, sith He that raised him once was able to raise him again.

But because they never read of any man in the scripture before that ever after his death raised again himself (for of raising other they had read), therefore, if they slew Christ too, they

1. mentioned before.   2. decrees.   3. instructions.
4. moral conduct.   5. furious.

thought they should make all the matter safe. Whereupon as
Saint John in the eleventh chapter of his gospel remembereth:[6]
"The bishops and the pharisees gathered together a council and
said: 'What do we? This man doth many miracles, and if we
leave Him thus, all shall believe in Him, and then shall the
Romans come and destroy both our town and our people.' "[7]
Thus the wily wretches, lo, the mischievous deed that they went
about[8] for the maintenance of their own worldly winning[9] and
in revenging of their own private malice, that would they color
under the pretext of a great zeal unto the commonwealth of all
the people. And in this saying, they very well wist that they lied.
For the Romans nothing rought[1] what or on whom the Jews
believed, whose true belief in one God they counted for superstition. And for nothing cared they among the Jews but that the
emperor of Rome should be their chief temporal governor and
have them his tributaries, and that they should have no king but
under him and at his assignment. Now that Christ went about no
temporal authority, nor would take upon Him as king[2] (albeit
indeed He was king), was well enough known unto them by that
He not only fled fro being king when the people would have
made Him king, but also refused to be so much as a judge or an
arbitror in a temporal matter concerning the dividing of a
private inheritance between two brethren, saying to the tone,
"Who hath appointed me judge or divider between you?"[3]

But yet for all this one of that council, called Caiphas (which
was bishop for that year), well allowed[4] their false lying motion
and was angry that it went not farther straight unto Christ's
death; and therefore himself sharply, by the authority of his office, reproved them and said unto them: "You know nothing"—
as though he would say: "You be fools, you consider not that it is
expedient for you that one man die for the people, and not all
the people to perish." These words, as the evangelist saith, he
spake not of himself, but like as[5] though he were an evil bishop,

6. mentions.   7. John 11 : 47–48.   8. *went about:* undertook.
9. gain.   1. *nothing rought:* cared not at all.
2. *take . . . king:* undertake the office of king.
3. Luke 12 : 13–14.   4. sanctioned.   5. *like as:* just as.

yet he was a bishop, so, though he meant but to further his malicious purpose, yet God so framed his words that unware[6] to himself they should be a very true profitable prophecy, signifying that that one man, our Savior Christ, should die for all the people, and not only for that people, but also, as Saint John farther saith, to gather together in one the children of God that were dispersed abroad. And from that day dided they purpose to kill our Savior Christ.[7] For which, for a while, our Savior forbare to walk abroad among the Jews, withdrawing Himself into the city of Ephraim, with His disciples, near unto the desert, because the bishops and the pharisees had given a commandment that if any man might wit[8] where He were, he should show them that they might make Him be taken.

But yet for to declare that this withdrawing of Christ was to give His disciples ensample, according to His own commandment[9] to fly from persecution when they conveniently can—lest in temerarious and foolhardy offering themself thereto their bold pride might turn into cowardice and take a foul shameful fall—that their instruction was (I say) the cause of His withdrawing, and not any fear of Himself, He declared well on Palm Sunday after, when He letted not openly to ride into the city, with His disciples about Him, where, without dread of His enemies, all the people received Him with procession and reverence, where all the people cried out as He went: *Hosanna filio David, benedictus qui venit in nomine Domini: Hosanna in altissimis.*[1] (Hosanna to the son of David, blessed is He that is come in the name of our Lord: Hosanna in the high places.) *Hosanna* in Hebrew signifieth "I beseech Thee save me."

But when the bishops, the priests, and the scribes, and the pharisees heard and saw this, and that the people came so many with Him, and among them so many of those that had seen Lazar both quick[2] and dead and four days buried too, and after yet now alive again, they thought again upon the killing of Lazar and our Savior too. And because they durst[3] at that

6. unaware.   7. For the whole episode, see John 11 : 49–53.
8. know.   9. Matt. 10 : 23.   1. Matt. 21 : 9.   2. living.
3. dared.

time not meddle with Him for fear of the people, some of the pharisees would have had Him cease[4] that voice of the people Himself, and said unto Him, "Master, make Thy disciples here hold their peace,"[5] as though that cry were but the cry of His disciples and not the common voice of the people. But our Savior soon answered them far of another fashion and said unto them, "Though these would hold their peace, the very stones shall cry it out."[6] And this word proved true upon the Good Friday following. For when the bishops, the priests, the scribes, and the pharisees had made the people leave off crying out of Christ's praise, and also turned them to the crying out against Him to have Him crucified, then, after all their cruelty spent out upon His death, the very stones in their manner cried Him out for Christ when, as the gospel saith: *Velum templi scissum est a summo usque deorsum, et petrae scissae sunt, et monumenta aperta sunt, etc.*[7] (And the veil of the temple rived from the height down unto the ground, and the stones brake, and the graves opened, and after that out of them rose many holy men's bodies.) But, as I began to tell you, when Christ came riding into Jerusalem so royally upon Palm Sunday, His enemies said unto themself: "You see we prevail nothing. Lo, all the world is fallen to Him."[8] And upon this arose this new council taken upon the Wednesday after (whereof our present lecture speaketh), in which there were gathered together against Christ the princes of the priests and the ancients of the people into the palace of Caiphas, that was (as you have heard) bishop for that year, to devise and study the means to take and destroy our Savior.

Where the gospel saith "the princes of the priests" ye shall understand that it was ordained in the law that there should be but one prince of the priests—bishop, or chief priest—and he to continue his office during his life. But afterward, by ambition of the priests, usurpation and covetise of the kings, the right order of the making or choosing of the bishop was changed, and they

4. still.   5. Luke 19 : 39.   6. Luke 19 : 40.
7. Matt. 27 : 51–52.   8. John 12 : 19.

were put in and put out by the kings, sometime for pleasure, sometime for displeasure, and sometime for money too, so that instead of one, now were they waxen[9] many. The ancients of the people were seventy, which, by Moyses at the special commandment of God, were (as it appeareth in the eleventh chapter of Numeri) institute[1] and ordained to be judges over the people, and, in great causes wherein their sentences varied, to refer the matter unto the chief priest and stand to his determination in the matter.[2] This number was still continued in Jerusalem and these were their ordinary judges upon the people; and these were those whom he calleth here the ancients of the people.

Here was, as you see now, a solemn great assembly, but then consider whereabout: about nothing else but to seek the ways and the means how they might by some wile take and put an innocent unto death. So may we see that every great council is not alway a good council, but as two or three be a good council that come together in God's name to commune[3] and counsel about good, and among them is God (witnessing our Savior[4] where He saith, "Wheresoever are two or three gathered together in my name, there am I too myself in the mids of them"[5]), so when men assemble them together to devise and counsel about mischief and wretchedness, the mo that are at it the worse is the council and the less to be regarded, be their personages in the sight of the world never so seemly[6] and their authority never so great—as these that here assemble about the death of Christ were the chief heads and rulers of the people, and specially the chief of the spiritualty,[7] so that those to whom it specially belonged to provide for an innocent's surety, they were these, lo, that specially gathered together to compass[8] an innocent's death. Out of such council God keep every good man. For that holy king and prophet, David, speaking of blessedness, putteth in the beginning of all his psalter for a principal blessedness: *Beatus vir*

9. become.   1. established.   2. Num. 11 : 16–17.
3. speak.   4. *witnessing . . . Savior:* as our Savior testifies.
5. Matt. 18 : 20.   6. stately.   7. clergy.   8. contrive.

qui non abiit in consilium impiorum[9] (Blessed is that man that hath not gone into the council of wicked men), that is to wit, that unto their wicked council hath not been partner nor given his assent. For likewise as God is in the mids of the good council, so in the midst of an evil council is there undoubtedly the devil.

But why went they about[10] so busily[1] to take Him by some wily train rather than boldly by force? The gospel showeth the cause: "For they were afeard of the people." His living was so holy, His doctrine was so heavenly, His miracles were so many and so marvelous, that, though the priests, the scribes, and the pharisees that bare the rule[2] deeply desired His death for their malicious anger and envy, yet the people of their own minds so highly did esteem Him that, if He had been taken in their company, they would not have failed to fight for Him. And therefore agreed this great assembly that they would not take Him on the holy day, *ne forte tumultus fiat in populo*[3] (lest there should arise some seditious business[4] among the people). The people they feared, but God they feared not at all. And as the prophet saith: *Illic trepidaverunt timore, ubi non fuit timor*[5] (There trembled they for dread, where the dread was not). For as for the people, they mought[6] percase[7] by policy have founden[8] the mean to master, but God might they never master. The wavering people they found the mean on the morrow so to turn against Christ, that as fast[9] as they honored Him and lauded Him within five days before, and not long afore[10] that would fain[1] have made Him king, as fast on the morrow they mocked Him and cried out to have Him crucified. But God, when all this great council had done their uttermost, the Godhead (I say) of Christ Himself (for His Father and Himself and their Holy Ghost are all three but one God) raised up His dead body again and, maugre[2] their

---

9. Ps. 1 : 1.   10. *went . . . about:* did they undertake.
1. carefully.   2. *bare the rule:* held the authority.
3. Matt. 26 : 5 and Mark 14 : 2.   4. commotion.
5. Ps. 13 : 5 (*AV*, 14 : 5).   6. might.   7. perhaps.
8. found.   9. earnestly.   10. before.   1. gladly.
2. in spite of.

men whom they set to keep His grave, He rose and went out thorough the hard stone, and after sent such a vengeance upon them all that from their misused liberty they be fallen ever since in every part of the world into perpetual thralldom.

And on this great assembled council against Christ, that thought themself so strong and their wily devices so wise that they would, with the provision of that assembled council, utterly destroy the innocent, are also well verified the words of the prophet: *Qui habitat in caelis irridebit eos, et dominus subsannabit eos.*[3] (He that dwelleth in heaven shall laugh them to scorn, and our Lord shall make them a mow.[4]) For soon after was their council dissolved, and their council house drawn down, and all the city destroyed, and He whom they killed with their council in despite of their council liveth and reigneth in heaven, while the foolish wretched wily counselors (such as die in their sin) lie weeping and wailing, the devil's burning prisoners, in the deep dungeon of hell.

The prayer.

Gracious God, give me Thy grace so to consider the punishment of that false great council that gathered together against Thee, that I be never to Thy displeasure partner, nor give mine assent to follow the sinful device of any wicked council.

The fourth lecture.

"But there entered Satanas into Judas, whose surname is Scariot, one of the twelve. Then went he to the princes of the priests and to the chief priests to betray Him to them. And he had communication with the princes of the priests and with the rulers in what manner he should betray Him to them. And he said unto them: 'What will you give me, and[5] I shall deliver Him to you?' And they, when they heard him, were well apaid[6] and promised and covenanted with him to give him money, and ap-

3. Ps. 2 : 4.   4. derisive grimace.   5. if.   6. pleased.

pointed to give him thirty groats. And he made them promise,
and fro that time forth he sought opportunity how that he might
at most commodity[7] betray Him out of presence[8] of the people."

Upon these words (good Christian people) is there given us
the occasion to speak yet of the third cause of Christ's passion,
that is to wit, upon what occasion the false traitor Judas was first
moved to fall to this heinous treason. For the perceiving
whereof, we must here repeat you one thing that was done a few
days before. As it is remembered in the twenty-sixth chapter of
Saint Matthew, and in the fourteenth of Saint Mark, and in the
twelfth of Saint John, our Savior six days before the feast of
pascha went into Bethania, where He had before raised Lazarus
fro death to life.[9] There had He supper prepared for Him, in
the house of Simon, the leper whom Christ had cured. Martha
served them, and Lazarus was one of the guests that sat at the
supper. Then came there Mary Maudlen, sister unto Lazarus
and Martha, and she took a pound-weight of ointment of nardus,[10] truly made and very dear, and therewith anointed she
Christ's feet, and wiped them with the hairs of her head. And
over that she brake the alabaster in which she brought it, and
poured all the remnant on His head. And all the house smelled
sweet of the savor of that sweet ointment.

Then Judas, which after fell to the treason and betrayed his
master, grudged[1] therewith and was wroth therewith and said:
"Wherefore was not this ointment sold for three hundred pence
and given to poor folk? It might have been sold for a great deal,
yea, more than for three hundred pence, and given to poor
folk." And thus said the thief, not for anything that he cared for
poor folk, but, as the gospel saith, because he was a thief and
bare[2] the purse, into which he would fain have had the price of
that ointment so that he might thereof, after his customable[3]
manner, have stolen out a part. Our Savior mildly answered for

7. advantage.   8. the company.
9. Matt. 26 : 6–15, Mark 14 : 3–10, and John 12 : 1–8.
10. spikenard, aromatic balsam.   1. complained.   2. held.
3. usual.

Mary Maudlen and said: "Why reprove you this woman? As for poor men you shall have ever with you, but me shall ye not ever have." And then opened He the mystery secretly wrought by God in the open work of her good affection, that where she did it to show how glad she was of His presence there, as the manner was that folk at feasts with pleasant sweet odors used to glad[4] their guests, God wrought therein, as our Savior there declared, the signification of His burying. For the manner then was in that country to anoint the dead corpse with sweet odors, as we dress the winding sheet here with sweet herbs and flowers.

And then whereas the rude, grudging words of Judas were spoken to her reproof, and in manner of her rebuke, our Savior on the tother side even there openly showed that for that deed should she forever, with the preaching of that gospel, be renomed and honored thoroughout all the world—so pleasant is to God the good affection of the heart declared by the frank[5] outward deed. For Him must we serve, though specially with the mind (which if it be not good vitiateth all together[6]), yet are we bound to serve Him also with body and goods and all, for all have we received of Him. But Judas, the covetous wretch, when he saw that this ointment was not sold so that he might steal a piece of the price, and then saw our Savior allow[7] her devotion in the deed and disallow his finding of that fault, as mildly as his Master touched him, yet could not the proud beast bear it, but beside his covetise fell unto malice too. And the devil took his time[8] and entered into his heart, and thereunto did put the suggestion of his horrible treason, and made him to devise and determine that the money which he lost by the anointing of his Master he would get it up again by the betraying of his Master. And thereupon came he to this assembly that we speak of now, and unsent-for presented himself unto them to help forward their ungracious[9] council.

And therefore, good reader, here we may well consider that

4. gladden.   5. generous.   6. *all together:* everything.
7. approve.   8. *took his time:* chose the right time.
9. wicked.

when men are in device about[1] mischief,[2] if they bring their
purpose properly[3] to pass, cause have they none to be proud
and praise their own wits. For the devil it is himself that bringeth
their matters about much more, a great deal, than they. There
was once a young man fallen in a lewd mind toward a woman,
and she was such as he could conceive none hope to get her, and
therefore was falling to a good point[4] in his own mind to let that
lewd enterprise pass. He mishapped[5] nevertheless to show his
mind to another wretch, which encouraged him to go forward
and leave it not. "For begin thou once man[6] the matter," quod
he, "and never fear it, let the devil alone with the remnant, he
shall bring it to pass in such wise as thyself alone canst not
devise how." I trow[7] that wretch had learned that counsel of
these priests and these ancients, assembled here together against
Christ at this council. For here you see that while they were at
their wits' end how to bring their purpose about in the taking of
Christ, and were at a point to defer the matter and put it over
till some other time, the devil sped them[8] by and by. For he entered into Judas' heart, and brought him to them to betray Him
forthwith out of hand.[9]

And therefore at his first coming, he went roundly[1] to the
matter and said unto them: "What will ye give me and I shall
deliver Him to you?" Here shall you see Judas play the jolly[2]
merchant, I trow. For he knoweth how fain all this great council
would be to have Him delivered. He knoweth well also that it
will be hard for any man to deliver Him but one of His own disciples. He knoweth well also that of all the disciples, there would
none be so false a traitor to betray his Master but himself alone.
And therefore is this ware, Judas, all in thine own hand. Thou
hast a monopoly thereof. And while it is so sought for and so
sore desired, and that by so many, and them that are also very
rich, thou mayest now make the price of thine own ware thyself,

---

1. *in device about:* contriving.   2. evil.   3. completely.
4. resolution.   5. had the misfortune.   6. manage.
7. believe.   8. *sped them:* made them succeed.
9. *out of hand:* at once.   1. bluntly.   2. arrogant.

even at thine own pleasure; and therefore ye shall, good readers, see Judas wax now a great rich man with this one bargain.
But now the priests and these judges were on the tother side
covetous too; and as glad as they were of this ware, yet while it
was offered them to sell,[3] they thought the merchant was needy,
and that to such a needy merchant a little money would be welcome, and money they offered him, but not much. For thirty
groats they said they will give, which amounteth not much above
ten shillings of our English money. Now would we look that the
fool would have set up[4] his ware, namely being such ware as it
was, so precious in itself that all the money and plate in the
whole world were too little to give for it. But now what did the
fool? To show himself a substantial merchant and not an huck-
ster, he gently[5] let them have it even at their own price.

I wot it well that, of the valure[6] of the money that Judas had,
all folk are not of one mind, but whereas the text saith *triginta
argenteos*,[7] some men call *argenteus* a coin of one valure and some
of another. And some put a difference between *argenteus* and
denariús, and say that *denarius* is but the tenth part of *argenteus*.
But I suppose that *argenteus* was the same silver coin which the
Romans at that time used stamped in silver, in which they expressed the image of the emperor's visage and the superscrip-
tion of the emperor's name, and was in Greek called *drachma*,
being in weight about the eighth part of an ounce. For of such
coin there are yet many remaining both of Augustus' days and
Tiberius' and of Nero's too. So that if the coin were that (for
greater silver coin I nowhere find that the emperor coined at
that time), then was Judas' reward the valure of ten shillings of
our English money, after the old usual groats used in the time of
King Edward the third, and long before and long after.

The ointment was of nardus[8] of the true making, as the gospel declareth in this word, *nardi pistici*.[9] And that ointment truly
made was very costly, which was the cause that the true making

3. for sale.   4. *set up:* raised the price of.   5. generously.
6. value.   7. Matt. 26 : 15.   8. spikenard, aromatic balsam.
9. John 12 : 3.

was less used, and folk for the great cost thereof used another
making thereof that was called counterfeit ointment of nardus.
But this was of the true making, and was (as the gospel saith)
precious, and that so farforth[10] that Judas valued it at three
hundred deniers, which I take for three hundred pieces of the
selfsame coin that was called *argenteus*. For if it were but a coin
(as some take it) that were worth but the tenth part of that, then
had all the ointment not been much above the valure of four
groats, which had been no such thing as had been likely that the
evangelists would have called precious. And therefore I reckon
that ointment to have been esteemed by Judas at an hundred
shillings. And now was his reward ten shillings, which is the
tenth part of that hundred shillings, as thirty groats is the tenth
part of three hundred. And thus hath he by the betraying of his
Master's body the tenth part of the valure of that ointment
whereof he lost his advantage by the anointing of his Master's
body.

Now if it be, as some doctors reckon, that he minded to win as
much by his treason as he reckoned for his own part lost in that
ointment, then seemeth it after this count and reckoning that, of
such as came in his keeping, he was after his customable[1] manner wont to steal the tenth. And then was Judas a figure of two
false shrews[2] at once: the tone the parishen[3] that stealeth his
tithe from his curate, to whom his duty were to pay it in God's
stead; the tother yet the worse thief of them both, the evil curate
himself, which, when he receiveth it, misspendeth upon himself
such substance thereof as above his own necessary finding[4] God
putteth him in trust to bestow upon the poor needy people.

It is a world[5] also to mark and consider how the false wily
devil hath, in everything that he doth for his servants, ever more
one point of his envious property,[6] that is to wit, to provide (his
own purpose obtained) that they shall have of his service for

10. *so farforth:* to such an extent.   1. usual.   2. rascals.
3. parishioner.   4. support.   5. *It . . . world:* It is a marvel.
6. *envious property:* attribute of envy.

their own part as little commodity as he can, even here in this world. For like as[7] he gat here unto[8] Judas no more advantage of his heinous treason (the occasion of his final destruction) but only this poor ten shillings—whereas if his Master Christ had lived, and he still carried his purse, there is no doubt but that he should at sundry times have stolen out for his part far above five times that—so fareth he[9] with all his other servants.

Look for whom he doth most in any kind of filthy fleshly delight, or false wily winning,[1] or wretched wordly worship; let him that attaineth it in his unhappy service make his reckoning in the end of all that feast and count well what is come in and what he hath paid therefore—that is to wit, lay all his pleasures and his displeasures together—and I dare say he shall find in the end that he had been a great winner if he never had had any of them both, so much grief shall he find himself to have felt, far above all his pleasure, even in those days in which his fantasies were in their flowers and prospered, beside[2] the pain and heaviness of heart that now in the end grudgeth[3] and grieveth his conscience, when the time of his pleasure is passed and the fear of hell followeth at hand.

Let us therefore leave the devil's false, deceitful service and take nothing at his hand. For he nothing giveth but trifles, nor never giveth half an inch of pleasure without an whole ell[4] of pain. And yet had Judas not the wit to disdain their simple niggardous[5] reward, but continued for it in his treason still, till he had wretchedly done it. And from that time of that reward promised him, with which yet (as it seemeth) they would not trust him till they had the ware in their own hand, he studied and sought the time in which he might peaceably deliver our Lord, when the people were out of the way.

In this, as the great clerk[6] Origen declareth, this Judas was a

7. *like as:* just as.   8. *gat . . . unto:* obtained here for.
9. *fareth he:* he behaves.   1. gain.   2. besides.   3. troubles.
4. unit of length, roughly equivalent to a yard.   5. niggardly.
6. scholar.

figure also of many other Judas.[7] For in many places when the
people be out of the way and gone aside from the faith, then
shall there some false wretch that hath been with Christ many a
fair day, and hath been His disciple, and among other true disciples hath faithfully preached the truth, come forth in the devil's name among the people and, for wretched worldly winning
to be gotten by their favor, shall falsely betray the truth and
cause to be spitefully killed the faithful true doctrine of Christ.
But woe may that wretch be by whom the truth is betrayed.

A prayer.

O my sweet Savior Christ, whom Thine own wicked disciple,
entangled with the devil, through vile wretched covetise betrayed, inspire, I beseech Thee, the marvel of Thy majesty with
the love of Thy goodness so deep into mine heart that, in respect of the least point of Thy pleasure, my mind may set alway
this whole wretched world at nought.

The fifth lecture.

"Before the feast of the pascha, Jesus, knowing that His hour
came on to go out of this world unto His Father, whereas He
had loved those that were His, unto the end He loved them."

In these words the holy evangelist Saint John, whom Christ so
tenderly loved that on His breast he leaned in His last supper,
and to him secretly He uttered[8] the false dissimuled[9] traitor,
and into whose custody He commended on the cross His own
dear, heavy[1] mother, and which is (for the manifold tokens of
Christ's special favor) specially called in the gospel, *discipulus ille
quem diligebat Jesus*[2] (the disciple that Jesus loved), declareth here
what a manner of faithful lover our holy Savior was, of whom

7. Origen presents the typological significance of Judas in his commentary on Matt. 26 : 14–16 (*Patrologiae cursus completus: series graeca*, ed. J. P.
Migne, 161 vols. [Paris, 1857–66], *13*, 1726–27).
8. revealed.   9. dissembling.   1. sorrowful.
2. John 19 : 26. See also John 13 : 23.

himself was so beloved. For unto those words he putteth and forthwith joineth the rehearsing of His bitter passion, beginning with His maundy, and therein His humble washing of His disciples' feet, the sending forth of the traitor, and after that His doctrine, His prayer, His taking, His judging, His scourging, His crucifying, and all the whole piteous tragedy of His most bitter passion. Before all which things he setteth these fore-rehearsed[3] words to declare that all these things that Christ did, in all this He did it for very love. Which love He well declared unto His disciples by many manner means at the time of His maundy, giving them in charge[4] that in loving each other they should follow the example of Himself. For He, those that He loved, He loved unto the end, and so would He that they should. He was not an unconstant lover that doth, as many do, love for a while and then upon a light occasion[5] leave off and turn from a friend to an enemy, as the false traitor Judas did. But He still so persevereth in love unto the very end, that for very love He came to that painful end; and yet not only for His friends that were already His, but for His enemies, to make them friends of His, and that not for His benefit but only for their own.

And here shall we note that, whereas the gospel saith in this place and divers other that Christ should go out of this world unto His Father (as where He said, "Poor men shall ye alway have, but me shall you not alway have"[6]), it is not meant that He shall be no more with His church here in the world nor come no more here till the day of doom. For Himself promised and said, "I am with you all the days even unto the end of the world."[7] He is here in His Godhead, He is here in the blessed sacrament of the altar, and sundry times hath here, since His ascension, appeared unto divers holy men. But those other words, as Saint Hierome saith (and Saint Beda too), are understanden[8] that He will not be here in corporal conversation[9] among us, as He was

3. already mentioned.   4. *in charge:* as a commandment.
5. *upon . . . occasion:* for a trivial reason.
6. John 12 : 8. See also Mark 14 : 7.   7. Matt. 28 : 20.
8. interpreted.   9. *corporal conversation:* bodily presence.

before His passion among His disciples, with whom He commonly did eat and drink and talk.[1]

Let us here deep consider the love of our Savior Christ, which so loved His unto the end, that for their sakes He willingly suffered that painful end, and therein declared the highest point of love that can be. For as Himself saith: *Majorem amorem nemo habet, quam ut animam suam ponat quis pro amicis suis.*[2] (A greater love no man hath than to give his life for his friends.) This is indeed the greatest love that ever any other man had. But yet had our Savior a greater. For He gave His, and I said before, both for friend and foe.

But what a difference is there now between this faithful love of His and other kinds of false and fickle love used in this wretched world. The flatterer feigneth to love thee, for that he fareth well with thee. But now if adversity so minish[3] thy substance[4] that he find thy table unlaid, farewell, adieu, thy brother flatterer is gone, and getteth him to some other board,[5] and yet shall turn sometime to thine enemy too and wait[6] thee with a shrewd[7] word.

Who can in adversity be sure of many of his friends when our Savior Himself was at His taking left alone and forsaken of His? When thou shalt go hence, who will go with thee? If thou were a king, will not all thy realm send thee forth alone and forget thee? Shall not thine own flesh let thee walk away, naked, silly soul, thou little wotest whither? Howbeit if thou die in the devil's danger, some fleshly lover of thine may soon after hap to follow thee, some such as in lecherous love hath borne thee filthy company. But if such a lover of thine happen there to come to thee, there will there be no love touches between you, but cursing and banning[8] shall you lie together wretchedly burning forever, where each of you shall be an hot faggot of fire to your filthy fellow.

1. The interpretations of Saint Jerome and Saint Bede can be found in the *Glossa ordinaria,* one of the biblical glosses available in the glossed Bibles of More's period.

2. John 15 : 13.   3. reduce.   4. wealth.   5. table.
6. lie in wait for.   7. abusive.   8. damning.

Let us every man, therefore, in time learn to love, as we should, God above all thing and all other thing for Him. And whatsoever love be not referred to that end, that is to wit, to the pleasure of God it is a very vain and an unfruitful love. And whatsoever love we bear to any creature whereby we love God the less, that love is a loathsome love and hindereth us from heaven. Love no child of thine own so tenderly but that thou couldest be content so to sacrifice it to God as Abraham was ready with Isaac, if it so were that God would so command thee. And sith God will not so do, offer thy child otherwise to God's service. For whatsoever thing we love whereby we break God's commandment, that love we better than God—and that is a love deadly and damnable. Now, sith our Lord hath so loved us for our salvation, let us diligently call for His grace that against[9] His great love we be not found unkind.[1]

A prayer.

O my sweet Savior Christ, which, of Thine undeserved love toward mankind so kindly wouldest suffer the painful death of the cross, suffer not me to be cold nor lukewarm in love again toward Thee.

9. in return for.   1. lacking in natural gratitude.

The second chapter.

Of the sending of Saint Peter and Saint John, the first day of the unleavened loaves, specified in the twenty-sixth of Saint Matthew, the fourteenth of Saint Mark, the twenty-second of Saint Luke, and the thirteenth of Saint John.[2]

"The first day of the unleavened loaves, when the paschal lamb was offered, in which the paschal lamb must needs be killed, there came the disciples to Jesus and say to Him: 'Whither wilt Thou that we go and make ready for Thee, that Thou mayest eat the paschal lamb?' And He sendeth of His disciples Peter and John, saying, 'Go you and make ready for us the paschal lamb that we may eat it.' But they said: 'Where wilt Thou that we shall make it ready?' And He said unto them: 'Go you into the city to a certain man. Lo, as you shall be entering into the city, there shall meet you a man bearing a pot of water. Follow you him into the house into which he entereth. And ye shall say to the goodman[3] of the house: "The Master saith to thee, 'My time is near, with thee I make my paschal.[4] Where is my refection,[5] where is my place where I may eat my paschal with my disciples?' " And he shall show you a great supping place paved,[6] and there make you it ready.' And His disciples went and came into the city. And, as they went, they found as Jesus had said unto them. And they made ready the paschal lamb. When the

2. See p. 54, n. 4.   3. master.   4. Passover.
5. place of refreshment.
6. More appears to mean "prepared" (*stratum* in the Vulgate, Mark 14 : 15 and Luke 22 : 12), although this meaning of "paved" is not recorded in the *OED*.

evening was come, He came with the twelve. And when the hour was come, He set down at the table, and the twelve apostles with Him."

The homily or lecture upon the second chapter.

I have before, good Christian readers, showed you in the exposition of the first chapter the ordinance[7] and institution of the feast of the paschal lamb and of the feast of the unleavened bread, and how the offering of that lamb was a figure of the offering up of Christ, the very unspotted lamb, that should be offered up to cleanse and wash away the spots of our sin with the innocent blood of Himself that had no spot of sin of His own. The paschal lamb was commanded to be sacrificed and eaten after the equinoctial[8] in vere,[9] the fourteenth day of the month. And on the morrow, and so forth seven days after (that is to wit, beginning the fifteenth day), was the feast of the unleavened bread, during which space they were commanded that they should have no leaven in their house.

Ye must understand also that though the first day of the feast of the unleavened loaves was the fifteenth day, yet likewise as we begin every feast from the noon before, so did the Jews begin that first day of the feast of the unleavened loaves in the evening before, when they might see the moon and the stars appear in the element.[1] And so, though the eating of the paschal lamb was the fourteenth day of the month, and the first day of the feast of the unleavened loaves was on the fifteenth day, yet by reason that the same first day of the feast began at the evening before (that is to wit, in the evening of the fourteenth day, in which evening the paschal lamb was to be sacrificed and eaten), these two feasts were, as you see, coincident together. For the tone fell in the beginning of the other. And for this cause were each of them called by the both names, that is to wit, by the name of "the feast of the paschal" and also by the name of "the feast of the unleavened bread." For sith the feast of the paschal lamb was

7. ordained usage.   8. equinox.   9. springtime.   1. sky.

the chief feast and was also the beginning of the tother, all the feast of the unleavened loaves was called "the paschal." And again because the first day of the feast of the unleavened loaves, though it were the fifteenth day of the month, yet, sith it began (I say) in the evening of the fourteenth day (at such time as the paschal lamb was sacrificed and eaten), the feast of the paschal lamb was also called "the feast of the unleavened bread" and "the first day of the feast of the unleavened bread."

And for this cause do both Saint Matthew and Saint Mark call the Sheer Thursday[2] in which Christ made His maundy the first day of the unleavened loaves, saying: "The first day of the unleavened loaves, in which the paschal lamb must be killed and sacrificed, the disciples came to Jesus and asked Him: 'Whither wilt Thou that we shall go to make ready the paschal lamb?' "[3] And, as I said, the Jews called also the feast of the unleavened bread "the feast of paschal." And specially they called and hallowed by that name of "paschal" the first day of the unleavened bread, which was the morrow after the eating of the paschal lamb.

And after that manner of their naming that day "the feast of paschal," Saint John in the thirteenth chapter of his gospel: *Ante diem festum Paschae, sciens Jesus quia venit hora ejus ut transeat ex hoc mundo ad patrem, etc.*[4] (Before the holy day of paschal, Jesus, knowing that His time was come that He should go out of this world unto His Father, and so forth.) Here, lo, Saint John calleth Sheer Thursday, in the evening of which day the paschal lamb was eaten, he calleth it (I say) by the name of "the day before that feastful[5] day of the paschal," because the Jews did celebrate the morrow (after the paschal eaten[6]) very solemnly, and called (as I have told you) that feast the feast of the paschal. And therefore Saint John here saying *Ante diem festum Paschae,* and calling Sheer Thursday "the day before the feastful day of paschal" (because

2. Maundy Thursday.
3. The quotation is an adaptation of Gerson's *Monotessaron,* composed of passages from Luke as well as Matthew and Mark.
4. John 13 : 1.   5. festal.   6. *i.e.,* was eaten.

the Jews so used to call the first day of the unleavened bread that began in the evening before, in which the paschal lamb was killed), used such a manner of speaking as we might call "Christmas Even" the day before the feastful day of Christmas.

I would not, good readers, stick so long upon the declaration of this point (as a thing wherein some shall peradventure take little savor[7]), saving that I thought it not a time all lost to let you know that, upon[8] the scripture in this point mistaken,[9] the church of Greece fell fro the church of the Latins in a point or twain. For, upon their own wrong construing this place of Saint John, they say that Christ did anticipate the time of eating His paschal lamb with His apostles, and (where the very day was the fourteenth day after their vernal equinoctial[10] in the evening) He did it (say they) the day before.[1]

And you shall understand that this is the cause for which they consecrate the body of Christ in leavened bread, contrary to the Latin church, which consecrateth in unleavened bread. For they say (and truth it is) that the feast of the unleavened loaves began the fifteenth day. And then (say they) He consecrated His blessed body at His maundy on the thirteenth day (that was, say they, Sheer Thursday), and therefore He consecrated then with leavened bread. Now to this we have showed you that the first day of that feast of unleavened bread began the feast in the evening before, that is to wit, on Sheer Thursday at night, and that Christ made then His maundy in the very time that was by the law appointed to the eating the paschal lamb. And sith He intended to fulfill the law, so was it most convenient that He should and most likely that He would—and so of truth He did, as the three evangelists, Saint Matthew, Saint Mark, and Saint Luke, plainly do declare. For they three agree together that it

7. enjoyment.   8. on the basis of.   9. wrongly understood.
10. equinox.
1. A passage concerned with the dating of the last supper—added here to the text by Rastell in *1557* on the basis of a letter written by More to his secretary, John Harris—has been omitted in this edition. See *CW 13,* 88/22–90/14, 91/14–22, and notes.

was in the first day of the unleavened bread and in which day
the paschal lamb must be killed. And so it appeareth by them
that, though the first day of that feast was the fifteenth day, yet
the feast of that fifteenth day began in the evening before in
which the paschal lamb was eaten, and eaten (as it appeareth
plainly) with unleavened bread.

And verily me thinketh[2] that if it so had been (as it was not)
that Christ had made His maundy a day before the time, yet
would not that sufficiently serve for the proof of their purpose[3]
that He consecrated in leavened bread. For though it be a good
proof that, sith He consecrated in the feast of the unleavened
loaves, He consecrated not in leavened bread (because the law
forbode them to have any leaven in the house), yet if He had
consecrated five days before that feast began, it would not prove
that He consecrated in leavened bread. For they might then and
at all times have unleavened bread, sith that was at no time forboden.

But surely the church of Greece was far overseen[4] in this
point and divers other, in which they partly knowledged[5] their
errors after and were reformed in general councils,[6] and yet returned of frowardness to their errors again, and in conclusion
we see whereto they be comen.[7]

But ye shall understand that, when I speak of the church of
Greece in this error, I speak but of the posteriors.[8] For the old
holy doctors of the Greeks were of the contrary mind, as appeareth in this point by the plain words of Saint Eusebius and
Saint Chrysostom both.[9] And that you may the more plainly perceive what peril it was unto them to fall to an opinion contrary to

---

2. *me thinketh:* it seems to me.   3. proposition.
4. *far overseen:* imprudently mistaken.   5. confessed.
6. *general councils:* Such as the councils of Lyons (1274) and Florence
(1438).
7. *be comen:* have come.   8. those later in time.
9. More may be thinking of quotations from Eusebius and Chrysostom
in the *Catena aurea,* a collection of patristic quotations on the four gospels made by St. Thomas Aquinas.

the church by construing the scripture after a few folks' fantasies,[10] those Greeks that began this opinion were fain in conclusion for the defense of their error to say that Saint Matthew, Saint Mark, and Saint Luke wrote in that point wrong all three, and that therefore Saint John wrote otherwise and corrected them—which untrue saying of theirs is so far out of all frame[1] that it is among Christian men more than shame to say it, that any of the four Evangelists should in the story write anything false, for then which of them might we trust, sith we can be no more sure of the tone than of the tother. But now let us proceed forth in the letter.[2]

"When His disciples had asked Him where His pleasure was that they should make ready the paschal for Him, He sent two of His apostles, that is to wit Peter and John, and said unto them: 'Go you and prepare the paschal lamb for us that we may eat it.' "

Our Savior, which said of Himself, *Non veni solvere legem sed adimplere* [3] (I am not come to break the law but to fulfill it), likewise as He would be circumcised first before He changed that sacrament into the more perfit sacrament of baptism, so, for the fulfilling of the old law, before He would offer up His own blessed body, the very unspotted lamb, upon the cross, and before also that He would institute the eating of His own blessed body in form of bread and wine in the blessed sacrament of the altar, He would first fulfill the precept of the law by the eating of the paschal lamb in time and manner appointed by the law, and so fulfill and finish the figure, and institute in the stead thereof the sacrament of highest perfection, the blessed sacrament of the altar, and offer up for the spots of our sin His own unspotted body as the most sweet sacrifice unto the Father upon the altar of the cross.

It followeth: "Then they said unto Him, 'Where wilt Thou that we shall make it ready?' And He said unto them: 'Go you

10. capricious speculations.
1. *so far . . . frame:* so remote from any kind of established order.
2. text.   3. Matt. 5 : 17.

into the city to a certain man. Lo, as you be entering into the city, there shall a man meet you bearing a pot of water; follow you him into the house into which he entereth, and you shall say to the goodman [4] of the house: "The Master saith to thee, 'My time is near, with thee I make my paschal. Where is my place where I may with my disciples eat the paschal?' " And he shall show you a great supping place on high paved,[5] and there do you make it ready.' "

In these words it appeareth well that our Lord, when He sent Saint Peter and Saint John unto the house where they should prepare His maundy, He would neither name them the dweller of the house nor tell them any known token of the house, of which thing divers of the old doctors conject[6] and tell divers causes. Some say He sent them to a man not named in token that God will come not only to men that are in the world famous and of great name but also to folk of none estimation in the count of the world nor of no name. Some other say (and both twain may well be true) that forasmuch as our Savior (to whom nothing was unknown) knew the promise of the false traitor Judas made unto the Jews upon the day before to betray Him, and that he went about ever after that to seek a time fit therefore where he might betray Him to them out of sight of the people, if He should have named the man or the place, the traitor mought[7] have caused Him and His disciples to be taken before His maundy made and His holy body consecrated in the blessed sacrament. And therefore, albeit that if the traitor had come and all the whole town with him, our Savior could have kept them all off with one word of His mouth or with one thought of His holy heart, yet this way liked His high wisdom as the most meet and convenient by which He would keep the traitor from the accomplishment of his traitorous purpose till the time should come in which Himself had determined to suffer it. And therefore our Savior used[8] Himself in this point wonderfully. For al-

4. master.   5. *on . . . paved:* prepared on high.
6. conjecture.   7. might.   8. conducted.

beit that the two disciples whom He sent were of all His apostles the most special chosen and most in trust and favor with Him, Saint Peter, which (as it appeareth in scripture and as the doctors say) specially loved Him, and Saint John, which (as the scripture sayeth and the doctors thereon) specially was beloved of Him, yet would He not take them aside and tell them the name of the man, lest He might thereby have given occasion of envy or suspicion to Judas, or peradventure grief to the remnant, if Christ should have seemed to trust them with that errand secretly with which He would trust none of them. He gave them therefore their errand in so strange a fashion that neither themself nor any of the other ten could wit[9] what to think therein. For He answered them as though He would say, "Where you shall prepare I will not tell you, nor who shall bring you thither I will not show you, but to let you see what I can do when me list,[10] such a token shall I tell you to bring you thither as neither no man knoweth nor no man can know but myself that am able at the time to make it so."

Then it followeth: "And His disciples went forth and came into the city, and they found as Jesus had said unto them and prepared there the paschal."

Here had His apostles and by them we too a proof of His glorious Godhead, secretly covered and unseen under the cloak of His seeming feeble manhead. And that not in this thing alone, but in this among many mo, some of the other kind of miracle, and some also like unto this. For as He did here show His disciples where they should meet the man with the water pot and then what He would have them do further, and that His bidding should surely be fulfilled and obeyed, so did He on the Palm Sunday before, when He sent His disciples and told them where they should find the ass and the colt tied, and bode[1] them take them boldly without any leave of the owner, and, whosoever would say aught unto them therefore,[2] they should say that

9. know.   10. *me list:* it pleases me.   1. commanded.
2. because of it.

their Master must occupy[3] them. A much like manner of message He gave His two apostles now, telling them where they should meet with a strange man and so forth what they should do further.

Now who but God could surely send men on such manner messages in which they should be sure to find such things as are unto all creatures unsure and uncertain, as things accompted[4] to fall under chance and hap?[5] And therefore, while they found everything come to pass as He had before told them, they might (and we may) surely know Him for God. For who could tell that the man with his pot of water walking on his errand and the two apostles going forth on theirs, neither party looking for other, should so begin to set forth and in such wise hold on their way that they should, at a place which neither of the both parties appointed, so justly[6] meet together? This could none do but He that not only beheld both parties at once but was able also to put in both their minds to set forth in time such as should serve therefore, and to moderate and measure their paces Himself in such wise as themself wist not why, and by His sure providence (seeming to themself hap, fortune, or chance) suddenly to meet together. This thing can there of himself none other do but He that hath the acts and the deeds of all creatures in His own hand, that of two sparrows being both not worth an halfpenny, not so much as the tone falleth, as our Savior saith, upon the ground without Him.[7]

Then it followeth further: "When the evening was come, Christ came with His twelve. And when the hour was come, He sat Him down at the table and His twelve apostles with Him."

Notwithstanding that the bishops and the pharisees had before given commandment (as appeareth in the eleventh chapter of the gospel of Saint John) that if any man wist where Christ were, he should give them knowledge that they might take Him,[8] and notwithstanding also that His own disciple Judas had

3. make use of.   4. considered.   5. fortune.   6. exactly.
7. Matt. 10 : 29.   8. John 11 : 56.

promised them to do that traitorous deed himself, yet our Savior, sith His time came on in which He was determined willingly to die, letted not to come into the city and came also not alone but with His twelve apostles waiting upon Him, whereby His coming was well likely to be noted. But He wist well enough what would befall, and that upon any marking of that coming He should not be taken. For He would not so be taken, nor would not so prevent[9] His traitor of his purpose, nor so disturb him of his promise, nor so make him leese his reward, but, benignly suffering him and taking patience with him, and yet offering him grace and kindness to win him, brought him to the maundy with Him. And therefore saith Saint Mark, "He came and His twelve with Him."[10] Whereby it should seem that Saint Peter and Saint John, after their errand done, resorted unto Christ again and made Him report of their speed,[1] and so came in company with the tother ten unto the maundy with Him.

Judas the traitor, in such places as the evangelists make mention of his going to the council and assembly of the priests to offer them his service in the treason, both[2] Saint Matthew, Saint Mark, and Saint Luke make specially mention that he was one of the twelve.[3] And here we see therefore by the evangelists not only mention that he came with our Lord but also that he sat at the supper with our Lord, and so for all the treason that the traitor wrought, yet was the traitor Christ's apostle still. And this point the evangelists again and again rehearse, not only to the shame of his traitorous falsehead,[4] in betraying such a Master with whom he was so taken forth[5] to be so near about Him, one of that few chosen number and so specially put in trust, but also that we should note well and mark thereby that the vice of a vicious person vitiateth not the company or congregation. For Christ with His twelve apostles were an holy company as a company, though one companion of the company was a very false, traitorous wretch. And for all his falsehead, both before that in

9. frustrate by acting before.   10. Mark 14 : 17.   1. success.
2. *i.e.,* all three.   3. Matt 26 : 14, Mark 14 : 10, Luke 22 : 3.
4. falsehood.   5. *taken forth:* advanced.

theft and then in treason too, Christ abode still with him among His other apostles, and his ungraciousness[6] letted[7] not but that of that company (as evil as he was) yet one he was. Nor now likewise the vices of vicious folk in Christ's church cannot let but that His Catholic Church, of which they be part, is, for all their unholiness, His holy Catholic Church, with which He hath promised to be unto the end of the world.

Upon this chapter among many things that men may take occasion to note, I note specially twain: one, the ensample that our Savior here giveth us to be diligent and studious in the keeping of His new law (which He hath ordained to endure in this world as long as the world shall last), while Himself was so diligent in the observing of the old law (which, given unto Moses, Himself came to change into so far the better and to deliver us fro the sore yoke thereof). But surely I fear me sore[8] that with a great part of Christian people the law of Christ is worse kept a great deal than was with the Jews the law of Moses at the coming of Christ, when it was kept worst. As for the sovereign points of patience and charity and contempt of the world, wherein our Savior saith in the sixth chapter of Saint Matthew that He would have His new church far pass and excel the old synagogue,[9] be so far, I fear me, let slip and forgotten that even in the very plain precepts we be more negligent than they. The Jews were in the keeping of the spirit of the law so negligent that God therefore, by the mouths of His prophets David and Isay, showed Himself to reject and set at nought[1] their outward ceremonies, sacrifices, and observances of their law, wherein He confessed them diligent, and said that with so little as they used of the tother, He had of them so much that He was full thereof fastidious[2] and weary. Not that those things misliked[3] Him, either done of their private devotion or for the fulfilling of the law, but for that they rested and satisfied their hearts in them, and both

6. wickedness.   7. prevented.
8. *I . . . sore:* I am severely afraid.   9. Matt. 6 : 2–6.
1. *set . . . nought:* have no esteem for.   2. disgusted.
3. were displeasing to.

left the better things undone and also did much evil too, trusting
that those outward works of their ceremonies and sacrifices
should recompense it, and afore God bear it out.[4] Which erroneous mind of theirs our Lord by the prophets reproved, declaring
that on their fasting days they would, while they fasted fro meat,
not fast fro sin but strive and chide and fight and sharply sue
their debtors. He bode them amend those faults and be charitable and forgive and give, and then would He better allow their
bare offering and sacrifice by word than now, with these fash-
ions used,[5] He would their sacrifice in offering up of their beasts
unto their no little cost. This tale that I tell you doth well appear
upon the forty-ninth psalm of David and upon the fifty-eighth
chapter of Isay, whose words to rehearse here were very long.

But now me think that we Christian folk wax in worse case.
For in the deeds of charity we walk, I fear me, nothing afore
them. And in those evil things we be nothing behind them. And
yet in the outward ceremonies also, I ween we be nothing
matches with them. For surely they did much more cost[6] and
used more devotion than we do. Of the cost there can no man
deny but that their offerings and their sacrifices were beside
their tithes far more chargeable[7] and costly to them than the
rites and ceremonies of Christendom are unto the Christian people. Of their diligence and devotion therein, we may well perceive, both by the places that I have spoken of (in which our
Lord rejecteth their diligence therein because of their negligence of charity and their froward,[8] malicious manners[9] beside) and also by many other places in the old law where the
commendable devotion of their costly ceremonies and sacrifices
appear. Their fastings were also very painful and precise,[1] and
ours negligent, slack and remiss, and now almost worn away.
Their sabbot days and their feasts kept they very solemn. How
slackly we keep ours in many places, and in what manner fash-

4. *bear it out:* make it supportable.
5. *with . . . used:* with the practice of these customs.
6. *did . . . cost:* expended much more money.   7. expensive.
8. perverse.   9. moral conduct.   1. strict.

ion, I cannot for sorrow and very shame rehearse. As for their faith, from those that among them held on the truth, the Jews were fallen into sects one or twain. But now if we should count and reckon the sundry sects which from the true faith are fallen about in divers parts of Almayne,[2] I fear me[3] we should find almost as many score. I can no more but pray God therefore that we may have the grace to follow the ensample of our Savior and observe His new law, which we be bounden to keep, as He observed the old law, which, though He came to change it, yet He would first fulfill it, for all that[4] He was not bound to keep it.

The tother thing that I note in this chapter is that it appeareth thereupon, as Theophilactus and Saint Bede say and Saint Chrysostom also,[5] that Christ had none house of His own, nor none of His apostles neither, as Himself said of Himself in the ninth chapter of Saint Luke: *Filius hominis non habet ubi caput suum reclinet.*[6] (The Son of Man hath not where to lay His head.) And therefore His apostles asked Him in what house He would eat His paschal. And our Savior again, to let them see that whoso for God's sake is content to lack an house shall not be disappointed when they should need it, sent them to another man's house, they neither wist whose nor where, and yet were they there welcome and well received.

In this we may take ensample also, that those that will be the disciples of Christ and followers of His apostles should not long to be great possessioners[7] and build up great palaces in this wretched wilderness of the world, wherein, to show that we have, as Saint Paul saith, "no dwelling city,"[8] our Savior and His apostles would have no dwelling house. One of the most special things to move us to the contempt of this world and to regard much the world to come is to consider that in that world we shall be forever at home and that in this world we be but wayfaring

2. Germany.   3. *I . . . me:* I am afraid.
4. *for . . . that:* even though.
5. More is perhaps alluding to passages quoted in the *Catena aurea* of St. Thomas Aquinas.
6. Luke 9 : 58.   7. owners.   8. Heb. 13 : 14.

folk. And verily though it be (as indeed it is) eath enough for any man to say the word that he is here but a pilgrim, yet is it hard for many a man to let it fall feelingly and sink down deep into his heart, which (against[9] that word slightly[10] spoken once in a year) useth to rejoice and boast many times in a day, by the space peradventure of many years together, what goodly places in this world he hath of his own, in every of which continually he calleth himself at home. And that such folk reckon themself not for pilgrims here, they feel full well at such time as our Lord calleth them hence. For then find they themself much more loath to part from this world than pilgrims to go fro their inn.

The prayer.

Almighty Jesus Christ, which wouldest for our ensample observe the law that Thou camest to change, and being maker of the whole earth, wouldest have yet no dwelling house therein, give us Thy grace so to keep Thine holy law and so to reckon ourself for no dwellers but for pilgrims upon earth, that we may long and make haste, walking with faith in the way of virtuous works, to come to the glorious country wherein Thou hast bought us inheritance forever with Thine own precious blood.

The third chapter.

Of the washing of the feet, specified[11] in the thirteen chapter of the gospel of Saint John.

"And when supper was done, when the devil had put into the heart of Judas, the son of Simon of Scariot, to betray Him, Jesus, knowing that His Father had given Him all things into His

9. in contrast to.   10. carelessly.   11. related in detail.

hands, and that He was come from God and goeth to God, ariseth fro supper and putteth off His clothes and took a linen cloth and did gird it about Him. Then He did put water into a basin and began to wash the feet of His disciples and wipe them with the linen cloth that He was gird withal.[1] Then cometh He to Simon Peter, and Peter saith unto Him: 'Lord, washest Thou my feet?' Jesus answered and said unto him, 'What I do thou knowest not now, but thou shalt know after.' Peter saith unto him: 'Thou shalt never wash my feet.' Jesus answered unto him: 'If I wash thee not, thou shalt have no part with[2] me.' Simon Peter said unto Him, 'Lord, not only my feet, but my hands and my head too.' Jesus saith unto him: 'He that is washed needeth no more but that he wash his feet, but is all clean. And you be clean, but not all.' For He knew who he was should betray Him. Therefore He said, 'You be not clean all.' Then, after that He had washed their feet, He took His clothes again. And when He was set down again at the table, He said unto them, 'Wot ye what I have done to you? You call me Master and Lord. And you say well, for so I am. Therefore if I have washed your feet, being your Lord and your Master, you owe[3] also one to wash another's feet. For I have given you an ensample that, likewise as I have done to you, so should you do too. Verily, verily, I say to you, the bondman is not more[4] than his lord, nor an apostle greater than he that hath sent him. If you know these things, blessed shall you be if you do these things.' "

The exposition.

The holy evangelist Saint John, in the beginning of the thirteenth chapter, beginning to speak of the last supper of our Lord, showeth that our Savior, *Cum dilexisset suos qui erant in mundo, in finem dilexit eos*[5] (Whereas He loved those that were His which were in the world, He loved them into the end), that is to wit, as some doctors say, "He loved them to the uttermost."

---

1. with.   2. *have . . . with:* have nothing to do with.
3. ought.   4. greater.   5. John 13 : 1.

For well ye wot the end of everything is the uttermost. And Christ loved His to the very uttermost, that is to wit, unto that extreme point of love beyond which no man could go. For He said Himself: *Majorem amorem nemo habet, quam ut animam suam ponat quis pro amicis suis.*[6] (Greater love can there no man have, than that a man give his life for his friends.) This kind of extreme kindness had Christ, not to His friends only, but to His enemies too. For he gave His own life for both twain. And therefore those that He loved He loved unto the end, that is to wit, unto the very uttermost.

Some doctors expoune those words, "He loved them to the end," that is to wit, not for a while and then cast them off, as many folk love in this world, but "He loved them to the end" so that when He should part out of this world (by a death so painful that the thinking thereof would make a man forget all his friends for heaviness, dread, and fear), He, the nearer He drew toward that painful, terrible death, the more He remembered His twelve apostles whom He had specially loved in the world, and the more tenderly took He thought for them when He was parting out of this world. And for to show that as Himself said, *Qui ad me venit non ejiciam foras*[7] (He that cometh to me, I will not cast him out), our Savior would not cast out Judas the traitor till he cast out himself, but, for all his traitorous purpose, tenderly went about to mend[8] him and brought him to the supper with Him.

Some expoune also those words, "He loved them into the end," to signify that the love that He bare them was not such a kind of love as worldly minded folk use to bear each to other, that is to wit, either for their own commodity to take pleasure by them, while that in this passage toward the end (that is to wit, the world to come) they be by the way walking with them, or else to do them some such kind of commodity as may serve them and stand them in some stead for their use in the way. But our Savior, those that He loved in the world, He loved not into the way

6. John 15 : 13.   7. John 6 : 37.   8. reform.

(that is to wit, not only unto their worldly commodities that are transitory and shall pass from them, which they shall leave behind them in the way) but He loved them into the end, that is to wit, toward the bringing of them to the end that He by His precious blood bought[9] them to.

And thus you see how all these expositions of the old holy doctors are very meet for the matter, which Saint John here beginneth to treat, which in this thirteenth chapter beginneth to enter toward the treating of Christ's passion, by which our Lord declared well that He loved unto the end, that is to wit, as I told you, to the uttermost. And first he beginneth therein to treat of His last supper, wherein He declared by many things, as shall after appear, that He loved His apostles to the end, that is to wit, that the nearer He drew to His death the more tenderly He remembered them. He declared also at that supper that He loved them into the end, that is to wit, into the world to come to the bliss of heaven, the end that He by His death prepared for them. This He declared specially at the last supper, both by the institution of the blessed sacrament and by the godly doctrine that He taught them to conduit[10] them thitherward, of which the very entry and open gate our Savior showed them in these words of the gospel that I have here before rehearsed you, as you shall well perceive by the perusing of the letter, which in this wise beginneth: "When the supper was done, when the devil had put into the heart of Judas, the son of Simon of Scariot, to betray Him," etc.

In these words, "when the supper was done," it is not to be taken that it was all done. For (as you see here) our Lord and all His apostles, after their feet washed, sat down at the table again. But you shall understand that the supper of the paschal lamb was done. For that was then eaten before that our Lord rose fro the table to go about the washing of the apostles' feet.

"Whereas the devil had put into the heart of Judas, the son of Simon of Scariot, to betray Him." By this, that the devil did put

9. redeemed.   10. guide.

that treason in his heart, is meant the secret suggestion of the devil by which he stirred the traitor Judas thereunto. By which we be learned[1] to know and consider that, when an ungracious[2] purpose falleth in our mind, we may well think that the devil is then even busy about[3] us, and not (as it is commonly said) at our elbow, but even at our very heart. For into the fleshly body can the devil enter and cast imagination[4] in our mind and offer us outward occasions also to illect,[5] stir, and draw us to his purpose. Judas was called not Scariot, but Iscariot, that is to wit, *Iscariotes,* "of a place named Iscariot."

"Jesus, knowing that the Father had given Him all things into His hands, and that He was come out fro God and goeth to God, riseth from the supper, and putteth off His garments, and took a linen cloth and gird[6] it about Him, and then put water into the basin, and began to wash the feet of His disciples, and wipe them with the linen cloth with which He was gird."

We need (I trust) to put no man in remembrance that our Savior Christ was as verily God as man. And therefore where the evangelist saith that He came out fro His Father and goeth again to His Father, it is not meant that His Godhead was at any time departed fro the Father; but by His going fro the Father was nothing meant but His being incarnate in the world, and His going again to the Father, the taking up of His manhead into heaven with Him. For by His coming into the earth He left not heaven but ever was, and ever is, and ever shall be, with His Father and their Holy Spirit both in heaven and in earth, and everywhere else at once. Nor by that He saith His Father had given Him all things into His hands is not meant that God the Father giveth anything unto the egal[7] God the Son. But like as He hath been eternally begotten of Him, so hath He had eternally egal dominion of all things with Him. I mean not only as much dominion, but also the selfsame dominion, in like manner[8] as He is egal God with His Father and the Holy Ghost not by being

1. taught.   2. wicked.   3. *busy about:* attentively occupied with.
4. a false image or idea.   5. entice.   6. girdled.   7. equal.
8. *in . . . manner:* in the same way.

another God as great but by being, albeit another distinct person, yet the selfsame God that they be.

And therefore the Father hath nothing in time given the Son but eternally before all time gave Him all (if a man may call it giving) by His only begetting.[1] Howbeit, Christ as man might receive of God's gift in time, as He was created in time. And therefore is there in these words expressed Christ's marvelous, excellent humility, as though the evangelist had in mo words declared it in this manner: our Savior Christ, whereas Judas had by the suggestion of the devil made promise to betray Him and continually persevered in that traitorous purpose, notwithstanding that He was very God and descended from heaven to be incarnate and should ascend thither again in the glorious body and soul of His blessed manhood, and that His Godhead had[2] ever[3] had of His Father by His eternal generation, and[4] to His manhood, by the unity of person with His Godhead, belonged also of all thing the whole dominion, so that with the traitor and all those to whom He should be betrayed He was able to do what Him list,[5] yet would He, not only to His other apostles but also to that very traitor too (whereby He should give his high, stubborn heart occasion to relent and repent and amend if it would be), so far humble Himself that, being their Master, their Lord, and their God, He would vouchsafe to do them lowly service in the washing, not of their heads or their hands, but even of their very feet, and wipe them too His[6] own hands. And therefore He would have nobody help Him therein, nor do a piece Himself for a countenance[7] and let another do the remnant, but He would put off His overgarments Himself, put the water into the basin Himself, wash all their feet Himself, and wipe their feet all Himself.

Then followeth it in the letter: "He came then unto Simon Peter, and Peter saith unto Him: 'Lord, washest Thou my

1. *by His . . . begetting:* solely by His begetting.
2. *i.e.,* he had.   3. always.   4. *i.e.,* and that.
5. *Him list:* He chose.   6. *i.e.,* with His.
7. *a countenance:* the sake of appearances.

feet?'" Saint Peter, having our Savior in such estimation and honor, as it well became Him to have, thought it in his mind un-meetly[8] that his Lord and Master should wash his feet. And therefore he said unto Him: "Lord, washest Thou my feet?" To whom our Savior said: "That that I do thou knowest not now. But thou shalt know afterward." As though He would say: "Though thou think it not convenient because thou canst not see for what cause I do it, yet I (all whose deeds are of such per-fection that I do nothing for nought) know a great cause neces-sary and convenient for which I do it, which thou canst not conject.[9] But when we have done, thou shalt know it, and there-fore suffer me first to do it."

But Saint Peter had so deep imprinted in his breast the mar-velous high majesty of the person of Christ, being the very Son of God, and with His almighty Father and His Holy Ghost egal[1] and one God, and therefore infinitely more in dignity above him than the heaven is in distance above the earth, could not, for all that word of our Savior, find in his heart to suffer Him do such simple, humble service unto him. And therefore with plain re-fusing thereof he withdrew his feet and answered our Savior in this wise: "Thou shall never wash my feet in this world." Our Lord, then—as He sometime did in other things touch[2] and temper the zeal of Peter, through fervor and heat somewhat un-discreet,[3] so to show him here that there could no virtue stand in stead[4] without an humble obedience, but that it would work unto damnation (seemed the thing never so good) if it were joined with disobedience against the will of God—spake sharply to him and said: "But if[5] I wash thee, thou shalt have no part with[6] me." When Saint Peter heard that word, he cast off his un-discreet courtesy and turned it unto perfect obedience, submit-ting himself whole unto the will of Christ, and said: "Lord, not only my feet, but also my hands and my head too." As though he would say: "Though I would for mine unworthiness be loath to

8. unfitting.   9. imagine.   1. equal.   2. rebuke.
3. imprudent.   4. *stand in stead:* be advantageous.
5. *But if:* Unless.   6. *no . . . with:* nothing to do with.

have Thy most excellent person do such simple service unto me, yet sith I see that for cause unknown unto me, of which it becometh me not to ask Thee a reckoning, Thou hast so determined to wash mine unworthy feet, that if I therein obey not Thine high pleasure I shall by disobedience fall in Thy displeasure and be departed[7] fro Thee and leese my part of Thy glory, I rather will be content to suffer Thee not only, Lord, to wash my feet, but over that mine hands and mine head too."

"Jesus answered and said unto him: 'He that is washed needeth not to wash but his feet, but is all clean.' " Forasmuch as Saint Peter offered himself to suffer to be of Christ's holy hands washed, not his feet only that are the lowest part but his hands also that are about the mids and his head too which is the highest part, by which three he signified himself content that Christ should wash all his whole body, Christ answered him that that thing were more than needed. For he that is washed once already by baptism is so clean washed altogether from all sin, both actual and original, that he never needeth to be all washed again, nor never shall be all washed again by baptism. For baptized shall no man be but once; the character and spiritual token by baptism imprinted in the soul is undelible and never can be put out. But in them that, for their unfaithfulness or for their evil living after their baptism, shall finally be damned, that token shall in their soul perpetually remain to their harm and shame, by which it shall evermore appear that they be neither paynims, Jews, nor Saracens, but (which worst is of all) false and unkind[8] Christian men. But there is none washed so clean by baptism but that (if he live) he shall have need to have his feet washed often. For by his feet are meant his affections.[9] For likewise as our feet bear our body hither and thither, so do our affections carry us to good works or bad. For look which way that our affections lead us and that way commonly walk we. And therefore said our Savior to Saint Peter when he offered to be all washed again both[1] feet, hands, and head, "He that is washed is all clean and

7. separated.   8. lacking in natural gratitude.   9. feelings.
1. *i.e.,* all three.

needeth to have no more washed but his feet," that is to wit, his
affections, "and then is he all clean." And with that our Savior,
considering the traitor Judas (the filthy feet of whose wretched,
covetous affection had carried him to the council of the Jews to
offer them his Master for money to sell, and from which traitorous affection Christ's great marvelous humanity, washing the
traitor's filthy feet, had not cleansed him), He said unto them all:
"You be clean, but yet all you be not clean," for He knew who it
was that should betray Him. And therefore He said: "All you be
not clean."

Upon the foresaid words of Christ unto Peter, "He that is
washed needeth but to wash his feet," and those words, "You be
clean," it appeareth, as the old holy doctors say, that the apostles
were before that all baptized and clean. But Judas had by his
filthy affection of his wretched covetise defiled himself by his
false treason again.

"Then after that He had washed their feet, He took His
clothes again, and when He was set at the table again, He said
unto them: 'Wot ye what I have done to you?' " Our Savior here
giveth us in these words a good occasion to perceive that His
outward works had, beside those visible apparent things which
every man might behold and see, such secret spiritual mysteries
meant and signified, and not only signified but also wrought and
done in them, that those spiritual things unseen were so much
the more principal parts of His deed that whoso know not them,
though they know His outward deed, yet may it be said that
they know not what He did.

So where our Savior healed a man in his body outwardly, and
inwardly also in his soul—whereof it is said, *Totum hominem
sanum fecit in sabbato* [2] (He made all the man whole in the sabbot
day, that is to wit, not the body only, for the body alone is not all
the man, but the soul too—they that looked on, though they wist
what he had outwardly done in the healing of the body, yet was
that inward work of His in healing of the soul so far passing[3]
that, that it may well be said they wist not what He did. And so

2. John 7 : 23.   3. surpassing.

was it in His works that He wrought in the blessed sacrament: as, when He consecrated His blessed body and blood in the form of bread and wine at this His last supper, had He not told them that point Himself, who could have told what He did?

And therefore here in the washing of His disciples' feet, albeit that they could not but both see and feel what He did, yet because His outward work therein was not in such a special manner His deed as was the inward mystery that He did and meant therein, He asked them: "Know you what I have done to you?" As though He would say: "I have done more than you know, for by the outward washing of your feet I have given you ensample of humility," which thing He declared unto them with most effectual words. For first, to the intent that they should consider of what weight and authority both His deed and His word should be with them, He plainly declared, taking occasion upon their own confession, that He was their very Lord and their very Master. And therefore He said unto them: "You call me Master and Lord, and you say well. For so I am indeed."

He was very Lord of them as of His creatures; He was very Master of them as of His disciples. Now putting this first in their remembrance for a foundation, thereupon He builded them a marvelous fruitful lesson with the declaration [4] of His former deed, saying unto them: "Therefore if I have washed your feet, being your Lord and your Master, you must also wash one another's feet." Then goeth He farther and declareth wherefore He washed their feet, as He before said to Saint Peter that He should know it afterward. And therefore now He telleth that He did it to give ensample [5] by His own deed unto them that they should each to other do the like. And therefore He said: "A sample [6] have I given you, that likewise as I have done to you, so should you do also, that is to wit, do each of you to other as I have done to you all."

Then goeth our Savior further yet and enforceth [7] His doctrine and His ensample with a strong mighty reason, saying:

4. elucidation.   5. example.   6. example.   7. reinforces.

"Verily, verily, I tell you, the bondman is not greater than his lord, nor a messenger more[8] than he that hath sent him." As though He would say: "Sith the bondman is no better than his lord, and I that am your creator am more highly Lord over you that are my creatures than any earthly lord is over his bondman, how should you disdain to wash your fellow's feet, when I your high Lord have not disdained to wash yours? And sith the messenger is not better than he that hath sent him, and all you be but mine apostles, that is to wit, but my messengers to do my message in preaching my word about the world, sith I that send you and therefore so far your better and yet have not disdained to wash your feet, there can none of you without very sinful and shameful pride disdain to wash the feet of his fellow."

And finally Christ knitteth[9] up all the whole matter with a very short substantial lesson: "If you know these things, blessed shall you be if you do these things." In which words our Savior well declareth that the bliss of heaven will not be gotten by knowing of virtue but by the use and doing thereof. For as no man can come at Canterbury by the bare knowledge of the way thither if he will sit still at home, so by knowing the way to heaven we can never the more come there but if we will walk therein. And therefore saith our Lord by the mouth of the prophet: *Beati immaculati qui ambulant in lege Domini. Non enim qui operantur iniquitatem in viis ejus ambulaverunt.*[10] (Blessed are they that are undefiled, that walk in the law of our Lord. But they that work wickedness walk not in His ways.) And our Savior saith[11] His own mouth that the knowledge without work not only doth no profit but also causeth increase of a man's punishment, in respect that[1] his punishment should be if, without his willful ignorance, his knowledge had been much less. For thus saith our Lord: "The bondman that knoweth not the will of his lord and doth it not shall be beaten with few stripes. But the bondman that knoweth his lord's will and doth it not shall be

8. greater.   9. sums.   10. Ps, 118 : 1 and 3 (*AV*, 119 : 1 and 3).
11. *i.e.,* says with.   1. *in respect that:* compared with what.

beaten with many stripes."[2] And therefore with this necessary, fruitful doctrine our Lord did knit up all and said: "If you know these things," that is to wit, "that my washing of your feet is done for your ensample, that sith I am indeed (as yourself do call me) your Lord and your Master, and that the bondman is not better than his lord, nor the messenger more than his master that sent him, you should not be so proud as to disdain to do as lowly service, each of you to other, as I have done to you all. If you know this and do it indeed, then shall you be blessed, or else for the bare knowledge shall you be but the worse."

Upon these words before rehearsed, had between our Savior and Saint Peter, that refused for reverence the thing that our Lord would do to him, holy doctors note that no man lawfully may for any private mind of reverence or devotion to God do the thing that God forbiddeth nor leave the thing undone that God biddeth. For it is an undiscreet[3] devotion, and an unreverent reverence, and no right humility, but an unperceived pride to stand stiff[4] against God's will and disobey His pleasure. For as the scripture saith: "Better is obedience than sacrifice."[5] Nor never shall God's precepts be obeyed if every man may boldly frame himself[6] a conscience with a glose[7] of his own making after his own fantasy put unto God's word. For of such manner dealing, whereby folk will of their private devotions, against the commandment of God, follow their own way, may these words of the scripture be verified: *Est via quae videtur hominibus justa, et novissima ejus tendit ad infernum.*[8] (There is a way that unto men seemeth just, and the last end thereof leadeth unto hell.)

King Saul thought, after his own mind, that he did very well when he kept and spared the goodly oxen for sacrifice. But while he brake in his so doing the commandment of God, this false-framed[9] devotion holp[1] him not but that he lost his king-

2. Luke 12 : 47–48.   3. imprudent.

4. *stand stiff:* remain stubborn.   5. 1 Kings 15 : 22.

6. *frame himself:* devise for himself.   7. interpretation.

8. Prov. 14 : 12.   9. *false-framed:* falsely contrived.   1. helped.

dom therefore. Saint Peter here thought he did well when he for reverence toward Christ would not suffer Him wash his feet. But our Savior showed him that, if he would for any such framed reverence of his own stand obstinately disobedient unto God's pleasure, he should have no part with Him. And therefore, while Christ was presently conversant[2] with him, He was the interpreter of His own precept. And King Saul should not have followed his own wit, but should have asked the prophet by whom that precept came to him. And in like wise, if a man doubt of the sentence and understanding of anything written in the scripture, it is no wisdom for him then to take upon him such authority of interpretation himself, as that he shall therein boldly stand unto[3] his own mind, but lean unto the interpretation of the old holy doctors and saints and unto that interpretation that is received and allowed by the universal church, by which church the scripture is comen to our hands and delivered unto us, and without which we could not (as Saint Austin saith) know which books were holy scripture.[4]

Our Savior here saith: "I have given you a sample, that, likewise as I have done to you, so should you do also." Would God that all the prelates, and all curates, and all preachers, yea, and fathers and mothers, and all masters of households too, would here of our Savior take ensample for to give good ensample. There are many that can be well content to be preaching, some to show their cunning[5] and some to show their authority. But would God they would use the fashion that our Savior used, that is to wit, the things that they bid other men do, do it first themself. The scripture saith of our Savior, *Cepit Jesus facere et docere*[6] (Jesus began to do and to teach), so that He not only taught men to do this or that, but He gave them also the sample and did the thing first Himself. To stir us to fast, He not only taught us what fashion we should use in fasting, but also for our ensample fasted

2. *presently conversant:* in personal and familiar contact.
3. *stand unto:* persist in.
4. See Augustine, *Contra epistolam Manichaei,* V (*PL 42, 176*).
5. knowledge.   6. Acts. 1 : 1.

forty days Himself. To stir us to wake and pray, He not only taught us by word, but used also by night to go forth into the Mount of Olivet and there to wake and pray by night Himself, by which custom the traitor knew where to find Him. To set nought by the royalty[7] of the world He not only taught us by word, but also by His poor birth, and all the course of His poor life, He gave us the ensample Himself. To stir us to patience and suffering of tribulation, He not only taught us and exhorted us by word, but gave us the ensample by His own cross, His own passion, and His own painful death. And surely, albeit that the best is (for him that hath a good thing taught him by one whom he seeth do the contrary himself) to do as he is well taught and not follow the lewd[8] sample of his evil deed, yet is our common condition such that, whereas word and deed both be scant able to draw us to do good, every one of the both is able enough to draw us to nought.[9] And therefore he that biddeth other folk do well and giveth evil ensample with the contrary deed himself fareth[10] even like a foolish weaver that would weave apace with the tone hand and unweave as fast with the tother.

The ensample of Christ in washing the apostles' feet, with His exhortation unto them by His ensample to do the like, bindeth not men to follow the literal fashion thereof in washing of folks' feet as for a rite or a ceremony or a sacrament of the church—howbeit, much it hath been ever since and yet in every country of Christendom in places of religion used it is, and noble princes and great estates[1] use that godly ceremony very religiously. And none I suppose nowhere more godly than our sovereign lord the king's grace here of this realm, both in humble manner washing and wiping and kissing also many poor folks' feet after the number of years of his age, and with right liberal and princely alms therewith.

And surely if the interpretation of the scripture were not by the spirit of God put in the whole corps[2] of the Catholic Church,

---

7. magnificence.   8. wicked.   9. wrongdoing.   10. acts.
1. *great estates:* persons of high social rank.   2. body.

he that would upon his own head stick upon the letter of the gospel and his own exposition thereto might contend that the washing of the feet were a sacrament unto which our Savior bound His church of necessity. But, as the universal church believeth, so is it not. Howbeit, in time and place convenient, it is (as Saint Austin saith) a thing of the more perfection if we not only do not disdain in our hearts but do it also in deed with our hands as our Lord did with His.[3]

When our Lord said, "You be clean but not all," He meant that the congregation and company of His twelve apostles, as a congregation and a company, was a clean company, though Judas, one of the company, was not clean. For many a right honest company is there that hath yet some not honest among them. And so is the Catholic Church called *sancta ecclesia,* "holy church," because that out thereof[4] there is none holiness, and for those that are holy therein, which are alway many, both priests and laymen too, though there be therein beside many bad of both sorts also.

Finally, where our Savior saith, *Si haec scitis, beati eritis si feceritis ea*[5] (If you know these things, you shall be blessed if you do them), two things in those words He giveth us warning of: the tone, that without faith there can be no good work that can be meritorious touching[6] the bliss of heaven; the tother, that have we the faith never so great, yet if we will not work well our faith shall fail of the bliss. And therefore to give us warning of the necessity that we have of faith, He said not these words alone, "If you do this you shall be blessed," but He began with these words, "If you know these things." Now the knowledge of those things that pertain to such kind of well doing as shall stand us in stead toward[7] salvation, that knowledge have we not but by faith. As the apostles there, though they saw Him wash their feet, yet that He did it to give them a sample of humility, and that such humility should be requisite to help them to heaven,

3. See Augustine's *In Johannis evangelium tractatus,* 58, 4 *(PL 35,* 1794).
4. *out thereof:* apart from it.   5. John 13 : 17.   6. as regards.
7. *stand . . . toward:* be of use to us with regard to.

and to be rewarded there, this knew they not but by the faith that they gave therein unto Christ's word. For, *Fides ex auditu, auditus autem per verbum Dei.*[8] (Faith, saith Saint Paul, cometh of hearing, and the hearing thereof is by the word of God.) Therefore, as I say, our Lord began their blessedness with faith. For faith is the very gate and first entry toward heaven: *Accedentem ad Deum oportet credere.*[9] (He that is coming to God must give credence and believe.) For if a man that believeth not do the selfsame thing either by chance or of some other affection,[10] which thing done by a faithful man in faith were meritorious, that deed done by the faithless is not meritorious at all. But yet, though faith be the first gate into heaven, he that standeth still at the gate and will not walk forth in the way of good works shall not come where the reward is. And therefore our Savior left[1] not with these words, *Si haec scitis beati eritis* (If you know these things you shall be blessed), but went further and, to make up His tale perfect, He added, *si feceritis ea* (if you do them).

I fear me there be many folk that, for delight of knowledge or for a foolish vainglory to show and make it known how much themself know, labor to know the law of God (and know it right well indeed, and can well preach it out again) that shall yet see many a poor simple soul with a gross plain faith (with no learning but good devout affection, walking the way of good works in this world) sit after full high with our Lord in heaven, when those great clerks[2] wandering here in evil works shall, for all their great knowledge and for all gay[3] preaching in the name of Christ, hear our Lord say to them (as in the thirteenth chapter of Saint Luke He saith He will say to such): *Discedite a me operarii iniquitatis.*[4] (Walk you from me you workers of wickedness.)

And for conclusion, all the work (with this ensample of His and all His declaration[5] thereupon) our Savior instructeth and exhorteth His apostles to, is the work of humility. For likewise as pride threw down the devil out of heaven, so shall there never

8. Rom. 10 : 17.   9. Heb. 11 : 6.   10. inclination.
1. stopped.   2. scholars.   3. brilliant.   4. Luke 13 : 27.
5. elucidation.

none ascend but with meekness thither. And sith the devil that fell himself by pride is ever most busy to tempt every man to the same sin (and specially those that he seeth aspire toward any excellence in spiritual kind of virtue or that he espieth put in prelacy[6] and authority over other men, whereby he hopeth to find a gate open to enter), our Savior therefore to keep against the ghostly[7] enemy that gate well warded[8] and sure, in sundry places again and again giveth His apostles (whom He made prelates and spiritual governors of His flock) special counsel against the prick[9] of pride, and with words and with this ensample of washing their feet His[1] own hands, exhorteth them by meekness and humility to compt[2] and reckon and use themself[3] as far under other as Himself doth in order[4] and authority prefer[5] and enhance[6] them above, and would that we should of duty for their degree do great honor unto them, and that they should themself of[7] meekness as fast[8] again put it fro them.

The prayer.

Almighty Jesus, my sweet Savior Christ, which wouldest vouchsafe Thine[9] own almighty hands to wash the feet of Thy twelve apostles, not only of the good but of the very traitor too, vouchsafe, good Lord, of Thine excellent goodness, in such wise to wash the foul feet of mine affections that I never have such pride enter into mine heart as to disdain either in friend or foe, with meekness and charity for the love of Thee, to file[1] mine hands with washing of their feet.

6. ecclesiastical power.   7. spiritual.   8. guarded.
9. goad.   1. *i.e.,* with His.   2. consider.
3. *use themself:* conduct themselves.   4. rank.   5. promote.
6. exalt.   7. *i.e.,* out of.   8. earnestly.   9. *i.e.,* with Thine.
1. defile.

The fourth chapter.

Of the institution of the sacrament, written in the twenty-sixth of Saint Matthew, the fourteenth of Saint Mark, and in the twenty-second of Saint Luke.

The first lecture upon the blessed sacrament.

"And as they were sitting at the table and eating, Jesus saith, 'With desire have I desired to eat the paschal with you before I suffer. I say to you that fro this time I shall not eat it, till it be fulfilled in the kingdom of God.' As they were at supper Jesus took bread, gave thanks, and blessed and brake it, and gave it to His disciples, and saith: 'Take you and eat you. This is my body, the which for you shall be delivered. This do you for the remembrance of me.' Likewise, taking the chalice after that He had supped, gave thanks and gave it them, saying: 'Take and divide it among you, and drink of this all. This is my blood of the New Testament. This is the chalice, the New Testament in my blood, which for you and for many shall be shed for remission of sins. I say verily to you that I shall not drink from henceforth of this generation[2] of the vine, until that day when I shall drink it new[3] with you in the kingdom of my Father God.' And they drank all thereof."

Albeit, good readers, that I have rehearsed you this chapter in such wise as the right famous clerk Master John Gerson rehearseth in his work called *Monotessaron*, gathered of the words of all the three evangelists, Saint Matthew, Saint Mark, and Saint Luke, and in a convenient order, linked and chained ensuingly[4] together, yet seemeth me[5] that for the beginning the thing shall

2. fruit. 3. anew. 4. in due sequence.
5. *seemeth me:* I think.

somewhat the better appear if we rehearse the words of Saint Luke somewhat more full, which words he writeth upon the end of the eating of the paschal lamb and before the institution of the blessed sacrament of the altar. For in his twenty-second chapter thus beginneth he this matter: *Et cum facta esset hora, discubuit, et duodecim apostoli cum eo. Et ait illis: Desiderio desideravi hoc pascha manducare vobiscum antequam patiar. Dico enim vobis, quia ex hoc non manducabo illud, donec impleatur in regno Dei. Et accepto calice gratias egit, et dixit: Accipite et dividite inter vos. Dico enim vobis quod non bibam de generatione vitis donec regnum Dei veniat.*[6] (And when the hour was come, He sat down at the table, and His twelve apostles with Him. And He saith unto them: "With desire have I desired to eat this paschal lamb with you before I suffer. For I tell you that fro this time I shall not eat it till it be fulfilled in the kingdom of God." And the cup taken, He gave thanks and said: "Take you and divide you it among you. For I say to you that I shall not drink of the generation of the vine till the kingdom of God come.")

These words hath Saint Luke whole[7] together of the finishing of the old paschal before he entereth into the rehearsing of the new paschal, whereof the old was a figure, that is to wit, before he beginneth to rehearse the institution of the blessed sacrament of the altar, of which he beginneth to speak forthwith after these words ended.

In the beginning of these words, written in the twenty-second chapter of Saint Luke, our Savior expresseth the great desire that He had to eat the paschal lamb at that time with His apostles, saying: *Desiderio desideravi hoc pascha manducare vobiscum antequam patiar.*[8] (With desire have I desired to eat this paschal lamb with you before my passion.) These words "with desire have I desired" are spoken after the manner of Hebrew speech, in which speech our Savior spake at the time Himself. For the Hebrews to express a thing vehemently use oftentimes, as it appeareth in sundry places of scripture, to double a word, some-

6. Luke 2 : 14–18.   7. all.   8. Luke 22 : 15.

time by the participle and the verb, sometime by the noun and the verb, as our Savior did here, saying, "with desire have I desired," that is to wit, "very sore[9] have I desired," or "very desirously have I longed for to eat this paschal lamb with you."

Two causes there were for which our Savior so sore longed at that time to eat the paschal lamb with His disciples. The tone appeareth upon that[1] I have showed you before, that is to wit, because that (as Saint John saith): *Cum dilexisset suos qui erant in mundo, usque in finem dilexit eos.*[2] (Whereas He had loved His that were in the world, He loved them to the end.) And therefore, sith He was now so near drawing to His passion, which He had determined to suffer on the morrow, He, like a most tender lover, longed with that last supper to make them His farewell at His departing fro them.

Wherein, as I before have said, appeared His wonderful loving heart. For had He been after the manner of other men (sith Himself saw His passion drawing so near, to which He should be so violently taken so shortly upon[3] His supper, and that passion so bitter as Himself well wist it should, of which He was so feared[4] and for which He was so sorrowful within so few hours after), He would have taken little pleasure or comfort in the company of His apostles nor list to make them a supper at that time.

But He loved them so tenderly that all the pain, sorrow, dread, and fear that was toward[5] Him could not so master and overwhelm His kind, loving affection toward them, but that the desire and longing to make His last supper with them so much increased greater as He surely saw that His bitter passion drew nearer. And that was therefore (as I say) one of the causes for which He said unto them at the eating thereof, "With desire have I desired," that is to say, "Sore[6] have I longed to eat this paschal lamb with you before my passion."

9. eagerly.   1. what.   2. John 13 : 1.   3. after.
4. afraid.   5. approaching.   6. eagerly.

The tother cause for which He longed so sore to eat that paschal lamb with them was because that He longed for the time in which He should, with His bitter passion, pay the price of our redemption and restore the kind of man unto the inheritance of the kingdom of heaven. And because that He would, before the offering up of His own blessed body (the very lamb, innocent and immaculate) unto the Father, institute the new paschal (the very eating of the selfsame holy, unspotted lamb, His own blessed body and blood, to be continually sacrificed, offered up unto the Father, and eaten in remembrance of His bitter passion under the form of bread and wine), He would, as was convenient, before the institution of the new very paschal, reverently finish the old paschal that was the figure thereof.

And therefore at the last supper, to declare the desire that He had so to do (that is to wit, to institute His new paschal by the finishing of the old), He said unto them: "With desire have I desired to eat this paschal lamb with you before my passion." And for to declare the more clearly that the cause of His desire was to the intent that He would finish it and offer up Himself the very lamb, whereof the tother was the figure, and would by that pleasant sacrifice bring the nature[7] of man into the kingdom of heaven, He therefore said farther unto them: *Dico enim vobis, quia ex hoc non manducabo illud, donec impleatur in regno Dei.*[8] (I say verily to you, that from this time I shall eat that no more till it be performed[9] in the kingdom of God.)

The fulfilling or performing of the sacrifice of the paschal lamb, being a figure, was the offering of His own blessed body in sacrifice, by which the nature of man was restored unto the kingdom of heaven. And by that new offering up of that innocent lamb so offered (which offering was the verity) was that old offering of the paschal lamb in Jerusalem (that was the figure) fully performed and thereupon took his full perfection in the kingdom of heaven.

But here must we consider that our Savior, in saying that He

7. race.   8. Luke 22 : 16.   9. fulfilled.

would eat the old paschal lamb no more till it were performed in the kingdom of heaven, did not mean that after that the figure were performed and had his perfection in heaven, He would then use or have used the same figure again in earth, but He meant that He would no more eat it at all. For this word *donec* in Latin (that is to say, "until" in English), when it limiteth[1] a time before which it denieth a certain thing to be done, doth not alway mean or imply (though sometime it do) the doing of the same thing after that time. As when the gospel saith, *Non cognovit eam, donec peperit filium suum primogenitum*[2] (Joseph knew not her till she had brought forth her first-begotten son), meaneth not that he knew her after. Nor where the prophet speaketh as in the person of the Father unto Christ, *Sede a dextris meis, donec ponam inimicos tuos scabellum pedum tuorum*[3] (Sit on my right hand till I put Thine enemies for a footstool under Thy feet), the prophet there meaneth not that when the enemies of Christ be thrown under His feet He shall then sit on the Father's right hand no longer. Nor here in like wise our Savior meant not that, after the verity fulfilled and perfited[4] in the kingdom of God, He would use or have used the figure here still in earth.

And that appeareth plain by two things. One, by this word *impleatur,* "till it be fulfilled." For, sith it was but a figure, and He said He would use it no more till it were fulfilled, He must needs mean that He would use it no more at all. For, being but a figure, it had no cause of use after that it was by the verity fulfilled.

And therefore as touching[5] the paschal lamb, when our Savior said, "I will from henceforth eat this no more till it be fulfilled in the kingdom of God," was as much as to say, "after this I will never eat it more," after such manner of speaking as one might say that looked for to die or that were entering into the Charterhouse,[6] "I will never eat flesh more in this world," or thus, "I trust to be in heaven ere I eat any more flesh," or such other

1. fixes definitely.   2. Matt. 1 : 25.
3. Ps. 109 : 1 (*AV*, 110 : 1).   4. perfected.   5. pertaining to.
6. A Carthusian monastery in London. The Carthusians were a very austere order.

kind of speaking like, not meaning that he would eat flesh in another world, but that he would eat none here, and consequently never eat flesh more.

The tother thing, by which it appeareth plain that our Savior intended not to have the figurative old paschal lamb any longer continue, is that He forthwith instituted the verity thereof, the new sacrifice, His blessed body and blood, the blessed sacrament of the altar.

But before the institution of His own Christian sacrament, to the intent it should appear that He would fully finish the old paschal of the Jews (and as who say wash it away), Himself with His apostles, as for a final end thereof, after the eating thereof, drank thereunto. Whereof Saint Luke proceedeth farther and saith: *Accepto calice gratias egit, et dixit: accipite et dividite inter vos.*[7] (He took the cup and gave thanks and said: "Take and divide among you.")

Our Savior as man gave thanks unto God the Father that the old sacrifice of the paschal lamb was now come to an end and that He was now come to the institution of the new sacrifice, His own blessed body in the holy sacrament of the altar.

Then our Lord commanded them to take and divide the cup of wine among them and drink all thereof, as the farewell of the old paschal. And then said He farther unto them: *Dico enim vobis, quod non bibam de generatione vitis, donec regnum Dei veniat.*[8] (I say to you that I shall not drink of the generation of the vine till the kingdom of God come.)

The kingdom of God He calleth here the state of His glory after His resurrection, in which He rose immortal, impassible,[9] and glorious.[1] Afore which time He said here unto them that He would drink no wine, as though He would say: "Such drink as I now drink with you to the old sacrifice of the paschal lamb will I drink no more till I arise again in my glory after my passion."

But after His resurrection, He did verily eat and drink with

7. Luke 22 : 17.   8. Luke 22 : 18.   9. incapable of suffering.
1. glorified.

them again, as appeareth plain by the evangelists, and as Saint
Peter beareth witness where he saith: *Qui manducavimus et bibimus
cum illo postquam resurrexit a mortuis.*[2] (We have eaten and
drunken with Him after that He was arisen fro death.)

After this done, our Savior Christ by and by, in the stead of
that old sacrifice of the paschal lamb so ended, did institute the
new sacrifice and the only sacrifice to be continued in His
church, the blessed sacrament of the altar. Which new sacrifice,
instead of that old sacrifice and of all the old sacrifices which
among the Jews fore-figured the very fruitful[3] sacrifice of
Christ's blessed body upon the cross, should, in His own church
of Jews and Gentiles together, continually with the selfsame
body and blood offered in the mass under the form of bread
and wine, represent that sacrifice in which on Good Friday
Christ once for ever offered the selfsame body and blood in
their proper form to the Father upon the cross.

And therefore, after the old sacrifice of the paschal lamb
clearly finished, as ye have heard, ere ever they rose fro the
board, our Savior forthwith went in hand[4] with the instituting of
that that should be the new sacrifice, the blessed sacrament of
the altar, His own holy body and blood under form of bread and
wine.

The manner of which institution, in the gospel of Saint
Matthew, Saint Mark, and Saint Luke, is rehearsed in this wise:
"Jesus took bread, gave thanks and blessed it, and brake it, and
gave it His disciples, saying: 'Take you and eat you. This is my
body, which shall be delivered for you.'"

First our Savior, in the beginning of this excellent work, gave
thanks and blessed the bread to give us ensample, as saith Saint
Bede, that in the beginning of every good work we should give
thank to God. Then He brake it and gave it unto them Himself
to signify, saith Saint Bede, that He gave Himself to His passion
of His own free will.[5] But to the intent they should well under-

2. Acts 10 : 41.   3. beneficial.   4. *went in hand:* proceeded.
5. More may have found the references to Bede in the *Catena aurea,* a
biblical gloss selected by St. Thomas Aquinas.

stand that this holy sacrament that Himself instituted in His own
holy person wonderfully far passed the old sacrifice of the paschal lamb instituted by the ministry of Moses in the old law, lest
they might peradventure take it for a far less thing than it
was—as they should have had a great cause to do if it had been
none other substance than the substance of bread, as to their
eyen[6] it seemed (for then had the lamb, which was a living, sensible[7] creature, been of the proper nature[8] much more excellent
than the unsensible substance of bread)—our Savior therefore,
to give them sure knowledge how great a gift it was that He
there gave them and how incomparably far above all the merit
of man to receive (that they should thereby consider how deeply
they were bounden and beholden to Him therefore, and with
devout thanks inwardly remember His inestimable bounty
therein), He gave them knowledge that though it was bread
when He took it in hand and that to their bodily senses seemed
yet bread still, yet it was now His own very body indeed. And
therefore He said unto them: "Take you and eat you. This is my
body." As though He might say: "Think not that for my special
new sacrifice, that I institute to represent forever in mine own
church (till I return to the general judgment) my most precious
passion, I give you a thing of more base nature than was the
thing that was wont to be sacrificed to fore-figure it in the short[1]
and soon passing synagogue—which you might think if my sacrifice of representation were but unsensible bread, where their
fore-figuring sacrifice was celebrated in a living creature, a fair,
unspotted lamb. But I will that you shall understand and know
that the thing which I give you here to eat is of a nature above
all measure more excellent. For though it seem bread, yet is it
flesh. And though it seem dead, yet is it living. The lamb,
though it was quick[2] taken to the sacrifice, yet was it eaten dead.
But this shall you eat quick, and it shall rest and abide quick in
you. And the lamb did feed and nourish your bodies; but this

6. eyes.   7. endowed with sensation.
8. *of the . . : nature:* of its own nature.
1. of brief duration.

shall feed and nourish your souls. For this is mine own body, and not my dead body, but animated and living with my soul. And mine own body shall never be separated fro my Godhead, so that if you receive and eat virtuously the tone into your body, you receive the tother graciously[3] into your souls."

In these few compendious[4] words of our Savior, "This is my body," is all this long tale included, and many a long, holy process more. And albeit that in those words alone He told them the thing plain enough, and notwithstanding that He had also declared them before that He would give them His own body to eat, inculking[5] that point into them with many words at length, mentioned in the sixth chapter of Saint John, yet to make them the more clearly perceive that this was the thing that He then told them of, He said not only, "This is my body," but He farther also added thereunto, "which shall be delivered for you"— as though He would say: "If any would be so far fro believing of the truth, that rather than believe this to be my very body, he would seek a glose[6] against mine own word and say that by this word, 'my body,' I meant but a sign or a figure or a token of my body, to put all such folk out of doubt I say that this which I give you here to receive and eat is the sameself body that shall be delivered for you to the Jews and to[7] Gentiles and by them to the cross and to the death."

Now to the intent that it should appear plain that He gave them not His body for that only time, as a special show of kindness to their own persons alone, but that they should perceive that He did it to begin and institute a new sacrament, instead of the old paschal, which should endure in His church in the stead of the tother there finished, He said unto them: *Hoc facite in meam commemorationem*[8] (This do you in the remembrance of me)—as though He would say to them: "Likewise as the synagogue of the Jews have hitherto used for a figure of my passion the old sacrifice of the paschal lamb, so do you use in my

3. by means of divine grace.   4. concise.   5. inculcating.
6. interpretation.   7. *i.e.,* "to the."   8. Luke 22 : 19.

church from henceforth in remembrance of my passion this new sacrifice of mine own body, that shall suffer that passion and be sacrificed once for ever upon the cross"—which sentence of our Savior's words is also declared by Saint Paul in the eleventh chapter of his first epistle to the Corinthies,[9] of which we shall speak hereafter.[10] But first shall we peruse the words of our Savior Himself.

After that He had thus given them His own blessed body to eat in the form of bread, He gave them likewise His blessed blood to drink in the form of wine, whereof it followeth in the gospel: "And likewise taking the chalice after supper, He gave thanks and gave it to them, saying: 'Take you and drink all you of this. This is my blood of the New Testament. This is the chalice, the New Testament in my blood, which for you and for many shall be shed into the remission of sins.' "

Our Savior at the converting and turning of the wine into His own precious blood, which He should so shortly after shed for our sins upon His painful cross, murmured not nor grudged[11] not at the remembrance of His bitter passion, but was glad, and gave God the Father thanks that He vouchsafed to suffer Him by His pain to pay our ransom and buy our souls from pain, as say Saint Remigius and Saint Chrysostom. And our Savior in His so doing (saith Saint Chrysostom) teacheth us what pain soever we suffer, to suffer it in such wise as we give God thank therefore.[1]

"And after His thanks given to God, He gave the chalice to His apostles and commanded them all drink thereof, saying: 'This is my blood of the New Testament. This is the chalice, the New Testament in my blood.' "

In these words our Savior showed them what thing it was that He gave them to drink in the chalice, that is to wit, that it was His own blood, saying, "This is my blood of the New Testament," as Saint Matthew rehearseth it, or, "This is the chalice,

9. Corinthians.   10. See 1 Cor. 11.: 25.   11. complained.
1. More probably refers to passages by Remigius and Chrysostom in the *Catena aurea* of Aquinas.

the New Testament in my blood," as Saint Luke rehearseth it, either for that our Savior spake both the tone words and the tother, or else for that both of the tone words and the tother the sentence is all one. For in the twenty-fourth chapter of Exodi is it specified[2] how that Moses in the confirmation of the old law put half the blood of the sacrifice into a cup, and the tother half he shed upon the altar, and, after the volume of the law read, he besprinkled the blood upon the people and said unto them: *Hic est sanguis foederis, quod pepigit Dominus vobiscum super cunctis sermonibus his.*[3] (This is the blood of the league[4] that our Lord hath made with you upon all these words.) And so was the Old Testament ratified and confirmed with blood. And in like wise was the New Testament confirmed with blood, saving that for to declare the great excellency of the New Testament brought by the Son of God above the Old Testament brought by the prophet Moses, whereas the Old Testament was ratified with the blood of a brute beast, the New Testament was ratified with the blood of a reasonable man, and of that man that was also God, that is to wit, with the blessed blood of our holy Savior Himself. And the selfsame blood gave our Lord here unto His apostles in this blessed sacrament, as He plainly declared Himself, saying, *Hic est sanguis meus novi testamenti*[5] (This is my blood of the New Testament), or, *Hic est calix novum testamentum in meo sanguine, qui pro vobis et pro multis fundetur in remissionem peccatorum.*[6] (This is the chalice, the New Testament in my blood, which shall be shed for you and for many for remission of sins.)

Here you see that by the words of our Savior rehearsed by Saint Matthew, and upon His words rehearsed by Saint Luke, our Lord very plainly declared unto His apostles that in that cup was the same blood of His own with which He could ratify His New Testament, and which blood should be shed upon the altar of the cross for the remission of sins, not of themself alone but also of many mo.

2. related in detail.   3. Exodus 24 : 8.   4. covenant.
5. Matt. 26 : 28, Mark 14 : 24.
6. The passage follows Gerson's *Monotessaron* in combining Matt. 26 : 28 and Luke 22 : 20.

When our Lord said, "This is the cup of the New Testament in my blood, which shall be shed for you and for many into remission of sins," He declared therein the efficacy of the New Testament above the Old in that the old law in the blood of beasts could but promise the remission of sin afterward to come. For as Saint Paul saith: "It was impossible that sin should be taken away with the blood of brute beasts."[7] But the new law with the blood of Christ performeth the thing that the old law promised, that is to wit, remission of sins. And therefore our Savior said, "This is the chalice, the New Testament in my blood," that is to wit, "to be confirmed in my blood, which shall be shed into remission of sins."

His words also declared the wonderful excellence of this new blessed sacrament above the sacrifice of the paschal lamb in these words: *Pro vobis et pro multis* (For you and for many). For in these words our Savior spake (saith Saint Chrysostom) as though He would say: "The blood of the paschal lamb was shed only for the first begotten among the children of Israel, but this blood of mine shall be shed for remission of sin of all the whole world." And so was it, according as Saint Chrysostom saith, shed for the sin of the whole world.[8] For sufficient it was for the sin of the whole world and as many mo too.

But it was effectually shed for those only that shall take the effect thereof, which are only those that shall be saved thereby, which shall be as Saint Remigius saith,[9] and as the truth is, not the apostles only but also many other of many regions, according to the foresaid words of our Savior: "This is the chalice, the New Testament in my blood, which shall be shed for you and for many into remission of sins."

Then likewise as He had before said (as you have heard rehearsed by Saint Luke) that, when He had with His disciples drunken after the paschal lamb, He would drink no more of the

7. Heb. 10 : 4.
8. More practically translates a passage from Chrysostom in the *Catena aurea* of Aquinas.
9. More is probably alluding to a passage from Remigius in the *Catena aurea* near the passage from Chrysostom translated above.

generation[10] of the vine till the kingdom of God were come, so
said He here again to them after the institution of His holy
blessed sacrament: *Dico enim vobis quia non bibam amodo de hoc
genimine vitis, usque in diem illum cum illud bibam novum vobiscum in
regno Patris mei Dei.*[1]

These words divers doctors do declare diversely. Some take
this saying of our Savior rehearsed by Saint Matthew and Saint
Mark to be the selfsame that Saint Luke rehearseth,[2] and that
they were spoken only after the institution of the sacrament, and
that Saint Luke observed the verity of the saying and not observed the time. And of this mind seemeth Master Gerson to
have been, as appeareth by his rehearsing of the matter.

But divers other doctors take them as spoken at diverse times,
the tone after the paschal finished, the tother after that at the institution of the blessed sacrament. And so seemeth it most plain
to appear upon the words of Saint Luke. And albeit that the first
words rehearsed by Saint Luke and these other rehearsed by
Saint Matthew and Saint Mark may be both understanden in one
sentence and as one thing twice said—that is to wit, that in both
the times of that saying our Savior meant that He would no
more drink with His apostles (after that time in which they
should then depart after that supper) until Himself were risen
again fro death, and His body forever immortal and impassible[3]
(which glory of His He called the kingdom of His Father), after
which entry thereinto by His resurrection, He would both eat
and drink with them again, and so would drink with them the
wine new[4] in the kingdom of His Father (that is to wit, Himself
being in the kingdom of His Father should drink the wine with
them in a new manner, that is to wit, when He should be forever
immortal and impassible), and that He would no more drink of
that kind of wine of which He consecrated, and which He
turned into His blessed blood, till His passion were passed and
His new life comen[5]—albeit (I say) that I deny not but that thus
they may be taken (and by some of the old holy doctors thus are

10. fruit.   1. Matt. 26 : 29, Mark 14 : 25.   2. See Luke 22 : 18.
3. incapable of suffering.   4. anew.   5. come.

declared indeed), yet are they by divers others of those old holy doctors expouned divers other wise, and (as it seemeth) may well be declared thus.

In the words rehearsed by Saint Luke when our Savior said, *Dico enim vobis quod non bibam de generatione vitis, donec regnum Dei veniat* [6] (I say verily to you that I shall not drink of the generation of the vine till the kingdom of God come), our Savior meant in these words that not only not after the supper but also not after the time of that draft there drunken to the paschal lamb, He would drink no more of the generation of the vine till the kingdom of God were come, that is to wit, that He would before His resurrection drink no more wine after that draft of wine which He drank next before those words spoken. And so did He then by those words also teach them to know and perceive well afterward that the wine, which (before His other words that Saint Matthew and Saint Mark rehearse spoken at the institution of the blessed sacrament) was in the chalice, and which wine He there converted into His own precious blood, was, at the time of the drinking thereof, not wine but His own holy blood under the form of wine, which thing they were (I say)—besides His other plain words: "This is my blood of the New Testament, which shall be shed for you and for many into remission of sins"—well showed and taught, in that He told them before the drinking of that (of which as I shall after show He drank Himself with them) that before His resurrection, which was not then comen, He would drink no wine.

Now in His second words rehearsed by Saint Matthew and Saint Mark—which words He spake at the institution of the blessed sacrament, when that (after the wine turned into His blood and taken to His apostles) He said: *Dico autem vobis, quia non bibam amodo de hoc genimine vitis, usque in diem illum cum illud bibam novum vobiscum in regno Patris mei Dei* [7]—in these words

6. Luke 22 : 18.
7. Matt. 26 : 29 and Mark 14 : 25. "I say verily to you that I shall not drink henceforth from this fruit of the vine until that day when I will drink it with you new in the kingdom of my Father, God."

(gathered together in one out of the gospel of the two foresaid evangelists) our Savior meant that He would after that draft no more drink with them of His own blessed blood, which He drank with them then, until His bitter passion and His glorious resurrection were performed. For after His glorious resurrection it is very probable, both upon these words and some other places of the scripture too, that He not only did eat with them common meat but also did consecrate and eat with them the blessed sacrament also.

Now that He should call here His own blessed blood by the name of the generation of the vine is nothing to be marvelled, while we see it in the common manner of holy scripture to call His blessed body and blood by the former names of the thing which He converted into them, as God in the scripture calleth Adam earth because he was made of the earth, saying: *Terra es et in terram reverteris.*[8] And the scripture calleth the serpent into which the rod of Aaron was turned by the name of a rod or a yard,[9] while it was not a rod but a serpent: *Virga Aaron devoravit virgas magorum Egiptiorum.*[1] And over this our Savior in those second words, as some holy doctors declare, by the vine meant Himself, which afterward unto His apostles He declared Himself, saying in the fifteenth chapter of Saint John: *Ego sum vitis vera.*[2] (I am the very vine.)

And so may every way these words of our Savior (spoken after the conversion of the wine into His blessed blood) be well thus understand:[3] "I say verily to you that I shall not, fro this time in which I drink now thereof with you, drink again of the generation of the vine, that is to wit, of my blood which I have here consecrated, and into which I have here converted and turned the generation of the vine (that is to say, the wine that came of

8. Gen. 3 : 19. "For dust thou art, and unto dust thou shalt return."
9. stick.
1. Exod. 7 : 12. "The rod of Aaron swallowed up the rods of the magicians of Egypt."
2. John 15 : 1.   3. understood.

the vine and was in the chalice before) until that day when," etc.

Or else, after those other holy doctors that expound the vine to be Himself, they may be well understanden thus: "I say verily to you that I shall not, fro this time in which I drink thereof with you now, drink anymore of this generation of the vine that we now drink of, that is to say, of mine own blood of the New Testament (as I have told you), which is the generation of that vine of which these other words of mine are verified, *Ego sum vitis vera,*[4] 'I am the very vine' (for of mine own body is mine own blood)—of this generation of the vine will I no more drink after this time until that day in which I shall drink it with you new, that is to wit, when it shall be new in the kingdom of my Father God (that is to say, that I being in the kingdom of God, my very natural Father,[5] that is to wit, after my resurrection when my body shall be forever immortal and impassible and in eternal glory), until that day will I not after this time drink anymore of this generation of the vine, that is myself, which am the very vine. And then after that will I drink it again with you, at which time it shall be new."

Now that with those words this exposition, by which they be understanden not of wine but of His blessed blood, most properly should agree, it appeareth both by divers other things that well may be gathered upon the circumstance[6] of the matter and also upon this latter saying of our Savior compared with the former. For in the former, He said that He would, after that draft of wine that He drank to the paschal lamb, drink no more wine till after His resurrection. And now had He drunken wine again after that and before His resurrection, if that which He drank the second time had been wine (as it was not, but was only His own blessed blood). And therefore is it very probable that, in His second saying, by these words, "this generation of the vine," He meant not any wine, but the blessed blood of Himself.

Also in the words that He spake before of the paschal lamb

4. John 15 : 1.   5. *my . . . Father:* the true Father of my nature.
6. context.

(when He said He would eat the paschal lamb after that no more till it were fulfilled and perfited[7] in the kingdom of God) He meant that the Mosaical sacrifice of the paschal lamb, that was the only figure,[8] He would never eat more. But the very paschal lamb that was the verity of that figure, that is to wit, His own blessed body and blood, after that the figure were by His new sacrament instituted, and (by His passion suffered and by His glorious body risen again fro death) fulfilled in the kingdom of God, that would He then eat again with them in the blessed sacrament under the form of bread, as He now would when He instituted it, and as He did after indeed. And so are these words of the chalice understanden in like wise of His blessed blood in the sacrament, which it seemeth that He by those words in like wise promised to drink again with them after His resurrection.

Finally, for this exposition, I note this word *novum,* that is to say, "new." Where our Savior in the said latter saying saith: *Dico autem vobis, quia amodo non bibam de hoc genimine vitis, usque in diem illum cum illud bibam novum vobiscum in regno Patris mei Dei*[9] (I say verily to you that from henceforth I shall not drink of this generation of the vine, until that day when I shall drink it with you new in the kingdom of my Father God), in these words, I say, I note and mark this word *novum,* "new." For, albeit that divers doctors expound it, *novum, id est novo modo* (new, that is to wit, in a new manner), because our Lord after His resurrection did both eat and drink with His disciples such common meat and drink as He was before wont to do, but yet in a new manner (that is to wit, now immortal and impassible, and not for the necessary food of the body, but for the proof of that He was risen with His very body), albeit, I say, that some doctors expound that word *novum* thus, yet seemeth me that the tother exposition is much more apt and consonant thereunto. For this word *novum* seemeth not there to be put for an adverb, but is a noun adjective, and therefore it signifieth some kind of newness in the

7. perfected.   8. *the . . . figure:* merely a type.
9. Matt. 26 : 29 and Mark 14 : 25.

drink itself, whereas by that exposition all the newness is in the drinker (that is to wit, in the person of Christ) and in the act of drinking, as done for a new cause, but no manner of newness in the drink itself at all.

For in the common wine that our Savior drank with them after His resurrection was there none other manner of newness than there was therein before. And therefore, as I said, this other exposition that I have here showed seemeth much more agreeable unto the text, that is to wit, that after that time He would no more drink with them His own blessed blood, which He drank with them then in the blessed sacrament, until that day when He should in the kingdom of God His Father drink that blood with them new. For after His glorious resurrection that holy blood of His and all His blessed body was waxen new, that is to wit, of a new condition, other than it was at that time in which they received it in the blessed sacrament.

For, albeit that His body, so delivered them at that time, suffered not, nor by their eating and receiving into their bodies was not pained, yet was it such that afterward it did suffer pain and death upon the cross. But when they received it again sacramentally after His ressurection, then was it in eternal glory so confirmed, and in such wise immortal and impassible, that it should never die nor never suffer pain after. And so, though there were in His blessed body and His blood given them in the sacrament before His passion such a secret wonderful glory of impassibility for the time (as was in His body for the time a visible, open glory at His marvelous transfiguration), yet in the sacramental receiving after His glorious resurrection it had that point of newness which it had not actually before, that is to wit, without loss, minishment,[1] or intermission,[2] eternal enduring of impassible and immortal glory.

And so should (as I say) that generation of that vine, that is to wit, the blessed blood of His own holy person which He drank with them, consecrated of the generation of the common vine

1. diminution.   2. cessation.

and in the likeness and form of common wine, be new after His
glorious resurrection, before which time He there told them that
He would drink no more thereof after that time, in which at His
maundy in the first institution He and all they did drink thereof
together, of which their drinking with Him Saint Mark maketh
mention, saying, *Et biberunt ex eo omnes* [3] (and they drank thereof
all), that is to wit, all the twelve apostles.

That all the apostles drank thereof appeareth well by these
words, at the least wise as many as were present at the time, and
that were they all twelve. For though some have doubted and
some also thought that Judas was gone before, yet is it the most
common sentence [4] of all the old holy men, and most received
for the truth among all Christian people, that the traitor received it too, whereof we shall have occasion to speak after in
other places.

But now that our Savior did receive and eat His own blessed
body, and drink His own blessed blood in the blessed sacrament
at His maundy with His apostles Himself, if any man doubt, it
seemeth me [5] that His own holy words afore rehearsed will well
declare it, in which words He said that Himself would drink no
more thereof till He would drink it with them new in the kingdom of God, that is to wit, in His glory as I have before showed
you.

And that He called His glory the kingdom of God appeareth
both by other places of scripture and also by His own words,
where, intending to show to some of his disciples (that is to wit,
Saint Peter, Saint James, and Saint John) a sight and show of His
glory in His transfiguration, He said: *Sunt quidam de hic stantibus
qui non gustabunt mortem, donec videbunt regnum Die.* [6] (There be
some here standing that shall not taste the death till they shall
see the kingdom of God.)

Besides this, likewise as He did Himself both eat and drink
with them of the old paschal lamb that was but the figure, so is it
none other to be thought but that in the instituting of this new

3. Mark 14 : 23.   4. judgment.   5. *it . . . me:* it seems to me.
6. Mark 8 : 39. See also Matt. 16 : 28.

blessed sacrament, the verity of that figure, He did Himself eat and drink with them too. And that He so did indeed holy Saint Chrysostom declareth, which in an homily upon these words of Christ, *Bibite ex hoc omnes* (Drink you of this all), saith thus: *Ne autem hoc audientes turbarentur, primum ipse sanguinem suum bibit, inducens eos sine turbatione in communionem mysteriorum.*[7] (Lest that they hearing that word should be troubled therewith, He drank His blood first Himself, inducing them into the communion of the sacraments without abashment or trouble.) Holy Saint Hierome also in his book against the great heretic Helvidius writeth in this wise: *Sic igitur Dominus Jesus fuit conviva et convivium, ipse comedens et qui comeditur.*[8] (So therefore was our Lord Jesus both the guest and the feast. He was both the eater, and was also He that was eaten.)

Now forasmuch as we shall somewhat farther enter into the treating of this blessed sacrament, let us pray Him that hath instituted it that we may in such wise treat thereof that it may both in the writer and the reader stretch to[9] the fruit[1] of their souls.

The prayer.

Our most dear Savior Christ, which after the finishing of the old paschal sacrifice hast instituted the new sacrament of Thine own blessed body and blood for a memorial of Thy bitter passion, give us such true faith therein and such fervent devotion thereto that our souls may take fruitful, ghostly[2] food thereby.

The second lecture upon the blessed sacrament.

So excellent is (good Christian readers) this holy blessed sacrament above all other, that neither is there any man able to enter,[3] pierce,[4] and perceive so many great wonderful things as are to be noted therein, nor those that of the old holy doctors

---

7. More is probably quoting Chrysostom from the *Catena aurea* of Aquinas.
8. More is probably also quoting Jerome from the *Catena aurea*.
9. *stretch to:* serve for.   1. advantage.   2. spiritual.
3. penetrate.   4. see thoroughly into.

are already noted, and of all Christian regions already received
and believed, able (as the dignity of the thing requireth) well to
declare or worthily to speak of. For in this holy sacrament is the
very body and the very blood of Him of whom all other sacraments receive their virtue and strength. For it is (as you have
heard of Christ's own words) the selfsame sacred body of Christ,
and the selfsame blessed blood of His, that was delivered and
shed for our sin.

Now albeit that there are in divers countries of Christendom
some (and hard it is to find any country so fortunate as to be
clear and clean without) that labor in this blessed sacrament to
subvert the very true Christian faith—and would make men
ween that those plain words of Christ, "This is my body" (etc.),
were otherwise meant than they were indeed, and that our Savior in His so saying did not affirm nor intend that the thing
which He gave His apostles to eat and to drink was His very
body and His very blood, but that they were still bread and wine
which He called then (say they) by the names of His body and
His blood because He would institute them for to stand as
tokens of His body and His blood for perpetual remembrance of
His passion—albeit there lack not, I say, some that labor to bring
good faithful folk out of the true belief into this erroneous
mind, yet is it not my present purpose to dispute the matter with
them but to show and set forth the truth before the eyen [5] of the
reader, that he may rather of the truth read, increase in faith,
and conceive devotion, than with much time bestowed in the
reading of their erroneous fallacies misoccupy his ears and heap
up in his heart a dunghill of their devilish vanities.

Howbeit somewhat of theirs is it, good readers, in my mind
necessary that you know, to the intent you may the better beware of their wiliness. Three special engines [6] use these manner
of folk with which they busily with all their might oppugn [7] the
inexpugnable [8] person of our Savior Christ, enforcing themself [9]

5. eyes.   6. instruments of warfare.   7. attack.
8. impregnable.   9. *enforcing themself*: striving.

by force to put out His glorious body out of the blessed sacrament.

First, using the name of sacrament of Christ's body with us, whereby good simple folk would ween they meant as we do, they misuse the meaning of that word against us, and in corners[1] corrupt some well-minded men before they perceive the train of their crafty purpose. For they make them ween that, sith we call it all the blessed sacrament of Christ's body and blood, therefore it is none other but a bare sacrament only, that is to wit, a token, a figure, a sign or memorial of His body and His blood crucified and shed, and not His own very body and His blood indeed.

Secondly, they say that those words of Christ may be well and conveniently expounded in such wise as they may serve to prove the sacrament a figure. And upon that they conclude that, sith they may be so expounded conveniently by an allegory, there is no necessity to expound them otherwise, nor that those words should not be so taken and declared as to say that they signify that in the sacrament is Christ's blessed body indeed.

Thirdly, they enforce[2] that reason[3] with the expositions of old holy men, which have expounded those words in an allegory[4] sense and have in their writings called this blessed holy housel[5] by the name of a sacrament, a sign, a memorial, and a figure. By which words of those old holy saints those new folk labor to blear the unlearned reader's eye and make him therewith ween that those old holy men, in that they called it a sign, a token, or a figure, did well declare that they took it not for the very body indeed, for that body cannot be (they say) by no mean a figure of itself.

These three are, I say, good reader, their three special darts. For I deny not but that they use mo: as the words of scripture, whereby they would prove Christ's body not in earth because He said before His ascension to heaven that they should not have Him here still in earth (but He meant of His corporal conversa-

1. *in corners:* in secluded places.   2. reinforce.
3. explanation.   4. allegorical.   5. eucharist.

tion[6] as they had Him before), and where they would also by the
words of scripture prove the blessed sacrament bread (but the
custom of the scripture is so common in that point to call a
thing, not as it is, but as it was, or as it seemeth, whereof I have
told you a sample or two before, that all the hold they can take
thereof slippeth out of their hand).

I deny not also but that they lay against[7] the sacrament and
say that Christ's blessed body is not there, because they say it
cannot. For it cannot be (they say) in so many places at once. But
now sith the truth is that Himself saith it is there, and in His so
saying so meant in very deed (as both before is proved and yet
shall hereafter), all that reason of theirs (that it cannot be so)
hath to any Christian man (that taketh Christ for God) no manner taste of any reason at all. For it standeth, you see, well upon
this ground only, that God is not able to perform His word.

Therefore albeit that (as I say) they say such other things too,
yet are those three things that I have rehearsed you[8] the special
things, and in effect the only things, with which they have their
special hope to deceive unlearned folk.

Now purpose I not yet, in this present treatise upon the passion, to enter much in dispicions[9] with them upon these three
points neither. For that thing would require an whole volume
alone (the labor whereof, if God hereafter give me time and opportunity thereto, I purpose not to refuse); but I will in effect,
for this while, only rehearse you some of those things that holy
cunning[1] men before my days have of this holy blessed sacrament, concerning this matter, left us behind them in writing.
Which things, if the reader diligently consider, shall (I trust) be
able somewhat to serve and suffice him to spy the fallacies and
soil[2] the subtleties of all those folks' false arguments and objections by himself.

Consider now, good readers, and remember that—sith this excellent high sacrament, under a form and likeness so common

6. *corporal conversation:* bodily presence.   7. *lay against:* attack.
8. *rehearsed you:* mentioned to you.   9. disputations.
1. learned.   2. refute.

and so simple in sight, covertly containeth in it a wonderful secret treasure, and signifieth and betokeneth also manifold marvelous mysteries—the holy cunning fathers afore our days have had much ado to find names enough and convenient with which they might in any wise insinuate[3] and show so many such manner things of this blessed sacrament as are partly contained therein and partly signified thereby. And therefore, by the secret instinct[4] of the Spirit of God, by which the Catholic Church of Christ is in such things led and ruled, the old holy virtuous fathers have not only called (upon effectual causes[5]) this holy sacrament by sundry diverse names, to signify thereby sundry singular things thereof, but have also, for the same intent (upon divers effectual respects that they saw and considered therein), called some two sundry things both by one common name.

For the better perceiving whereof we must mark and consider that in this blessed sacrament there are two things actually and really contained: one that is a very bodily substance and that is the very blessed body and blood of our Savior Himself; the tother that is not any substance but accidents, that is to wit, those accidents that were before in the bread and wine (which bread and wine are converted by the almighty power of God into the very body and blood of Christ). Those accidents, I say, of whiteness, redness, hardness, softness, weight, savor, and taste, and such other like, remain and abide in the blessed sacrament, and by the mighty power of almighty God they remain without the body of which they be the accidents, which—while they be now neither accidents in the bread and wine (sith bread or wine none is there), nor accidents unto the blessed body and blood of Christ (which two things are the only corporal substance that are there) and accidents are not naturally, nor the mind of a living man cannot well imagine how any accident can be but in a bodily substance whereunto it is accident and whereupon it dependeth—much folly were it therefore much to muse thereupon how,

3. impart to the mind subtly.   4. prompting.
5. *upon effectual causes:* for valid reasons.

and in what wise, and wherein these accidents abide and are conserved. But that question with many such other mo—wherewith a proud curious mind hath carried many a man out of faith—let us remit unto God. For as He only can make those miracles, so can He only tell how.

Now albeit that an accident, by a general manner of speaking, is a thing (sith it is not nothing), and in such wise I mean by this word "a thing" when I say there are in the blessed sacrament two things; yet, forasmuch as the name of "sacrament" properly signifieth a sign or token, which betokeneth an holy thing, the "thing" of a sacrament is properly called that holy thing that the sacrament betokeneth—as in baptism the washing of the body with water, signifying the washing of the soul by grace, is properly the sacrament, and the washing of the soul fro sin is called the "thing" of the sacrament, that is to say, the thing that the sacrament or sacramental sign (I mean the washing in the water) betokeneth.

Now in this holy sacrament of the altar (which hath, as reason is,[6] above all other sacraments sundry special prerogatives[7]) there are two sacraments or sacramental signs of sundry kinds: the tone an outward sacrament or sacramental sign sensible (as baptism hath, and confirmation, and the tother four), the tother an inward sacrament or sacramental sign unsensible,[8] which none of the remnant[9] have. The outward sensible sacrament or sacramental sign is the form of bread and the form of wine. The inward sacrament and sacramental sign unsensible is the very blessed body of Christ under that form of bread and the very blessed blood of Christ under the form of wine.

Now are there likewise in this blessed sacrament (above the nature also of all the tother six) two things of the sacrament, or two sacramental things (that is to wit, two things that are by the two sacramental signs betokened). And those two things, though they be both secret and unsensible, yet are they of diverse

6. *as reason is:* in conformity to reason.
7. divinely given privileges.   8. imperceptible to the senses.
9. others.

sundry kinds too. For the tone is both by the sacrament (that is to wit, by the sacramental sign) signified and also in the sacrament contained. The tother is only by the sacrament signified, but in the sacrament it is not contained. The thing of the sacrament that is both signified and contained is the very body and the very blood of our Savior Himself, therein actually and really present. The thing of this blessed sacrament that is signified thereby and not contained therein is the unity or society of all good holy folk in the mystical body of Christ.

For this must we now first understand, that the first kind of sacrament that we spake of (that is to wit, the outward sacramental signs) be sacraments (that is to wit, signs and tokens) of both these two sacramental things: that is to wit, of the very natural body of Christ that is in the sacrament contained, and also of the society of all saints in the mystical body of Christ that is not contained in it but signified and betokened by it. For the outward sacramental signs (that is to wit, the form of bread and wine) betoken the very natural body and blood of Christ being in the sacrament. For as the holy doctors declare, likewise as bread specially refresheth and sustaineth the body—whereof the scripture saith: *Panis confirmat cor hominis* [1] (Bread strenketh [2] a man's heart)—and wine gladdeth the heart—whereof the scripture saith also: *Vinum laetificat cor hominis* [3]—so the very blessed body and blood of Christ in the sacrament, received worthily, [4] doth specially above all other sacraments refresh, make strong, and confirm the soul in grace, and so fulfilleth [5] in some good folk the soul with spiritual consolation that the soul is in a certain manner of an heavenly drunkenness. In proof whereof our Savior saith of His body in the sacrament: *Panis quem ego dabo caro mea est; qui manducat hunc panem vivet in aeternum.* [6] (The bread that I shall give is my flesh; he that eateth this bread shall live everlastingly.) And of His blessed blood in the sacrament He saith

1. Ps. 103 : 15.   2. strengthens.
3. Ps. 103 : 15. "Wine gladdens the heart of man."
4. with a fitting disposition.   5. fills to the full.
6. John 6 : 52, 59.

by the mouth of the prophet: *Calix meus inebrians quam praeclarus est?*[7] (My cup that maketh men drunk, how noble it is?)

These outward sacramental signs (the form of bread and wine) do also signify and betoken unto us the tother sacramental thing (or the tother thing of the sacrament), that is to wit, that thing of the sacrament that is signified by the sacrament but not contained therein—that is to wit, the society of all saints in the mystical body of Christ. For likewise as the bread, which is in this holy sacrament turned into Christ's very body (of which bread the form still remaineth), was made of many corns[8] of wheat into one loaf and the wine that is converted into His blessed blood (of which wine the form remaineth) was made of many grapes flowing into one wine, so be all holy saints gathered together in one, into the unity of Christ's holy mystical body, as Saint Paul toucheth in his epistle to the Corinthies,[9] saying: *Unus panis et unum corpus multi sumus; omnes qui de uno pane, et de uno calice participamus.*[1] (We many be one bread and one body, as many as be partakers of one bread and one cup.)[2]

The tother kind of sacrament or sacramental sign (that is to wit, the sacrament or sacramental sign secret and unsensible[3]) is, I say, the very natural body and blood of our Savior in the form of bread and wine. For His very body and His very blood in these forms so known and seen unto us, not by our senses but by the truth of our faith, do betoken and represent unto us the self-same body and the selfsame blood crucified and shed upon the cross. For our Savior at His last supper, at the institution of the blessed sacrament, did ordain, institute, and appoint them to sig-

---

7. Ps. 22 : 5.   8. grains.   9. Corinthians.
1. 1. Cor. 10 : 17.
2. At this point More directed that a passage be inserted from St. Augustine (*In Joannis evangelium, tractatus 26, PL 35,* 1614–15) to support the symbolic significance of bread uniting many grains and wine many grapes. Rastell (*English Works,* 1557) gave the Latin and translated it (with less skill than one would have expected from More). Both the Latin and the translation are omitted here.
3. imperceptible to the senses.

nify, betoken, and represent unto His church under those forms the selfsame body crucified and the selfsame blood also shed for remission of man's sins at His bitter passion.

And therefore when our Savior gave His blessed body in form of bread unto his apostles, saying unto them: *Hoc est corpus meum, quod pro vobis tradetur* [4] and *Hic est sanguis meus qui pro vobis et multis effundetur in remissionem peccatorum* [5] (This is my body, which shall be delivered for you; this is my blood, which for you and for many shall be shed into remission of sins), He said unto them farther, *Hoc facite in meam commemorationem.* [6] (This do ye in the remembrance of me.) So that there we may see that He there instituted the same body of His that should be delivered for us unto death and the same blood that should be shed for our sins to be in His church continually consecrate [7] and celebrate [8] as a monument and a memorial representing to us Himself.

Now in what wise those secret invisible sacraments (His own very natural blessed body and blood) under those visible sacraments (those forms of bread and wine) should signify, betoken, and represent unto us Himself (that is to say, the same body and blood in their proper form), the apostle explaineth in the eleventh chapter of his first epistle to the Corinthies, saying: *Quotienscumque manducabitis panem hunc et calicem bibetis, mortem domini annunciabitis donec veniat.* [9] (As often as you shall eat this bread and drink this cup, you shall show the death of our Lord till He come.) Here we see that, whereas our Savior in His own words ordained His own very body and blood in the sacrament to signify, betoken, and represent Himself unto our remembrance, Saint Paul showeth here that it is the remembrance of Him as in His passion; and so betoken His body and His blood in the sacrament the selfsame body in his [1] own likeness hanging on the cross and the selfsame blood in the proper likeness on the same shed for our sin. The selfsame unsensible sacrament also, the

4. Luke 22 : 19. Cf. Matt. 26 : 26, Mark 14 : 22.
5. Matt. 26 : 28. Cf. Mark 14 : 24, Luke 22 : 20.
6. Luke 22 : 19.   7. consecrated.   8. celebrated.
9. 1 Cor. 11 : 26.   1. its.

natural body of Christ that is under the sensible sacrament of
bread, signifieth and betokeneth the tother aforesaid sacramental thing, that is to wit, the society of saints. For like as the natural body of Christ is many members in one natural body, so is
that society of saints many lively[2] members in the unity of
Christ's mystical body.

And thus we see, good Christian readers, that the outward
sensible sacraments (the forms of bread and wine) be in such
wise figures, tokens, and sacramental signs, that they be only sacramental signs and not sacramental things. And on the tother
side, the secret sacramental thing which is both by the outward
sensible sacraments and by the secret unsensible sacraments signified and not contained (that is to wit, the society of saints in
the unity of Christ's body mystical) is only the thing of the sacrament, or the sacramental thing, and not a sacramental sign, neither sensible nor unsensible (for it is signified only and signifieth
not). But the very natural body and blood of Christ, in the form
of bread and wine, be both sacramental signs, because they signify, and also sacramental things, because they be signified.

Yet must we further know that, albeit we speak only of the
blessed body and blood of Christ, that are verily present in form
of bread and wine, yet is there with them the soul of our Savior
also. For His blessed body and blood in the sacrament, though
they seem dead—for the more full representation and figuring
of the same body and blood remaining dead on the cross after
His holy soul given up to the Father, whereby His bitter passion
was fully performed and finished—yet be they not dead in the
sacrament, but quick and animated with His blissful soul, which
after the return thereof and copulation[3] again with His immortal and impassible body never departed after from it nor never
shall.

There is with it also, beside His blessed soul, His almighty
Godhead. For the Godhead from the first time of His incarna-
tion never departed neither fro the soul nor fro the body. But

2. living.   3. union.

when they two were by death departed [4] and severed asunder, the Godhead—that is to wit, the almighty natural Son of the almighty Father, the second person in Trinity (of which Father and Son the third almighty person of the coeternal Trinity proceeded)—was still in unity of person, both with the blessed soul delivering the old fathers in hell, and with the body lying dead in the sepulcher too.

Moreover, albeit that the blessed blood is consecrate [5] severally under the form of wine, to signify and represent unto us that in the passion (of which the blessed sacrament is a memorial) the blood was severed fro the body, yet is there in the blessed sacrament both the blood with the body that is in the form of bread, and the body with the blood that is under form of wine— that is to wit, the body (under the form of bread) immediately, as by the form of bread most specially signified, and the blood by concomitance, because the body is never without it; and likewise, under the form of wine the blessed blood immediately, because there by that form of wine the blood is chiefly signified, and the whole blessed body is there with it by concomitance, because that the blood, since His glorious resurrection, never was, nor is, nor never shall be separate from His whole blessed body.

If men ask then the question, what we may think of the holy blood of Christ out of the sacrament, continually kept and honored in divers places and with many great miracles approved, [6] me thinketh it may be answered in two manner wise without any peril of our faith. For I see no necessity to say that all the blood that Christ had in His body at any time here in earth is in His body now. And so may some part of His very holy blood that hath been sometime in His blessed body be now remaining in earth. And also, sith His blessed body may be where it will, His very glorious blood may be by miracle in sundry places sensible, where it pleaseth Himself, and His blessed body invisible therewith.

4. separated.   5. consecrated.   6. attested to.

In a crucifix stricken[7] God may also create new blood, which is
none of His.[8] And over this, the blissful soul of Christ and His
almighty Godhead also be both twain, I say, not immediately
contained in the sacrament, because they be neither immediately
signified by those sensible sacramental signs (the forms of bread
and wine), nor be there as secret unsensible signs appointed to
signify any other things (as the blessed body and the blood be),
but be therefore there by concomitance, because fro the body and
the blood neither the soul nor the Godhead is at no time since
the resurrection asunder.

And by concomitance are there also both the Father and the
Holy Ghost. For sith the Godhead of the Son and the Godhead
of them both is all one self[9] Godhead, neither of them both can
be severed from Him, but it must needs be that where He is,
there be they both, not only by a general manner of being (by
which each of them is ever with any of all the things that they
have created), but also by that special manner of being by which
(whatsoever manner that be) any of those three persons is with
Himself, except the only personal distinction.[10] It seemeth also
that by concomitance, though not a concomitance following of like
necessity (yet by a certain concomitance following of convenient
congruity), there is everywhere evermore about this blessed sacrament a glorious heavenly company of blessed angels and
saints, as divers holy doctors declare.

Now forasmuch as under any of the two outward sensible sacraments (the forms either of the bread or the wine) the whole
inward unsensible sacrament (the very body and blood of Christ)
is, as I have showed you, verily and fully contained, and also
under every part thereof (be it divided into never so many),
therefore whosoever worthily do receive his holy housel[1] under
any one of those two forms only[2] doth verily and sufficiently re-

---

7. struck.   8. *none of His:* not His own blood.   9. same.
10. *except . . . distinction:* except that the distinction among the persons
remains. (Thus, the Father is with the Son as the Son is with Himself, except that the Father is a distinct person from the Son whereas the Son is
not personally distinct from Himself.)
1. eucharist.   2. alone.

ceive both the blessed body and blood of our Savior and therewith His blessed soul and His Godhead too, yea, and all the
whole Trinity together. And albeit that of old time lay people
did commonly receive their housel under both the forms, yet alway
fro the beginning did they sometime receive it some under the
tone form and some under the tother alone, as by the old writings of the old holy saints it doth in divers places appear. Howbeit, when they received their housel under the tone kind alone,
it was most commonly under the form of bread, because that
under that form it was most able both to be carried without peril
of spilling and longest to be kept without peril of turning.[3]

Upon which thing so long ago begun and used, it came to that
point afterward that for divers inconvenience,[4] which many
times mishapped[5] in the blessed blood under the form of wine
when the common people were houseled[6] under both the forms,
the whole people thorough[7] Christendom fell in a custom uni-
form all in one fashion to receive their holy housel (that is to wit,
the very whole body of Christ and blood both) under the form
of bread only—of which custom no man hath heard or read any
beginning, which thing alone may well suffice to make indifferent[8] men perceive that it began even forthwith after Christ's
death and that the leefulness[9] thereof was known and taught by
the tradition of the apostles themself. For surely if it had not
been known for leeful[1] of old, the whole people of all Christendom would never have taken it up of new,[2] being a thing of neither pleasure nor winning, nor being nothing forced unto it (for
law was there none made to command it).

Howbeit, when that the country of Boheme, falling into many
heresies, began not only to do the contrary, receiving it under
both the forms (wherein the body of Christendom would not
have sticked[3] to suffer them as a thing leeful to them that
would[4]), but also took upon them farther to reprove and reproach for damnable the common long-continued custom of the

3. spoiling.   4. unfortunate occurrences.
5. happened unfortunately.   6. given communion.
7. throughout.   8. impartial.   9. lawfulness.   1. lawful.
2. anew.   3. been reluctant.   4. wished to.

whole corps[5] of Christendom—upon this demeanor of theirs, the general Council of Constance[6] condemned in their so doing their over-arrogant error. For upon that point of theirs, if the whole body of Christendom may damnably be deceived in matter concerning our faith or the use of the sacraments, then followeth there an inevitable confusion and nothing can there in the Catholic Church be sure: neither tradition, law, custom, nor scripture—neither to know how it is to be understanden nor yet so much as which the very books be, as holy Saint Austin (against the great heretics the Manichees) doth very clearly declare.[7]

Now is this custom (and long was, ere their heresies began in Boheme) so universal that neither lay nor priest, man nor woman, good nor bad, either otherwise used[8] in receiving the holy housel beside[9] the mass or anything repugned[1] thereat. Howbeit, though (as I say) this guise[2] and custom was universal both with lay people and priests, in being houseled of[3] another man's hand (as the priests be themself alway, save only when they say mass), yet did there never priest in the mass use to consecrate in the tone form alone. And the cause is because that in the mass the blessed sacrament is (as the old holy doctors all with one voice agree, and all the corps of Christendom with them fro the apostles' days) not only a sacrament but also a sacrifice that by the offering of the body and blood of Christ (under the forms of bread and wine upon the altar) representeth the sacrifice in which the selfsame body and blood (in their own proper form) was offered upon the cross.

And therefore, albeit that in each of the two forms is the whole sacrament, both for the thing that it signifieth and for the thing that it containeth, yet under the tone kind only was it never used to offer that holy sacrifice, but under the both twain together, that the thing should be correspondent unto the figure

5. body.
6. The Council of Constance (1415) condemned the Bohemian reformer John Huss to death.
7. See above, p. 115, n. 4.   8. practiced.   9. outside of.
1. resisted.   2. practice.   3. by.

(for this holy sacrifice was forefigured in the offering of Mel-
chizedek,[4] that offered both bread and wine).

Yet is there also put into the wine, before the consecration, a little water alway, whereof we find no word written in the gospel,
nor any plain place in all the scripture for it. And yet may it not be
leefully[5] left out, as all the old holy doctors teach us. And divers
causes they lay[6] of that institution,[7] partly for that out of the
holy heart of Christ, when it was pierced with the spear, there
issued both blood and water.[8] And some allege that it is done for
to signify the joining of the people with Christ (for, as it appeareth in the Apocalypse, by water is signified people[9]). And finally, some holy saints say that it is done because that our Savior
Himself, at His maundy, tempered His wine with water. And all
these may be good causes, with the truth and the will of God
well known. But else I verily believe that no good man (upon
any of these considerations or any other), when he should consecrate, would presume or adventure[1] to put water into his
wine—where the gospel of the institution[2] speaketh of no water
at all (but only of wine alone)—and therefore it well and clearly
appeareth, both by this point and divers other mo (as in the very
words and manner of consecration), the rites and the manner of
this holy sacrament were more at large showed and more fully
taught by Christ's apostles by mouth than afterward written by
their pen.

And so appeareth it also by Saint Paul, which first taught it the
Corinthies without any book written thereof, and, after writing
them somewhat thereof, saith yet finally, *Caetera quum venero ipse
disponam.*[3] (The remnant I will order when I come myself.) And
never wrote he those orders after[4] that he took farther at his
coming, as far as ever I could hear proved. Origen saith also
(and divers other old holy doctors) that many things of the mass
were taught by the apostles by tradition, without writing, by

4. Cf. Gen. 14 : 18.   5. lawfully.   6. present, allege.
7. established rule.   8. See John 19 : 34.   9. Rev. 17 : 15.
1. venture.   2. founding.   3. 1 Cor. 11 : 34.
4. afterward.

mouth.[5] Saint Denis also, in his book *De Ecclesiastica hierarchia,* saith that the apostles taught the manner of consecrating in the mass by mouth.[6]

Now because of these wonderful things, and many other wherein this most blessed sacrament so far excelleth all other, as that sacrament that not only signifieth and betokeneth but also verily and really containeth the holy and blessed blood of Him of whom all the other sacraments take their strength (for He is, as I have said, not only man but also God, and with His holy body and blood is also His holy soul, and with both His body and soul joined His unseparable Godhead, and of Him His Father and their Holy Spirit is all one Godhead and therefore there present all three)—for these causes, I say, for which this blessed sacrament so many manner ways differeth from all other, the old holy doctors have accustomed to speak of this holy sacrament in divers wise and, to signify and insinuate thereby the divers properties thereof, by sundry diverse names have been accustomed to call it.

Whereas the sacrament of baptism is not called "the sacrament" alone but "the sacrament of baptism," nor any of the remnant[7] without the addition of their own proper name (as the sacrament of confirmation, the sacrament of penance, and so forth the remnant), only this blessed sacrament is called and known by the name of "sacrament" alone, signifying and showing thereby that this blessed sacrament is the most excellent and of all holy sacraments the chief. And that I see not why it were, if it were not (as it is) the very body of Christ, for the sacrament of baptism is unto salvation of more necessity than it, and the sacrament of penance too.

This blessed sacrament of the body and blood of Christ is called also distinctly by the name of either form, *sacramentum panis et sacramentum vini* (the sacrament of bread and the sacrament of wine), because that the form of bread betokeneth and

5. See Origen's fifth homily on the Book of Numbers (*PG 12,* 603).
6. Dionysius (Denis), the pseudo-Areopagite, *PG 3,* 375, 378.
7. others.

immediately containeth the tone, and the form of wine the tother. And albeit that they be indeed two distinct sacraments (that is to wit, both two distinct sacramental outward signs, for neither is the form of bread the form of wine, nor the form of wine the form of bread, and two distinct sacramental inward signs too), and two distinct sacramental things also, of that kind of thing that is contained therein (for neither is the body the blood, nor the blood the body), yet is all together called by the name of "the blessed sacrament" in the singular number, *sacramentum altaris* (the sacrament of the altar); and yet is it never used at the altar but in both the forms. But for because that the very real thing that is contained under both those forms is one entire body—that is to wit, the very lively, natural, glorious body of our Savior Christ Himself, to the integrity whereof the blood of the same pertaineth, and whereof it is now an inseparable part—which blessed body and blood (though they, being in the sacrament under several forms, severally do signify and therefore be well and with good reason called several sacraments) be yet never severally separate asunder indeed; therefore to give us knowledge that all that is really contained in both these sacramental forms is one very real thing—that is to wit, the very blessed one entire body of Christ—all the whole, under the both forms together, is called by the name of "the sacrament of the altar" in the singular number.

It is called *sacramentum panis* (the sacrament of bread) and it is called also *panis* (that is to say, bread) because that of bread it was consecrated and that, after the bread converted and turned into the body of Christ, the form and accidents of the bread abide and remain (as I before have showed you[8] that in scripture a man is called "earth" because he was made of the earth, and in the scripture Moses' yard[9] was called still a yard when it was turned from a dead yard into a quick serpent that devoured all the serpents that the witches of Egypt had by their enchantment brought forth before Pharaoh their king). But yet, lest the

8. See above, p. 134.   9. stick.

naming it bread might make some men ween it were but bread indeed, it is called also plainly by the name of the thing that it is indeed, the body and blood of our Lord.

It is also called *sacramentum communionis* (the sacrament of communion) because that the thing that all the sacraments or sacramental signs (both outward signs and inward, both sensible and unsensible) do signify is, as I have showed you, the communion—that is to wit, the union together—of all holy saints in one society, as lively members in the mystical body of Christ. It is also called not only "the sacrament of communion" but over that "the communion" itself, which is called in Latin *communio* and *synaxis* in the Greek. And this blessed sacrament is called the communion—that is to say, the union or gathering together in one—because that this sacrament doth not only signify that communion but that the very real thing that is in this blessed sacrament (beside the signification thereof) doth also effectually make[1] it. For the blessed person of our Savior Christ, being verily both God and man, doth as God, of His almighty power, by His manhead as by His instrument (not an instrument dead and separate as are all His other sacraments, but by His instrument lively, quick, conjoined, unied,[2] and forever unseparable), in special manner—by grace that He giveth with the joining of His own holy body and blood unto them that effectually receive it—doth work, I say, this wonderful work of the communion of men together with God.

And over this, our Savior, that is in the sacrament, is not only the worker of this communion, but, sith that this communion is a gathering together of all saints into His own mystical body, this holy sacrament therefore, in which His own very body is, may be well called the communion. And so by their calling this blessed sacrament by the name of communion, the old holy doctors and all the congregation of all Christian people have and do put every man and woman of the same congregation in remembrance that in the blessed sacrament is the very body and blood,

1. effect.   2. united.

and by concomitance (as I have before declared) the very whole person, of our sovereign Lord and almighty Savior Christ, from whom (as I have said) neither His almighty Father nor their almighty Spirit either is or can be sundered.

This blessed sacrament is also called *eucharistia,* which in the Greek tongue signifieth "giving of thanks," to put us in remembrance how high hearty thanks we be bounden of duty to give unto God for this inestimable benefit. This holy sacrament is also called *sacrificium* (the sacrifice) because it is, as I have told you, the only sacrifice betaken[3] by Christ unto His Christian church, instead of the old paschal (which was the figure thereof), to be offered up while the world standeth:[4] instead of flesh and blood of beasts, the very flesh and blood of our Savior Himself, immortal and impassible under the forms of bread and wine, representing the most acceptable sacrifice of the same flesh and blood offered up, once for ever, mortal and passible[5] upon the cross at His bitter passion.

This holy sacrament is also called of the old holy doctors *cena dominica* (the supper of our Lord), by which name there are signified unto us two things. One is the excellency of this blessed sacrament, this new very paschal lamb, the sacred body of our Savior Himself, over and above the old paschal lamb of the Jews. For that paschal being but the figure, and this of that figure the verity, the figure passed[6] and finished, this only[7] verity—the blessed body and blood of Christ—beareth now the name alone of the supper of our Lord to signify the tother to be nothing in the respect of[8] this. The tother thing which that name signifieth and representeth unto us is the verity of the blessed body and blood of Christ in the sacrament. For it is called the supper of our Lord to put us in mind and to let us know that it is not another thing but the selfsame thing that our Lord gave there to His apostles: not another supper, but the selfsame supper. For His body is the selfsame body now that it was then, and His

3. granted.   4. continues.   5. capable of suffering.
6. *i.e.,* having been surpassed.   7. single.
8. *in the respect of:* in comparison with.

blessed blood the selfsame in like wise, and that was the supper that He last gave unto them after the paschal lamb eaten.[9] And that selfsame body and blood is the thing that He giveth us. And therefore is it called the supper of our Lord, to let us (as I say) perceive that the thing that we receive at God's board now is the very selfsame thing that the apostles received then, and that is not the same bread and the same wine that were then turned but the very selfsame body and blood into which they were then turned.

Finally, beside yet divers other names diversly signifying the manifold great graces thereof, it is, as I have said, both by the scripture and all the holy doctors plainly and clearly called by the proper name of the thing that indeed it is, that is to wit, *corpus domini et sanguis domini* (the body and blood of our Lord).

And likewise as by all these names afore rehearsed, and yet other mo, for the cause above remembered, this blessed sacrament is called by the old holy doctors and all the corps of Christendom, not in Latin only and in Greek, but in other vulgar tongues too, so in our English tongue is it also called the holy "housel"—which name of housel doth not only signify unto us the blessed body and blood of our Lord in the sacramental form, but also, like as this English word "God" signifieth unto us not only the unity of the Godhead but also the Trinity of the three persons, and not only their supersubstantial[1] substance but also every gracious property (as justice, mercy, truth, almightiness, eternity, and every good thing more than we can imagine), so doth unto us English folk this English word "housel," though not express, yet imply and under a reverent devout silence signify both the sacramental signs and sacramental things, as well the things contained as the things holily signified, with all the secret, unsearchable mysteries of the same. All which holy things right many persons—very little learned, but yet in grace godly minded, with heart humble and religious, not arrogant, proud,

9. *i.e.,* had been eaten.   1. transcending all substance or being.

and curious—under the name of holy housel, with inward heavenly comfort, do full devoutly reverence, as many a good, poor, simple, unlearned soul honoreth God full devoutly under the name of God that cannot yet tell such a tale of God as some great clerks can that are yet for lack of like devotion nothing near so much in God's grace and favor.

Here have I, good Christian readers, rehearsed you some of those many names by which, for the manifold mysteries contained therein and signified thereby, this blessed sacrament is called. And this have I done to the intent that if it hap[2] you at any time hereafter to hear or read any of these things that are said or written by them that use of some of these names to take occasion of oppugning[3] the truth, you may have ready before, at your hand, the fallacy of their sophism soiled.[4] As for ensample, because it is called (as it is indeed) the sacrament of Christ's body, that is to wit, a figure, a token, or a representation of His body, they labor to make men ween that it cannot be His very body indeed. But I have here before showed you in what wise it is a sacrament and doth betoken, and in what wise it is the thing of the sacrament and is betokened.

Howbeit, where we say that the very body in the form of bread betokeneth and representeth unto us the selfsame body in his own proper form hanging on the cross, they say that nothing can be a figure or token of itself, which thing I marvel much that any man taketh for so strange. For if there were but even in a play or an interlude[5] the personages of two or three known princes represented, if one of them now liked for his pleasure to play his own part himself, did he not there, his own person under the form of a player, represent his own person in form of his own estate? Our Savior (as Saint Austin saith), walking with His two disciples toward the castle of Emmaux in form of a wayfaring man, betokened and was a figure of Himself in form of His own person glorified, going out of corporal conversation

2. happened to.   3. attacking.   4. refuted.
5. short, comic play.

of this world by His wonderful ascension unto heaven.[6] And in like wise our Savior, appearing to Mary Magdalene in the form of a gardener, was a figure of Himself in His own proper form, planting the faith and other virtues in the garden of our souls.[7]

Now as you see, good readers, that these folk trifle in this point, so do they (as earnest and as great as the matter is) but in a manner utterly trifle in the remnant. As (for another sample) because the sacrament is called in scripture "bread," they say it is bread indeed. And surely if that argument be so sure as they would have it seem, the selfsame reason must of reason[8] serve sufficiently (sith it is in scripture as plainly called "flesh") to drive them to grant that it is very flesh indeed. Howbeit indeed, the most part of these that are fall[9] fro the right belief of the sacrament are not yet in that point fallen fully so foul but that they let not to confess that in the blessed sacrament is Christ's very flesh indeed. But then say they that it is very bread too. Howbeit, the custom of scripture in calling it bread though it be not bread, that have I twice touched before.[1]

But then say the tother sort (the far worse sort again) if the calling it bread in scripture prove it not bread indeed, then by the same reason the calling it flesh in scripture proveth it not flesh indeed. To that we say that, if it were but a bare word spoken, it might be taken for an allegory or some other trope or figure of common speaking. But in this point so many things in scripture agree together upon the very thing, that it is very clear and plain that in calling it bread the scripture meaneth not that it is bread, but calleth it by the name that it did bear before and that it seemeth still. But in calling it the body of Christ, though it useth (as it doth in many places) an allegorical sense beside, yet appeareth it, I say, plain upon[2] the circumstances that the scrip-

6. Luke 24 : 15, 13. Cf. Augustine's *Sermones* 235–36 (*PL 38*, 1118, 1121).

7. John 20 : 15. Cf. Augustine, *In Joannis Evangelium, Tractatus* 121 (*PL 35*, 1957).

8. *of reason:* in accordance with reason.   9. fallen.

1. See above, pp. 134, 155.   2. on the basis of.

ture meaneth that it is the very blessed body of our Savior Himself indeed. To this say they again, "Yea, but we can and do conster[3] all those texts another way with an allegory[4] sense and prove by the old doctors that our exposition is true."

To this we answer them and say, if you conster all those texts divers other good ways with your allegories—so that[5] you do not with any of those ways take away the true sense of the letter—we will not withstand[6] your allegories but will well allow them, for the old holy doctors did the same. But on the tother side, if with any of your allegorical expositions you deny the very literal sense beside, and say that the body of our Savior is not really under the form of bread in the sacrament, then say we that in your such expouning you plain expoun it false. For we say that such manner of your expositions is plain against the very sentence and the meaning of the text. And we say that in this point you report the old holy doctors untruly. For all the holy doctors and saints fro the apostles' days to your own declare the scripture clear against you. I will not here enter into the declaring of all the places of scripture, by which places (opened and explained with the circumstances of the letter) good Christian people may well and plainly perceive that the very meaning of the scripture is against these folk and proveth plain for the Catholic Church. For that were both a very long work and also a digression somewhat too long fro my present purpose, which is only to declare those words that I have already declared—that is to wit, the words of our Savior Himself, rehearsed by the three foresaid evangelists, Saint Matthew, Saint Mark, and Saint Luke, and spoken by our Savior at the institution of this blessed sacrament—and not to declare here all His other words that He spake thereof before—rehearsed in the sixth chapter of Saint John, where He said, *Panis quem ego dabo vobis caro mea est pro mundi vita*[7] (The bread that I shall give you is my flesh for the life of the world) and *Caro mea vere est cibus, et sanguis meus vere est potus*[8] (My flesh is verily meat and my blood is verily drink), with

3. construe.   4. allegorical.   5. *so that:* provided that.
6. oppose.   7. John 6 : 52.   8. John 6 : 56.

many mo plain words further—nor to declare the words of Saint
Paul either—where he saith in the eleventh chapter of the first
pistle[9] to the Corinthians, *Dominus Iesus in qua nocte tradebatur, ac-
cepit panem et gratias agens fregit et dixit: Accipite et manducate; hoc est
corpus meum quod pro vobis tradetur*[1] (Our Lord Jesus in the same
night that He was betrayed took bread and giving thanks brake
it and said, "Take and eat; this is my body, which shall be betrayed for you") and *Quicunque manducaverit panem hunc, et biberit
calicem domini indigne, reus erit corporis et sanguinis domini*[2] (Whosoever eateth this bread and drinketh the cup of our Lord unworthily[3] shall be guilty of the body and blood of our Lord) and,
by and by after, He saith also, *Probet autem seipsum homo, et sic de
pane illo edat, et de calice bibat; qui enim manducat et bibit indigne,
iudicium sibi manducat et bibit, non dijudicans corpus domini.*[4] (Let a
man examine and judge himself and so eat of this bread and
drink of the cup; for he that eateth and drinketh unworthily,
eateth and drinketh judgment and damnation to himself, not
discerning and esteeming the body of our Lord.) These places
of scripture, and yet other mo, plainly proving the presence of
Christ's very body and blood in the blessed sacrament, is not, as
I say, my present purpose to declare.

But yet to the intent you shall see that in the foresaid exposition of those words of our Savior at the institution of the blessed
sacrament, where He calleth it His own body and His own blood,
I have not told you a tale of mine own head, but that the old
holy doctors and saints, contrary to these new men's tale, do
plainly declare the same and plainly do affirm that in the blessed
sacrament is the very body and blood of our Savior Christ Himself, I shall rehearse you the plain words of some of them.[5]

Here have you, good Christian readers, heard the very plain
open words of divers of the old holy doctors, by which we may

---

9. epistle.   1. 1 Cor. 11 : 23–24.   2. 1 Cor. 11 : 27.
3. without proper regard.   4. 1 Cor. 11 : 28–29.
5. At this point More quotes (in Latin and English) passages from nine-
teen Latin and Greek Fathers (from St. Ignatius of Antioch to Theophy-
lactus of Bulgaria). They have been omitted here.

plainly perceive and see that they were of the selfsame belief of old that we be now, and which hath ever been the belief of Christ's whole church since the institution of the blessed sacrament unto this day. And many years was it ere ever any man began to doubt, but that as well Catholics as all other that were yet in sundry other points heretics agreed together all in one that in this blessed sacrament is the very body and the very blood of Christ. For like as it was known to the apostles by the teaching of our Savior Christ Himself, and so forth[6] unto the primitive church or congregation of Christian people that were gathered together in many parts of the world in the apostles' days, so was the selfsame truth taught by the apostles themself, first fully and thoroughly by mouth and tradition, or delivery without writing, and afterward by writing conveniently also. Of the understanding of which writing there could at that time no doubt or debate arise, forasmuch as the whole people knew the truth of the thing before the writing of the apostles and evangelists, by the faith that the apostles and evangelists had taught them before by mouth.

And so using and teaching the sacraments, and understanding without any difficulty the words of the scripture therein, by their fore-taught and fro time to time kept and continued faith, lived in unity and concord of belief concerning this blessed sacrament, no man gainsaying the very blessed body and blood to be therein, even after that many folk were fallen in many other points from the true Catholic faith. And this appeareth very plain, by that we see both[7] Saint Irenaeus confound the Valentinians, and Saint Hilarius confound the Arians, and Saint Austin confound the Manichees, by certain arguments grounded upon the verity of the very body and blood of our blessed Savior in this holy sacrament, which had been, you wot well, nothing to the purpose if those three sects of heretics had not agreed with those three holy saints, and with the Catholic Church, that in the sacrament is the very body and blood of Christ.

6. *so forth:* then onward.   7. *i.e.,* all three.

Howbeit, after that began there some (among their other heresies) to fall then unto some of these concerning the blessed sacrament. For when men began once to take the bridle in the teeth and run forth at rovers[8] out of the common trade[9] of the fore-taught and received (and by the whole Catholic Church believed and professed) faith, then could there not (nor yet can) with such manner of folk the letter of holy scripture be any bridle to refrain them back. For setting the autority of the whole corps of the known Catholic Church at nought[1] and challenging[2] the Spirit of God from the same, and ascribing that Holy Spirit, some to such a known church of heretics as themself assigned, and the more part of them ascribing that Spirit to an only[3] unknown church, and challenging yet nevertheless (contrary to their own position) the truth of understanding and interpreting of holy scripture (to which they confessed the inspiration of that Holy Spirit requisite) every man of them to himself—using[4] (I say) themself in this wise, the scripture could not hold them. For they would and did (and yet such folk do) deny for scripture which books of scripture they list, and such as they list to receive, interpret and conster[5] as they list. By reason whereof at sundry times sundry heresies sprung[6] and spread abroad, and—with great trouble of the good Catholic folk, and great decay of the true Catholic folk, and eternal destruction of their souls that took those wrong ways—flowered for a little while. Howbeit, our Lord (laud and thank be to Him) ever provided with His Holy Spirit that all these heresies were in short space by His Catholic Church condemned and suppressed. And so hath His Catholic faith in His Catholic Church, as well in this article of the blessed sacrament as in all the remnant, this fifteen hundred year continued and ever continue shall while this world last, what wrestling soever the infidels shall make with it.

Howbeit, men may gather upon the scripture that, like as Christendom hath now in some place lost many lands and in

8. *at rovers:* at random.   9. track.
1. *setting . . . at nought:* having no esteem for.   2. laying claim to.
3. single.   4. behaving.   5. construe.   6. sprang up.

some other win[7] many lands again, so shall it be, after the faith spread[8] so full round about it, that there shall be no land in any part thereof (in which part people are dwelling) but that they shall have heard of the name and faith of Christ. Which was not all done (as Saint Austin saith) in the time of the apostles themself, but, like these words of Christ (saith Saint Austin), *Qui vos audit, me audit*[9] (He that heareth you, heareth me), though they were spoken only to the apostles, were not yet only meant for the apostles' persons only but spoken to them in the name of the church as governors for the same—and therefore to those governors of the church also as to the world's end should succeed in their places—so this prophecy of *In omnem terram exivit sonus eorum, et in fines orbis terrae verba eorum*[1] (Into all the world is gone out the sound of them, and into the ends of the roundel[2] of the earth the words of them), which words were written by the prophet David many years ere the apostles were born (and yet prophesied by the verb of the pretertemps,[3] or time past, to signify that the thing prophesied should as surely succeed and be verified as though it were past already), were not meant that the thing should be fully performed by their own persons, but part in one time, part in other, by such as the governors of the Catholic Church, which should succeed in their places, should in times and opportunity convenient send forth about it and appoint thereunto.

But afterward, when it is all preached round about upon all parts of the earth, the time shall come when it shall so sore decay again, and the church by persecution so straited[4] into so narrow a corner, that, in respect of[5] the countries into which Christendom hath been and shall be dilated and spread before, it shall seem that there shall be then no Christian countries left at all. Whereof our Savior said: *Quum venerit filius hominis, putas*

7. won.   8. *i.e.,* has been spread.
9. Luke 10 : 16. Cf. Augustine's *De civitate Dei,* XVIII, 50; and *De natura et gratia* (*PL 44,* 249).
1. Ps. 18 : 5.   2. sphere.   3. past tense.   4. constricted.
5. *in respect of:* in comparison with.

inveniet fidem in terra? [6] (When the Son of Man shall come—that is to wit, at the day of doom to judge the world—trowest[7] thou that He shall find faith in the earth?) But that time shall be but short, for our Savior saith, *Propter electos breviabuntur dies illi;* [8] and then shall our Lord come soon after, and finish this present world, and reward every good man after his good works wrought in his true Catholic faith: *Reddet unicuique secundum opera sua.* [9] (He shall yield every man according to his works.) But yet such works we must understand as are wrought in faith, for as Saint Paul saith, *Sine fide impossibile est placere deo.* [10] (Without faith it is impossible to please God.)

But finally this Catholic faith of the presence of Christ's very body and blood in the blessed sacrament hath, as I have showed, been the faith of Christ's whole Catholic Church ever since Christ's first institution thereof until this present time, and ever shall be while the world endureth. Whereagainst[11] whoso wrestleth cannot fail in conclusion to take a very foul fall, as far down (except he repent) as from the place that he walketh on in earth into the deep pit of hell, from which fall our Lord of His goodness defend every Christian man.

The third lecture of the Sacrament.

I have in the first lecture (good readers) expouned you the words of our Savior at the institution of the blessed sacrament. And after have I in the second showed you somewhat of the sacramental signs and of the sacramental things that are either contained therein or signified thereby, and have also somewhat rehearsed you the very words of the old holy doctors, whereby we may plainly perceive that the old holy saints believed the presence of the very body and blood of Christ in the blessed sacrament in like wise as we do.

Now is it convenient that we somewhat speak in what manner

6. Luke 18 : 8.   7. believe.
8. Matt. 24 : 22. "For the elect's sake those days shall be shortened."
9. Matt. 16 : 27.   10. Heb. 11 : 6.   11. against which.

wise we ought to use [12] ourself in the receiving. We must understand that of this holy sacrament there are three manner of receiving. For some folk receive it only sacramentally, and some only spiritually, and some receive it both.

Only sacramentally do they receive it which receive the blessed sacrament unworthily.[13] For they verily receive the very body and blood of our blessed Savior into their body in the blessed sacrament in form of bread out of[1] the mass, or in form of bread and wine in the mass. For as holy Saint Austin saith of the false traitor Judas, though he was nought and received it at the maundy to his damnation, yet was it our Lord's body that he received.[2] But because they receive it in deadly sin (that is to wit, either in will to commit deadly sin again, or impenitent of that they have committed before), therefore they receive it not spiritually; that is to say, they receive not the spiritual thing of the sacrament, which (as I before have showed) is the sacramental thing that is signified thereby, that is to wit, the society of holy saints—that is to say, he is not by the spirit of God unied[3] with holy saints as a lively[4] member of Christ's mystical body.

For we must understand that Christ in giving His own very body into the very body of every Christian man, He doth in a certain manner incorporate all Christian folk and His own body together in one corporation mystical. And therefore saith Saint Paul: *Omnes de uno pane manducamus.*[5] (All we eat of one loaf.) Not that all the people eat of one material loaf, for there were among them distributed many, but he meaneth that that very thing that is there under the form of that loaf of bread is that one thing that the apostle and all they and all we too eat. And then saith he also: *Unus panis multi sumus.*[6] (We many be of one loaf.) And so are we, as I say, by the receiving each of us that loaf that is Himself mystically, all incorporate together and all made that one loaf. And therefore when our Lord in giving that

12. conduct.   13. without proper regard.
1. *out of:* apart from.
2. Augustine, *In Joannis evangelium, Tractatus 62 (PL 35,* 1801).
3. united.   4. living.   5. 1 Cor. 10 : 17.   6. *Ibid.*

loaf at the first institution unto His apostles that there represented His church said, "This is my body," in giving (I say) to His church His very body, He not by word but by His deed called (as Saint Cyprian saith in his sermon *De cena Domini*) His church His body too.[7]

But now, though that every Christian man so receiving is in a certain manner a member of His mystical body (the church) by this sacramental receiving, yet, for his receiving it in deadly sin, he receiveth it not spiritually; that is to say, though he receive Christ's holy flesh into his body, he receiveth not yet Christ's Holy Spirit into his soul. And therefore this manner of deadly receiving His quick flesh giveth no quickness or life unto the soul. And in such a receiver of Christ's flesh are these words of Christ verified: *Spiritus est qui vivificat, caro non prodest quicquam.*[8] (The flesh availeth nothing; the spirit is it that giveth life.)

And therefore I say that, without the spiritual receiving, the sacramental receiving nothing availeth. And not only that it nothing availeth, but over that it sore noyeth[9] and hurteth. For Saint Paul, after that he hath plainly told and showed the Corinthies that the thing which they did eat and drink was the body and blood of Christ, he said unto them, *Quicumque manducaverit panem et biberit calicem Domini indigne, reus erit corporis et sanguinis Domini, et judicium sibi manducat et bibit, non dijudicans corpus Domini.*[1] (Whosoever eat the bread and drink the cup of our Lord unworthily shall be guilty of the body and blood of our Lord, and eateth and drinketh judgment unto himself, for that that[2] he discerneth not the body of our Lord, that is to wit, considereth it not and useth it like as he ought to do, it being the body of our Lord as it is.)

Here we see that, notwithstanding that he that receiveth the

7. Ernaldus Abbas Bonaevallis, *Liber de cardinalibus operibus Christi* (*PL 189*, 1643). Chapter 6 of this work, which was attributed to Cyprian in More's time, is entitled *De cena domini, et prima institutione consummantis omnia sacramenta.*
8. John 6 : 64.   9. *sore noyeth:* grievously harms.
1. 1 Cor. 11 : 27–29.   2. *that that:* the fact that.

blessed sacrament receiveth the very body of our Lord, yet receiving it unworthily (and therefore not spiritually), though he be by the only[3] sacramental receiving of Christ's body incorporate as a member (in a certain manner) in the mystical body of His Catholic Church, yet, for lack of the spiritual receiving by cleanness of spirit, he attaineth not the fruitful thing of the sacrament, that is to wit, the society of saints; that is to say, he is not by the spirit of Christ animated and quickened and made a lively member in the pure mystical body, the fellowship and society of saints.

Some, as I said before, receive this blessed sacrament only spiritually and not sacramentally, and so do all they receive it which are in clean life and are at their high mass devoutly. For there the curate offereth it for him and them too. And although that only himself receive it sacramentally, that is to wit, the very body and blood under the sacramental signs (the forms of bread and wine), yet as many of them as are present at it and are in clean life receive it spiritually, that is to wit, the fruitful thing of the sacrament; that is to say, they receive grace, by which they be by the spirit of Christ more firmly knit and unied quick, lively members in the spiritual society of saints.

3. mere.

A TREATISE TO RECEIVE
THE BLESSED BODY
OF OUR LORD

A treatise to receive the blessed body of our Lord, sacramentally and virtually[4] both, made in the year of our Lord 1534 by Sir Thomas More, Knight, while he was prisoner in the Tower of London, which he entitled thus as followeth: To receive the blessed body of our Lord, sacramentally and virtually both.

They receive the blessed body of our Lord both sacramentally and virtually which in due manner and worthily receive the blessed sacrament. When I say "worthily" I mean not that any man is so good, or can be so good, that his goodness could make him of very right and reason[5] worthy to receive into his vile, earthly body that holy blessed glorious flesh and blood of almighty God Himself, with His celestial soul therein, and with the majesty of His eternal Godhead, but that he may prepare himself, working with the grace of God, to stand in such a state as the incomparable goodness of God will, of His liberal bounty, vouchsafe to take and accept for worthy to receive His own inestimable precious body into the body of so simple[6] a servant.

Such is·the wonderful bounty of almighty God, that He not only doth vouchsafe, but also doth delight to be with men, if they prepare to receive Him with honest and clean souls. whereof He saith: *Delitiae meae esse cum filiis hominum.*[7] (My de-

4. with spiritual effect.
5. *of . . . reason:* with a justifiable claim and in accordance with reason.
6. humble. 7. Prov. 8 : 31.

light and pleasures are to be with the sons of men.) And how can
we doubt that God delighteth to be with the sons of men when
the Son of God, and very almighty God Himself, liked not only
to become the Son of Man (that is to wit, the son of Adam, the
first man) but, over that, in His innocent manhood to suffer His
painful passion for the redemption and restitution of man.

In remembrance and memorial whereof He disdaineth not to
take for worthy such men as wilfully make not themself unworthy to receive the selfsame blessed body into their bodies, to the
inestimable wealth[8] of their souls. And yet of His high sovereign
patience, He refuseth not to enter bodily into the vile bodies of
those whose filthy minds refuse to receive Him graciously[9] into
their souls. But then do such folk receive Him only sacramentally and not virtually, that is to wit, they receive His very blessed
body into theirs under the sacramental sign, but they receive not
the thing of the sacrament, that is to wit, the virtue and the effect thereof (that is to say, the grace by which they should be
lively[1] members incorporate[2] in Christ's holy mystical body),
but, instead of that lively grace, they receive their judgment and
their damnation.

And some such, by the outrageous enormity of their deadly
sinful purpose, in which they presume to receive that blessed
body, deserve to have the devil (through the sufferance of God)
personally so to enter into their breasts that they never have the
grace after to cast him out, but like as a man with bridle and
spur rideth and ruleth an horse and maketh him go which way
he list[3] to guide him, so doth the devil by his inward suggestions[4] govern and guide the man, and bridle him from all good
and spur him into all evil, till he finally drive him to all mischief,
as he did the false traitor Judas, that sinfully received that holy
body, whom the devil did therefore first carry out about[5] the
traitorous death of the selfsame blessed body of his most loving

8. well-being.   9. through divine grace.   1. living.
2. incorporated.   3. desires.   4. temptations.
5. *carry out about:* take away to pursue.

Master (which he so late so sinfully received) and, within a few hours after, unto the desperate destruction of himself.

And therefore have we great cause, with great dread and reverence, to consider well the state of our own soul when we shall go to the board[6] of God, and as near as we can (with help of His special grace, diligently prayed for before) purge and cleanse our souls by confession, contrition, and penance, with full purpose of forsaking from thenceforth the proud desires of the devil, the greedy covetise[7] of wretched, worldly wealth, and the foul affection of the filthy flesh, and be in full mind[8] to persevere and continue in the ways of God and holy cleanness of spirit, lest that (if we presume so unreverently to receive this precious margarite,[9] this pure pearl, the blessed body of our Savior Himself, contained in the sacramental sign of bread) that like a sort[1] of swine rooting in the dirt and wallowing in the mire, we tread it under the filthy feet of our foul affections, while we set more by[2] them than by it, intending to walk and wallow in the puddle of foul, filthy sin; therewith the legion of devils may get leave of Christ so to enter into us as they gat[3] leave of Him to enter into the hogs of Genezareth,[4] and, as they ran forth with them and never stinted till they drowned them in the sea, so run on with us (but if[5] God of His great mercy refrain[6] them and give us the grace to repent), else not fail to drown us in the deep sea of everlasting sorrow.

Of this great outrageous peril, the blessed apostle Saint Paul giveth us gracious warning where he saith in his first epistle to the Corinthies:[7] *Quicumque manducaverit panem et biberit calicem Domini indigne, reus erit corporis et sanguinis Domini.*[8] (Whosoever eat the bread and drink the cup of our Lord unworthily, he shall be guilty of the body and blood of our Lord.) Here is (good

6. table.   7. covetousness.   8. *be . . . mind:* be fully disposed.
9. pearl.   1. herd.   2. *set more by:* value more highly.
3. got.   4. Matt. 8 : 28–32, Mark 5 : 11–14, Luke 8 : 32–33.
5. *but if:* unless.   6. restrain.   7. Corinthians.
8. 1 Cor. 11 : 27.

Christian readers) a dreadful and terrible sentence, that God here (by the mouth of His holy apostle) giveth against all them that unworthily receive this most blessed sacrament, that their part shall be with Pilate and the Jews, and with that false traitor Judas, sith[9] God reputeth[10] the unworthy receiving and eating of His blessed body for a like heinous offense against His majesty as He accompteth[1] theirs that wrongfully and cruelly killed Him.

And therefore to the intent that we may avoid well this importable[2] danger, and in such wise[3] receive the body and blood of our Lord, as God may of His goodness accept us for worthy (and therefore not only enter with His blessed flesh and blood sacramentally and bodily into our bodies but also with His Holy Spirit graciously[4] and effectually into our souls), Saint Paul, in the place afore-remembered,[5] saith: *Probet seipsum homo, et sic de pane illo edat, et de calice bibat.*[6] (Let a man prove himself, and so eat of that bread and drink of that cup.) But then in what wise shall we prove ourself? We may not go rashly to God's board,[7] but by a convenient[8] time taken before we must (as I began to say) consider well and examine surely what state our soul standeth in.

In which thing it will be not only right hard, but also peradventure impossible, by any possible diligence of ourself to attain unto the very full, undoubted surety thereof, without special revelation of God. For as the scripture saith: *Nemo vivens scit, utrum odio vel amore dignus sit.*[9] (No man living knoweth whether he be worthy the favor or hatred of God.) And in another place: *Etiamsi simplex fuero, hoc ipsum ignorabit anima mea.*[1] (If I be simple,[2] that is to say, without sin, that shall not my mind surely know.) But God yet in this point is of His high goodness content if we do the diligence[3] that we can to see that we be not in the

9. since.   10. considers.   1. accounts.   2. unbearable.
3. a way.   4. through divine grace.   5. mentioned before.
6. 1 Cor. 11 : 28.   7. table.   8. suitable.
9. Eccles. 9 : 1.   1. Job 9 : 21.   2. innocent.
3. *do . . . diligence:* do the utmost.

purpose of[4] any deadly sin. For though it may be that, for all our diligence, God (whose eye pierceth much more deeper into the bottom of our heart than our own doth) may see therein some such sin as we cannot see there ourself—for which Saint Paul saith: *Nullius mihi conscius sum, sed non in hoc justificatus sum*[5] (In mine own conscience I know nothing, but yet am I not thereby justified)—yet our true diligence done in the search God of His high bounty so farforth[6] accepteth that He imputeth not any such secret lurking sin unto our charge for an unworthy receiving of this blessed sacrament, but rather the strength and virtue thereof purgeth and cleanseth that sin.

In this proving and examination of ourself which Saint Paul speaketh of, one very special point must be to prove and examine ourself and see that we be in the right faith and belief concerning that holy blessed sacrament itself: that is to wit, that we verily believe that it is, as indeed it is, under the form and likeness of bread, the very blessed body, flesh and blood of our holy Savior Christ Himself, the very selfsame body and the very selfsame blood that died and was shed upon the cross for our sin, and the third day gloriously did arise again to life and, with the souls of holy saints fette out of hell, ascended and styed[7] up wonderfully into heaven, and there sitteth on the right hand of the Father, and shall visibly descend in great glory to judge the quick[8] and the dead, and reward all men after[9] their works. We must (I say) see that we firmly believe that this blessed sacrament is not a bare sign, or a figure,[1] or a token of that holy body of Christ, but that it is (in perpetual remembrance of His bitter passion that He suffered for us) the selfsame precious body of Christ that suffered it by His own almighty power and unspeakable goodness, consecrated and given unto us.

And this point of belief is, in the receiving of this blessed sacrament, of such necessity and such weight with them that have years and discretion that, without it, they receive it plainly to

4. *in . . . purpose of:* disposed to do.   5. 1 Cor. 4 : 4.
6. *so farforth:* to such an extent.   7. climbed.   8. living.
9. according to.   1. type.

their damnation. And that point believed very full[2] and fastly[3] must needs be a great occasion to move any man in all other points to receive it well. For note well the words of Saint Paul therein: *Qui manducat de hoc pane, et bibit de calice indigne, judicium sibi manducat et bibit, non dijudicans corpus Domini.*[4] (He that eateth of this bread and drinketh of this cup unworthily eateth and drinketh judgment upon himself, in that he discerneth not the body of our Lord.) Lo, here this blessed apostle well declareth that he which in any wise[5] unworthily receiveth this most excellent sacrament receiveth it unto his own damnation, in that he well declareth by his evil demeanor toward it, in his unworthy receiving of it, that he discerneth it not, nor judgeth it, nor taketh it for the very body of our Lord, as indeed it is. And verily it is hard,[6] but that[7] this point deeply rooted in our breast should set all our heart in a fervor of devotion toward the worthy receiving of that blessed body. But surely there can be no doubt, on the tother[8] side, but that, if any man believe that it is Christ's very body and yet is not inflamed to receive Him devoutly thereby, that man were likely to receive this blessed sacrament very coldly and far from all devotion if he believed that it were not His body but only a bare token of Him instead of His body.

But now, having the full faith of this point fastly grounded in our heart, that the thing which we receive is the very blessed body of Christ, I trust there shall not greatly need any great information[9] farther[10] to teach us, or any great exhortation farther to stir and excite us, with all humble manner and reverent behavior to receive Him. For if we will but consider, if there were a great worldly prince which for special favor that he bare[11] us would come visit us in our own house, what a business[12] we would then make, and what a work it would be for us to see that our house were trimmed up[1] in every point to the

2. fully.   3. firmly.   4. 1 Cor. 11 : 27–29.   5. way.
6. likely.   7. *but that:* that.   8. other.   9. instruction.
10. further.   11. bore.   12. to-do.
1. *trimmed up:* put in good order.

best of our possible power, and everything so provided and ordered, that he should by his honorable receiving perceive what affection we bear him and in what high estimation we have him, we should soon by the comparing of that worldly prince and this heavenly prince together (between which twain is far less comparison than is between a man and a mouse) inform and teach ourself with how lowly mind, how tender loving heart, how reverent humble manner we should endeavor ourself to receive this glorious heavenly king, the king of all kings, almighty God Himself, that so lovingly doth vouchsafe to enter not only into our house (to which the nobleman Centurio knowledged[2] himself unworthy[3]) but His precious body into our vile, wretched carcass, and His Holy Spirit into our poor simple soul.

What diligence can here suffice us, what solicitude can we think here enough, against[4] the coming of this almighty king, coming for so special gracious favor, not to put us to cost, not to spend of ours, but to enrich us of His, and that after so manifold deadly displeasures done Him so unkindly[5] by us, against so many of His incomparable benefits before done unto us? How would we now labor and foresee[6] that the house of our soul (which God were coming to rest in) should neither have any poisoned spider or cobweb of deadly sin hanging in the roof, nor so much as a straw or a feather of any light lewd[7] thought that we might spy in the floor, but we would sweep it away.

But forasmuch (good Christian readers) as we neither can attain this great point of faith, nor any other virtue, but by the special grace of God, of whose high goodness every good thing cometh—for as Saint James saith: *Omne datum optimum, et omne donum perfectum, de sursum est, descendens a Patre luminum*[8] (Every good gift, and every perfect gift, is from above, descending from the Father of lights)—let us therefore pray for His gracious[9]

2. confessed.
3. Cf. Matt. 8 : 8. The centurion's words preceded the giving of communion in the mass.
4. in preparation for.   5. ungratefully.   6. provide.
7. *light lewd:* trivial bad.   8. James 1 : 17.   9. conferring grace.

help in the attaining of this faith, and for His help in the cleansing of our soul against His coming, that He may make us worthy to receive Him worthily. And ever let us of our own part fear our unworthiness, and on His part trust boldly upon His goodness if we forslow[1] not to work with Him for our own part. For if we willingly upon the trust and comfort of His goodness leave our own endeavor undone, then is our hope no hope, but a very foul presumption.

Then when we come unto His holy board, into the presence of His blessed body, let us consider His high glorious majesty, which His high goodness there hideth from us and the proper form of His holy flesh covereth under the form of bread—both to keep us from abashment, such as we could not peradventure abide if we (such as we yet be) should see and receive Him in His own form such as He is, and also for the increase of the merit of our faith in the obedient belief of that thing (at His commandment) whereof our eyen[2] and our reason seem to show us the contrary.

And yet forasmuch as, although we believe it, yet is there in many of us that belief very faint and far fro[3] the point of such vigor and strength as would God it had, let us say unto Him with the father that had the dumb son, *Credo Domine, adjuva incredulitatem meam*[4] (I believe, Lord, but help Thou my lack of belief), and with His blessed apostles, *Domine, adauge nobis fidem.*[5] (Lord, increase faith in us.) Let us also with the poor publican, in knowledge of our own unworthiness, say with all meekness of heart, *Deus, propitius esto mihi peccatori.*[6] (Lord God, be merciful to me sinner that I am.) And with the centurion, *Domine, non sum dignus ut intres sub tectum meum.*[7] (Lord, I am not worthy that Thou shouldest come into my house.)

And yet with all this remembrance of our own unworthiness, and therefore the great reverence, fear and dread for our own part, let us not forget on the tother[8] side to consider His ines-

1. neglect.   2. eyes.   3. from.   4. Mark 9 : 23.
5. Luke 17 : 5.   6. Luke 18 : 13.   7. Matt. 8 : 8.
8. other.

timable goodness, which disdaineth not for all our unworthiness to come unto us and to be received of us.

But likewise as at the sight or receiving of this excellent memorial of His death (for in the remembrance thereof doth He thus consecrate and give His own blessed flesh and blood unto us) we must with tender compassion remember and call to mind the bitter pains of His most painful passion, and yet therewithal rejoice and be glad in the consideration of His incomparable kindness (which in His so suffering for us to our inestimable benefit He showed and declared toward us), so must we be both sore afeard[9] of our own unworthiness, and yet therewith be right glad and in great hope at the consideration of His unmeasurable goodness.

Saint Elizabeth, at the visitation and salutation of our blessed Lady (having by revelation the sure inward knowledge that our Lady was conceived with our Lord), albeit that she was herself such as else (for[10] the diversity between their ages) she well might,and would have thought it but convenient[1] and meetly[2] that her young cousin should come visit her, yet now, because she was mother to our Lord, she was sore amarvelled[3] of her visitation and thought herself far unworthy thereto, and therefore said unto her: *Unde hoc, ut veniat mater Domini mei ad me?*[4] (Whereof is this, that the mother of our Lord should come to me?) But yet for all the abashment of her own unworthiness she conceived throughly[5] such a glad blessed comfort that her holy child Saint John the Baptist hopped in her belly for joy, whereof she said: *Ut facta est vox salutationis tuae in auribus meis, exultavit gaudio infans in utero meo.*[6] (As soon as the voice of thy salutation was in mine ears, the infant in my womb leapt for joy.)

Now like as Saint Elizabeth by the Spirit of God had those holy affections,[7] both of reverent considering her own unworthiness in the visitation of the mother of God, and yet for all that so great inward gladness therewith, let us at this great high visita-

9. afraid.   10. because of.   1. suitable.   2. appropriate.
3. *sore amarvelled:* quite amazed.   4. Luke 1 : 43.
5. completely.   6. Luke 1 : 44.   7. inclinations.

tion, in which not the mother of God, as came to Saint Elizabeth, but one incomparably more excelling the mother of God than the mother of God passed Saint Elizabeth doth so vouchsafe to come and visit each of us with His most blessed presence that He cometh not into our house but into ourself—let us (I say) call for the help of the same Holy Spirit that then inspired her, and pray Him at his high and holy visitation so to inspire us that we may both be abashed with the reverent dread of our own unworthiness and yet therewith conceive a joyful consolation and comfort in the consideration of God's inestimable goodness, and that each of us, like as we may well say with great reverent dread and admiration, *Unde hoc, ut veniat Dominus meus ad me?* [8] (Whereof is this, that my Lord should come unto me?) and not only unto me but also into me, so we may with glad heart truly say at the sight of His blessed presence, *Exultavit gaudio infans in utero meo.* [9] (The child in my belly—that is to wit, the soul in my body, that should be then such a child in innocency as was that innocent infant Saint John—leapeth, good Lord, for joy.)

Now when we have received our Lord and have Him in our body, let us not then let Him alone and get us forth about other things and look no more unto Him (for little good could he [10] that so would serve any guest), but let all our business [11] be about Him. Let us by devout prayer talk to Him, by devout meditation talk with Him. Let us say with the prophet: *Audiam quid loquatur in me Dominus.* [1] (I will hear what our Lord will speak within me.)

For surely, if we set aside all other things and attend unto Him, He will not fail with good inspirations to speak such things to us within us as shall serve to the great spiritual comfort and profit of our soul. And therefore let us with Martha provide that all our outward business may be pertaining to Him, in making cheer to Him and to His company for His sake, that is to wit, to poor folk, of which He taketh every one not only for His disciple

---

8. Luke 1 : 43.   9. Luke 1 : 44.
10. *little . . . he:* he would lack good sense.   11. concern.
1. Ps. 84 : 9 (*AV*, 85 : 8).

but also as for Himself. For Himself saith: *Quamdiu fecistis uni de his fratribus meis minimis, mihi fecistis.*[2] (That that you have done to one of the least of these my brethren, you have done it to myself.) And let us with Mary also sit in devout meditation and hearken well what our Savior, being now our guest, will inwardly say unto us. Now have we a special time of prayer, while He that hath made us, He that hath bought[3] us, He whom we have offended, He that shall judge us, He that shall either damn us or save us, is of His great goodness become our guest, and is personally present within us, and that for none other purpose but to be sued unto for pardon and so thereby to save us. Let us not leese[4] this time, therefore, suffer not this occasion to slip, which we can little tell whether ever we shall get in again or never. Let us endeavor ourself to keep Him still,[5] and let us say with His two disciples that were going to the castle of Emmaus, *Mane nobiscum Domine*[6] (Tarry with us, good Lord), and then shall we be sure that He will not go from us, but if[7] we unkindly[8] put Him from us. Let us not play[9] like the people of Genezareth, which prayed Him to depart out of their quarters because they lost their hogs by Him, when instead of the hogs He saved the man out of whom He cast the legion of devils that after destroyed the hogs.[1] Let not us likewise rather put God from us by unlawful love of worldly winning[2] or foul filthy lust, rather than for the profit of our soul to forbear it. For sure may we be that when we wax such God will not tarry with us, but we put Him unkindly from us. Nor let us not do as did the people of Hierusalem which on Palm Sunday received Christ royally and full devoutly with procession, and on the Friday after put Him to a shameful passion; on the Sunday cried, *Benedictus qui venit in nomine Domini*[3] (Blessed be He that cometh in the name of our Lord), and on the Friday cried out, *Non hunc, sed Barabbam*[4] (We

2. Matt. 25 : 40.   3. redeemed.   4. lose.   5. always.
6. Luke 24 : 29.   7. *but if:* unless.   8. ungratefully.
9. act.   1. Matt. 8 : 34, Mark 5 : 17, Luke 8 : 37.   2. gain.
3. Matt. 21 : 9.   4. John 18 : 40.

will not have Him but Barabbas); on the Sunday cried, *Hosanna in excelsis,*[5] on the Friday, *Tolle, tolle, crucifige eum.*[6] Sure if we receive Him never so well nor never so devoutly at Easter, yet whensoever we fall after to such wretched sinful living as casteth our Lord in such wise out of our souls, as His grace tarrieth not with us, we show ourself to have received Him in such manner as those Jews did. For we do as much as in us is to crucify Christ again: *Iterum* (saith Saint Paul) *crucifigentes filium Dei.*[7]

Let us (good Christian readers) receive Him in such wise as did the good publican Zacchaeus, which when he longed to see Christ and because he was but low of stature did climb up into a tree, our Lord, seeing his devotion, called unto him and said: "Zacchaeus, come off[8] and come down, for this day must I dwell with thee."[9] And he made haste and came down, and very gladly received Him into his house. But not only received Him with a joy of a light[10] and soon sliding[1] affection, but that it might well appear that he received Him with a sure earnest virtuous mind, he proved it by his virtuous works. For he forthwith was contented to make recompense to all men that he had wronged, and that in a large[2] manner, for every penny a groat,[3] and yet offered to give out also forthwith the tone[4] half of all his substance unto the poor men, and that forthwith also, by and by,[5] without any longer delay. And therefore he said not, "Thou shalt hear that I shall give it," but he said, *Ecce dimidium bonorum meorum do pauperibus.*[6] (Lo, look, good Lord, the tone half of my goods I do give unto poor men.)

With such alacrity, with such quickness of spirit, with such gladness, and such spiritual rejoicing as this man received our Lord into his house, our Lord give us the grace to receive His blessed body and blood, His holy soul, and His almighty

5. Mark 11 : 10. "Hosanna in the highest."
6. John 19 : 15. "Away, away with him! Crucify him."
7. Heb. 6 : 6. "Crucifying the Son of God once more."
8. *come off:* come along.   9. Luke 19 : 5.   10. fickle.
1. passing.   2. generous.   3. coin worth four pence.
4. one.   5. *by and by:* immediately.   6. Luke 19 : 8.

Godhead both, into our bodies and into our souls, that the fruit of our good works may bear witness unto our conscience that we receive Him worthily, and in such a full faith and such a stable purpose of good living as we be bounden[7] to do. And then shall God give a gracious sentence[8] and say upon our soul, as He said upon Zacchaeus, *Hodie salus facta est huic domui*[9] (This day is health and salvation come unto this house), which that holy blessed person of Christ, which we verily in the blessed sacrament receive, through the merit of His bitter passion (whereof He hath ordained His own blessed body in that blessed sacrament to be the memorial), vouchsafe, good Christian readers, to grant unto us all.

7. obliged.   8. *gracious sentence:* merciful judgment.
9. Luke 19 : 9.

THE SADNESS OF CHRIST

The Sadness, the Weariness, the Fear, and the Prayer of Christ Before He Was Taken Prisoner. Matthew 26, Mark 14, Luke 22, John 18.

"When Jesus had said these things, they recited the hymn and went out to the Mount of Olives."[10]

Though He had spoken at length about holiness during the supper with His apostles, nevertheless He finished His discourses with a hymn when He was ready to leave. Alas, how different we are from Christ, though we call ourselves Christians: our conversation during meals is not only meaningless and inconsequential (and even for such negligence Christ warned us that we will have to render an accounting)[1] but often our table-talk is also vicious, and then finally, when we are bloated with food and drink, we leave the table without giving thanks to God for the banquets He has bestowed upon us, with never a thought for the gratitude we owe Him.

[Paul of Saint Mary, Archbishop of] Burgos,[2] a learned, holy man, and an outstanding investigator of sacred subjects, gives some convincing arguments to show that the hymn which Christ at that time recited with His apostles consisted of those six

---

10. Matt. 26 : 30. Here and in the *Treatise upon the Passion* More quotes from the *Monotessaron,* a gospel harmony by John Gerson (1363–1429), a French churchman and spiritual writer.

1. Matt. 12 : 36.

2. Usually called Burgensis. More refers to his *Additiones* to the *Postillae* of Nicholas de Lyra, both of which were included in the glossed Bibles of More's period.

psalms which, taken together, are called by the Jews "The Great Alleluia"—namely Psalm 112 and the five following it. For from very ancient times the Jews have followed the custom of reciting these six psalms, under the name "Great Alleluia," as a prayer of thanksgiving at the Passover and certain other principal feasts, and even now they still go through the same hymn on the same feastdays.

But as for us, though we used to say different hymns of thanksgiving and benediction at meals according to the different times of the year, each hymn suited to its season, we have now permitted almost all of them to fall out of use, and we rest content with saying two or three words, no matter what, before going away, and even those few words we mumble merely for form's sake, muttering through our yawns.

"They went out to the Mount of Olives," not to bed. The prophet says, "I arose in the middle of the night to pay homage to you,"[3] but Christ did not even lie down in bed. But as for us, I wish we could truly apply to ourselves even this text: "I thought of you as I lay in my bed."[4]

Moreover, it was not yet summer when Christ left the supper and went over to the mount. For it was not that much beyond the vernal equinox, and that the night was cold is clearly shown by the fact that the servants were warming themselves around charcoal fires in the courtyard of the high priest.[5] But this was not the first time that Christ had done this, as the evangelist clearly testifies when he says "as He customarily did."[6]

He went up a mountain to pray, teaching us by this sign that, when we prepare ourselves to pray, we must lift up our minds from the bustling confusion of human concerns to the contemplation of heavenly things.

Mount Olivet itself also has a mysterious significance, planted as it was with olive trees. For the olive branch was generally used as a symbol of peace, which Christ came to establish between

3. Ps. 118 : 62 (AV, 119 : 62).   4. Ps. 62 : 7 (AV, 63 : 6).
5. John 18 : 18.   6. Luke 22 : 39.

God and man after their long alienation. Moreover, the oil which is produced from the olive represents the anointing by the Spirit, for Christ came and then returned to His Father in order to send the Holy Spirit upon the disciples so that His anointing might then teach them what they would not have been able to bear had it been told them only a short time before.[7]

"Across the stream Cedron to the outlying estate named Gethsemane."[8]

The stream Cedron lies between the city of Jerusalem and the Mount of Olives, and the word "Cedron" in Hebrew means "sadness." The name "Gethsemane" in Hebrew means "most fertile valley" or "valley of olives." And so there is no reason for us to attribute it merely to chance that the evangelists recorded these place-names so carefully. For if that were the case, once they had reported that He went to the Mount of Olives, they would have considered that they had said quite enough, if it were not that God had veiled under these place-names some mysterious meanings which attentive men, with the help of the Holy Spirit, would try to uncover because the names were mentioned. And so, since not a single syllable can be thought inconsequential in a composition which was dictated by the Holy Spirit as the apostles wrote it, and since not a sparrow falls to the earth without God's direction,[9] I cannot think either that the evangelists mentioned those names accidentally or that the Jews assigned them to the places (whatever they themselves intended when they named them) without a secret plan (though unknown to the Jews themselves) of the Holy Spirit, who concealed in these names a store of sacred mysteries to be ferreted out sometime later.

But since "Cedron" means "sadness," and also "blackness," and since this same word is the name not only of the stream mentioned by the evangelists but also (as is sufficiently established) of the valley through which the stream flows and

7. John 16 : 12–13.
8. John 18 : 1, Matt. 26 : 36, and Mark 14 : 32.   9. Matt. 10 : 29.

which separates the city from the estate Gethsemane, these names (if their effect is not blocked by our drowsiness) remind us that while we are exiled from the Lord (as the apostle says)[1] we must surely cross over, before we come to the fruitful Mount of Olives and the pleasant estate of Gethsemane, an estate which is not gloomy and ugly to look at but most fertile in every sort of joy, we must (I say) cross over the valley and stream of Cedron, a valley of tears and a stream of sadness whose waves can wash away the blackness and filth of our sins. But if we get so weary of pain and grief that we perversely attempt to change this world, this place of labor and penance, into a joyful haven of rest, if we seek heaven on earth, we cut ourselves off forever from true happiness, and will drown ourselves in penance when it is too late to do any good and in unbearable, unending tribulations as well.

This, then, is the very salutary lesson contained in these place-names, so fittingly chosen are they. But as the words of holy scripture are not tied to one sense only but rather are teeming with various mysterious meanings, these place-names harmonize with the immediate context of Christ's passion very well, as if for that reason alone God's eternal providence had seen to it that these places should long beforehand have been designated by such names as would prove to be, some centuries later, preordained tokens of His passion, as the comparison of His deeds with the names would show. For, since "Cedron" means "blackened," does it not seem to recall that prediction of the prophet that Christ would work out His glory by means of inglorious torment, that He would be disfigured by dark bruises, gore, spittle, and dirt?—"There is nothing beautiful or handsome about his face."[2]

Then, too, the meaning of the stream He crossed—"sad"—was far from irrelevant as He Himself testified when He said, "My soul is sad unto death."[3]

---

1. 2 Cor. 5 : 6.   2. Isa. 53 : 2.   3. Matt. 26 : 38, Mark 14 : 34.

"And His disciples also followed Him."[4]

That is, the eleven who had remained followed Him. As for the twelfth, the devil entered into him after the morsel and made off with him,[5] so that he did not follow the master as a disciple but pursued Him as a traitor, and bore out only too well what Christ said: "He who is not with me is against me."[6] Against Christ he certainly was, since, at that very moment, he was preparing to spring his trap for Him, while the other disciples were following after Him to pray. Let us follow after Christ and pray to the Father together with Him. Let us not emulate Judas by departing from Christ, after partaking of His favors and dining excellently with Him, lest we should bear out that prophecy: "If you saw a thief you ran away with him."[7]

"Judas, who betrayed Him, also knew the place, because Jesus frequently went there with His disciples."[8]

Once again the evangelists take advantage of mentioning the betrayer to emphasize for us, and to recommend to us by such emphasis, Christ's holy custom of going together with His disciples to that place in order to pray. For if He had gone there only on some nights and not frequently, the betrayer would not have been so completely convinced he would find our Lord there that he could afford to bring the servants of the high priest and a Roman cohort there as if everything had been definitely arranged, for if they had found that it was not arranged, they would have thought he was playing a practical joke on them and would not have let him get away with it unscathed. Now where are those people who think they are men of stature, who are proud of themselves as if they had done something fine, if sometimes, on the vigil of a special feast, they either continue their prayers a little longer into the night or get up earlier for

4. Luke 22 : 39.   5. John 13 : 27–30.
6. Matt. 12 : 30, Luke 11 : 23.   7. Ps. 49 : 18 (*AV*, 50 : 18).
8. John 18 : 2.

their morning prayers? Our Savior Christ had the habit of spending whole nights without sleep in order to pray.

Where are those who called Him a glutton for food and wine because He did not refuse to go to the banquets of the publicans and did not think it beneath Him to attend the celebrations of sinful men?[9] Where are those who thought that, by comparison with the strict regimen of the pharisees, His morals were hardly better than those of the common rabble? But while these gloomy hypocrites were praying on the corners of the main thorough-fares so that they might be seen by men, He was eating lunch with sinners, calmly and kindly helping them to reform their lives. On the other hand, He used to spend the night praying under the open sky[10] while the hypocritical pharisee was snoring away in his soft bed. How I wish that those of us who are pre-vented by our own laziness from imitating the illustrious ex-ample of our Savior might at least be willing to call to mind His all-night vigils when we turn over on the other side in our beds, half asleep, and that we might then, during the short time be-fore we fall asleep again, offer Him thanks, condemn our sloth-fulness, and pray for an increase of grace. Surely if we set out to make a habit of doing even the least little bit of good, I feel cer-tain that God will soon set us forward a great way on the path of virtue.[11]

"And He said, 'Sit down here while I go over there to pray.' And He took Peter and the two sons of Zebedee with Him. He began to feel sorrow and grief and fear and weariness. Then He said to them, 'My soul is sad unto death. Stay here and keep watch with me.' "[12]

Commanding the other eight to stop somewhat lower down, He went further on, taking with Him Peter, John, and his brother James, the three whom He had always singled out from the rest of the apostles by a certain special privilege of intimacy.

9. Cf. Matt. 11 : 19.   10. Luke 6 : 12.   11. Cf. Matt. 13 : 23.
12. Matt. 26 : 36–38, Mark 14 : 32–34.

Now even if He had done this for no other reason than that He wanted to, no one ought to have been envious because of His generosity.[1] But still there were certain reasons for this which He might well have had in mind. For Peter was outstanding for his zealous faith and John for his virginity, and his brother James was to be the very first of all to suffer martyrdom in the name of Christ. Furthermore, these were the three to whom He had formerly granted the secret knowledge and open sight of His glorified body. It was only right, then, that those same three whom He had admitted to such an extraordinary vision and whom He had invigorated with a momentary flash of the eternal brilliance so that they ought to have been stronger than the others, should have assigned to them the role of His nearest supporters in the preliminary agony of His passion. But when He had gone on a little way, He suddenly felt such a sharp and bitter attack of sadness, grief, fear, and weariness that He immediately uttered, even in their presence, those anguished words which gave expression to His overburdened feelings.: "My soul is sad unto death."[2]

For a huge mass of troubles took possession of the tender and gentle body of our most holy Savior. He knew that His ordeal was now imminent and just about to overtake Him: the treacherous betrayer, the bitter enemies, binding ropes, false accusations, slanders, blows, thorns, nails, the cross, and horrible tortures stretched out over many hours. Over and above these, He was tormented by the thought of His disciples' terror, the loss of the Jews, even the destruction of the very man who so disloyally betrayed Him, and finally the ineffable grief of His beloved mother. The gathered storm of all these evils rushed into His most gentle heart and flooded it like the ocean sweeping through broken dikes.

Perhaps someone may wonder how it could be that our Savior Christ could feel sadness, sorrow, and grief, since He was truly God, equal to His all-powerful Father. Certainly He could not

1. Matt. 20 : 15.   2. Matt. 26 : 38.

have felt them if He had been God (as He was) in such a way as
not to be man also. But as a matter of fact, since He was no less
really a man than He was really God, I see no reason for us to be
surprised that, insofar as He was man, He had the ordinary feelings of mankind (though certainly no blameworthy ones)—no
more than we would be surprised that, insofar as He was God,
He performed stupendous miracles. For if we are surprised that
Christ felt fear, weariness, and grief, simply on the grounds that
He was God, why should we not also be surprised that He experienced hunger, thirst, and sleep, seeing that He was none the
less divine for doing these things? But here, perhaps, you may
object, "I am no longer surprised at His capacity for these emotions, but I cannot help being surprised at His desire to experience them. For He taught His disciples not to be afraid of those
who can kill the body only and can do nothing beyond that;[3]
and how can it be fitting that He Himself should now be very
much afraid of those same persons, especially since even His
body could suffer nothing from them except what He Himself
allowed?

"Furthermore, since we know His martyrs rushed to their
deaths eagerly and joyfully, triumphing over tyrants and tor-
turers, how can it not seem inappropriate that Christ Himself,
the very prototype and leader of martyrs, the standard-bearer of
them all, should be so terrified at the approach of pain, so shaken, so utterly downcast? Shouldn't He rather have been especially careful to set a good example in this matter, just as He had
always let His deeds precede His precepts,[4] so that others might
learn from His own example to undergo death eagerly for
truth's sake, and so that those who afterwards would suffer
death for the faith with fear and hesitation might not indulge
their slackness by imagining that they are following Christ's pre-
cedent?—whereas, actually, their reluctance would both detract
a great deal from the glory of their cause and discourage others
who observe their sadness and fear." Those who bring up these

3. Cf. Luke 12 : 4, Matt. 10 : 28.   4. Cf. Acts 1 : 1.

objections and others of the same sort do not scrutinize carefully
enough all the facets of this problem and do not pay enough attention to what Christ meant when He forbad His followers to
fear death. For He hardly intended it to mean that they should
never under any circumstances recoil from a violent death, but
rather that they should not, out of fear, flee from a death which
will not last, only to run, by denying the faith, into one which
will be everlasting. For He wished His followers to be brave and
prudent soldiers, not senseless and foolish. The brave man bears
up under the blows which beset him; the senseless man simply
does not feel them when they strike. Only a foolish man does
not fear wounds, but a prudent man does not allow any fear of
suffering to divert him from a holy way of life for that would be
to refuse lesser pains at the expense of plunging himself into far
more bitter ones.

When an afflicted part of the body is to be cut or cauterized,
the doctor does not try to persuade the sick man not to feel any
mental anguish at the thought of the pain the cutting or burning
will cause, but rather encourages him to bear up under it. He
admits it will be painful, but stresses that the pain will be out-
weighed by the pleasure of health and the avoidance of even
more horrible pain. Indeed, though our Savior Christ commands us to suffer death (when it cannot be avoided) rather
than fall away from Him through a fear of death (and we do fall
away from Him when we publicly deny our faith in Him), still
He is so far from requiring us to do violence to our nature by
not fearing death at all that He even leaves us free to flee from
punishment (whenever this can be done without injury to His
cause). "If you are persecuted in one city," He says, "flee to
another."[5] This permission, this cautious advice of a prudent
master, was followed by almost all the apostles and by almost all
the illustrious martyrs in the many succeeding centuries: there is
hardly one of them who did not use it at some time or other to
save his life and extend it, with great profit to himself and oth-

5. Matt. 10 : 23.

ers, until such a time as the hidden providence of God foresaw was more fitting.

On the other hand, some brave champions have taken the initiative by publicly professing their Christianity, though no one was trying to discover it, and by freely exposing themselves to death, though no one was demanding it. Thus God chose, according to His pleasure, to increase His glory sometimes by concealing the riches of the faith, so that those who set clever traps for His believers might be duped, sometimes by displaying them, so that those who cruelly persecuted His followers might be incensed by seeing all their hopes frustrated and finding, much to their outrage, that all their ferocity could not overcome martyrs who met death willingly. But God in His mercy does not command us to climb this steep and lofty peak of bravery, and hence it is not safe for just anyone to go rushing on heedlessly to the point where he cannot retrace his steps gradually but may be in danger of falling head over heels into the abyss if he cannot make it to the summit. As for those whom God calls to do this, let them choose their goal and pursue it successfully and they will reign in triumph.[6] He keeps hidden the times, the moments,[7] the causes of all things, and when the time is right He brings forth all things from the secret treasure-chest of His wisdom, which penetrates all things irresistibly and disposes all things sweetly.[8]

And so, if anyone is brought to the point where he must either suffer torment or deny God, he need not doubt that it was God's will for him to be brought to this crisis. Therefore, he has very good reason to hope for the best. For God will either extricate him from the struggle, or else He will aid him in the fight and make him conquer so that He may crown him with the conqueror's wreath. "For God is trustworthy," the apostle says. "He does not allow you to be tempted beyond what you can stand, but with the temptation He also gives a way out so that you may

6. Cf. Ps. 44 : 5 (AV, 45 : 4).   7. Cf. Acts 1 : 7.   8. Cf. Sap.
8 : 1.

be able to bear it."[9] Therefore, when things have come to the point of a hand-to-hand combat with the prince of this world, the devil,[10] and his cruel underlings, and there is no way left to withdraw without disgracing the cause, then I would think that a man ought to cast away fear and I would direct him to be completely calm, confident, and hopeful. "For," says the scripture, "whoever lacks confidence on the day of tribulation, his courage will be lessened."[1]

But before the actual engagement, fear is not reprehensible, as long as reason does not cease to struggle against fear—a struggle which is not criminal or sinful but rather an immense opportunity for merit. For do you imagine that, since those most holy martyrs shed their blood for the faith, they had no fear at all of death and torments? On this point I will not pause to draw up a list; to me Paul may stand for a thousand others. Indeed, if David was worth ten thousand soldiers in the war against the Philistines,[2] then certainly Paul can also be considered worth ten thousand soldiers in the battle for the faith against faithless persecutors. And so this bravest of champions Paul, who was so far advanced in hope and the love of Christ that he had no doubts about his heavenly reward, who said "I have fought the good fight, I have finished the race, and now there remains for me a crown of justice,"[3] which he longed for so ardently that he said "To me to live is Christ and to die is gain"[4] and "I long to be dissolved and to be with Christ,"[5] nevertheless this very same Paul not only managed skillfully to escape from the snares of the Jews by means of the tribune,[6] but also freed himself from prison by declaring that he was a Roman citizen,[7] and once again he eluded the cruelty of the Jews by appealing to Caesar,[8] and he escaped the hands of the impious King Aretas by being let down from the wall in a basket.[9]

9. 1 Cor. 10 : 13.   10. John 12 : 31, 14 : 30, 16 : 11.
1. Prov. 24 : 10.   2. See 1 Kings 18 : 7–8, 21 : 11, 29 : 5.
3. 2 Tim. 4 : 7–8.   4. Phil. 1 : 21.   5. Phil. 1 : 23.
6. Acts 23 : 6–10, 12–30.   7. Acts 22 : 25–29.
8. Acts 25 : 10–12.   9. 2 Cor. 11 : 32–33. Cf. Acts 9 : 25.

But if anyone should contend that he was looking to the fruit that was to be planted afterwards through his efforts, and that throughout these events he was not frightened by any fear of death, certainly I will freely grant the first point, but I would not venture to assert the second. For that most brave heart of the apostle was not impervious to fear, as he himself clearly shows when he writes to the Corinthians, "For even when we came to Macedonia, our flesh had no rest, but suffered all manner of affliction, conflicts without, fears within."[1] And in another place he wrote to the same persons: "I was with you in weakness and fear and much trembling."[2] And once again: "For we do not wish you, brethren, to be ignorant of the affliction which came upon us in Asia, since we were burdened beyond measure, beyond our strength, so that we were weary even of life."[3] In these passages do you not hear from Paul's own mouth his fear, his trembling, his weariness more unbearable than death itself, so that his experience seems to call to mind that agony of Christ and to present, as it were, an image of it? Go ahead now and deny if you can that Christ's holy martyrs felt fear at the terrible prospect of death. But, on the other hand, no amount of terror, however great, could deter this same Paul from his program of advancing the faith, and no advice from the disciples could persuade him not to go to Jerusalem (to which he felt he was called by the Spirit of God), even though the prophet Agabus had foretold that chains and certain dangers were awaiting him there.[4]

And so the fear of death and torments carries no stigma of guilt but rather is an affliction of the sort Christ came to suffer, not to escape. We should not immediately consider it cowardice for someone to feel fear and horror at the thought of torments, not even if he prudently avoids dangers (provided he does not compromise himself); but to flee because of a fear of torture and death when the circumstances make it necessary to fight, or

1. 2 Cor. 7 : 5.   2. 1 Cor. 2 : 3.   3. 2 Cor. 1 : 8.
4. Acts 21 : 10–13.

to give up all hope of victory and surrender to the enemy, that, to be sure, is a capital crime according to the military code.[5] But otherwise, no matter how much the heart of the soldier is agitated and stricken by fear, if he still comes forward at the command of the general, goes on, fights, and defeats the enemy, he has no reason to fear that his former fear might lessen his reward in any way. As a matter of fact, he ought to receive even more praise because of it, since he had to overcome not only the enemy but also his own fear, which is often harder to conquer than the enemy himself.

As for our Savior Christ, what happened a little later showed how far He was from letting His sadness, fear, and weariness prevent Him from obeying His Father's command and keep Him from carrying out with courage all those things which He had formerly regarded with a wise and wholesome fear. For the time being, however, He had more than one reason why He should choose to suffer fear, sadness, weariness, and grief— "choose" I say, not "be forced," for who could have forced God?[6] Quite the contrary, it was by His own marvelous arrangement that His divinity moderated its influence on His humanity for such a time and in such a way that He was able to yield to the passions of our frail humanity and to suffer them with such terrible intensity. But, as I was saying, Christ, in His wonderful generosity, chose to do this for a number of reasons.

First of all, in order to do that for which He came into the world—that is, to bear witness to the truth.[7] And then, although He was truly man and also truly God, still there have been some who, seeing the truth of His human nature in His hunger, thirst, sleep, weariness and suchlike, have falsely persuaded themselves that He was not true God—I do not mean the Jews and gentiles of His time, who rejected Him, but rather the people of a much later time who even professed His name and His faith, namely

5. *Codex Iustinianus* 12, 45, 1.
6. Cf. Isa. 53 : 7 and John 10 : 17–18.   7. John 18 : 37.

heretics like Arius and his followers, who denied that Christ was of one nature with the Father and thus embroiled the church in great strife for many years. But against such plagues as this Christ provided a very powerful antidote, the endless supply of His miracles.

But there also arose an equal danger on the other side, just as those who escaped Scylla had to cope with Charybdis. For there were some who fixed their gaze so intently on the glory of His signs and powers that they were stunned and dazed by that immense brightness and went so far wrong as to deny altogether that He was truly a man. These people, too, growing from their original founder into a sect, did not hesitate to rend the holy unity of the Catholic Church and to tear it apart with their disgraceful sedition. This insane belief of theirs, which is no less dangerous than it is false, seeks to undermine and subvert completely (so far as lies within their power) the mystery of mankind's redemption, since it strives to utterly cut off and dry up the spring (as it were) from which the stream of our salvation flowed forth, namely the death and passion of our Savior. And so, to cure this very deadly disease, the best and kindest of physicians chose to experience sadness, dread, weariness, and fear of tortures and thus to show by these very real signs of human frailty that He was really a man.

Moreover, because He came into the world to earn joy for us by His own sorrow, and since that future joy of ours was to be fulfilled in our souls as well as our bodies, so too He chose to experience not only the pain of torture in His body but also the most bitter feelings of sadness, fear, and weariness in His mind, partly in order to bind us to Him all the more by reason of His greater sufferings for us, partly in order to admonish us how wrong it is for us either to refuse to suffer grief for His sake (since He freely bore so many and such immense griefs for us) or to tolerate grudgingly the punishment due to our sins, since we see our holy Savior Himself endured by His own free choice such numerous and bitter kinds of torment, both bodily and mental—and that not because He deserved them through any

fault of His own, but rather in order to do away with the wicked
deeds which we alone committed.[8]

Finally, since nothing was hidden from His eternal foreknowl-
edge, He foresaw that there would be people of various temperaments in the church (which is His own mystical body)—that His
members (I say) would differ considerably in their makeup.[9]
And although nature alone, without the help of grace, is quite
incapable of enduring martyrdom (since, as the apostle says, "No
one can say 'Jesus is Lord' except in the Spirit"[10]), nevertheless
God does not impart grace to men in such a way as to suspend
for the moment the functions and duties of nature, but instead
He either allows nature to accommodate itself to the grace which
is superadded to it, so that the good deed may be performed
with all the more ease, or else, if nature is disposed to resist, so
that this very resistance, overcome and put down by grace, may
add to the merit of the deed because it was difficult to do.

Therefore, since He foresaw that there would be many people
of such a delicate constitution that they would be convulsed with
terror at any danger of being tortured, He chose to enhearten
them by the example of His own sorrow, His own sadness, His
own weariness and unequalled fear, lest they should be so dis-
heartened as they compare their own fearful state of mind with
the boldness of the bravest martyrs that they would yield freely
what they fear will be won from them by force. To such a person
as this, Christ wanted His own deed to speak out (as it were) with
His own living voice: "O faint of heart, take courage and do not
despair.[1] You are afraid, you are sad, you are stricken with weariness and dread of the torment with which you have been cruelly threatened. Trust me. I conquered the world,[2] and yet I suffered immeasurably more from fear, I was sadder, more
afflicted with weariness, more horrified at the prospect of such
cruel suffering drawing eagerly nearer and nearer. Let the

---

8. Cf. Isa. 53 : 5, 8, 12, and 2 Cor. 5 : 19–21.
9. See Eph. 4 : 4–16 and John 14 : 2.   10. 1 Cor. 12 : 3.
1. Cf. Isa. 35 : 4 and Ecclus. 7 : 9.   2. John 16 : 33.

brave man have his high-spirited martyrs, let him rejoice in imitating a thousand of them. But you, my timorous and feeble
little sheep, be content to have me alone as your shepherd,[3]
follow my leadership; if you do not trust yourself, place your
trust in me. See, I am walking ahead of you along this fearful
road. Take hold of the border of my garment and you will feel
going out from it a power which will stay your heart's blood
from issuing in vain fears,[4] and will make your mind more
cheerful, especially when you remember that you are following
closely in my footsteps (and I am to be trusted and will not allow
you to be tempted beyond what you can bear, but I will give
together with the temptation a way out that you may be able to
endure it)[5] and likewise when you remember that this light and
momentary burden of tribulation will prepare for you a weight
of glory which is beyond all measure.[6] For the sufferings of this
time are not worthy to be compared with the glory to come
which will be revealed in you.[7] As you reflect on such things,
take heart, and use the sign of my cross to drive away this dread,
this sadness, fear, and weariness like vain specters of the darkness. Advance successfully[8] and press through all obstacles,
firmly confident that I will champion your cause[9] until you are
victorious and then in turn will reward you with the laurel crown
of victory."[1]

And so among the other reasons why our Savior deigned to
take upon Himself these feelings of human weakness, this one I
have spoken of is not unworthy of consideration—I mean that,
having made Himself weak for the sake of the weak, He might
take care of other weak men by means of His own weakness.[2] He
had their welfare so much at heart that this whole process of His
agony seems designed for nothing more clearly than to lay down

---

3. Cf. Matt. 26 : 31, John 10 : 14–16, Jer. 17 : 16, and Zech. 13 : 7.
4. Mark 5 : 25–34, Luke 8 : 43–48.   5. 1 Cor. 10 : 13.
6. 2 Cor. 4 : 17.   7. Rom. 8 : 18.   8. Cf. Ps. 44 : 5 (*AV*, 45 : 4).
9. Cf. Isa. 19 : 20 and 63 : 1.
1. Cf. 2 Tim. 2 : 5, 1 Cor. 9 : 25, 1 Cor. 15 : 57, Heb. 11 : 6.
2. 1 Cor. 9 : 22.

a fighting technique and a battle code for the faint-hearted
soldier who needs to be swept along, as it were, into martyrdom.

For, in order to teach anyone assailed by a fear of imminent
danger that he should both ask others to watch and pray, and
still place his trust in God alone apart from the others, and likewise in order to signify that He would tread the bitter winepress
of His cross alone without any companion,[3] He commanded
those same three apostles whom He had chosen from the other
eight and taken on with Him almost to the foot of the mount, to
stop there and to bear up and watch with Him; but He Himself
withdrew from them about a stone's throw.[4]

"And going on a little way He fell face down on the earth and
prayed that, if it were possible, the hour might pass from Him.
And He said: 'Abba, Father, to you all things are possible. Take
this cup away from me, but yet not what I will, but what you will.
My Father, if it is possible, let this cup pass away from me; yet
not as I will, but as you will.' "[5]

First of all Christ the commander teaches by His own example
that His soldier should take humility as his starting point, since it
is the foundation (as it were) of all the virtues from which one
may safely mount to higher levels. For, though His divinity is
equal and identical to that of God the Father, nevertheless because He is also man, He casts Himself down humbly as a man,
face down on the earth before God the Father.[6]

Reader, let us pause for a little at this point and contemplate
with a devout mind our commander lying on the ground in
humble supplication. For if we do this carefully, a ray of that
light which enlightens every man who comes into the world[7] will
illuminate our minds so that we will see, recognize, deplore, and
at long last correct, I will not say the negligence, sloth, or apathy,
but rather the feeble-mindedness, the insanity, the downright
blockheaded stupidity with which most of us approach the all-

---

3. Isa. 63 : 3.   4. Luke 22 : 41.
5. Matt. 26 : 39, Mark 14 : 35–36.   6. Cf. Phil. 2 : 5–7.
7. John 1 : 9.

powerful God, and instead of praying reverently address Him in a lazy and sleepy sort of way; and by the same token I am very much afraid that instead of placating Him and gaining His favor we exasperate Him and sharply provoke His wrath.

I wish that sometime we would make a special effort, right after finishing our prayers, to run over in our minds the whole sequence of time we spent praying. What follies will we see there? How much absurdity, and sometimes even foulness will we catch sight of? Indeed we will be amazed that it was at all possible for our minds to dissipate themselves in such a short time among so many places at such great distance from each other, among so many different affairs, such various, such manifold, such idle pursuits. For if someone, just as an experiment, should make a determined effort to make his mind touch upon as many and as diverse objects as possible, I hardly think that in such a short time he could run through such disparate and numerous topics as the mind, left to its own devices, ranges through while the mouth negligently mumbles through the hours of the office and other much used prayers.

And so if anyone wonders or has any doubts about what the mind is doing while dreams take over our consciousness during sleep, I find no comparison that comes closer to the mark than to think that the mind is occupied during sleep in exactly the same way as are the minds of those who are awake (if those who pray in this way can be said to be awake) but whose thoughts wander wildly during prayers, frantically flitting about in a throng of absurd fantasies—with this difference, though, from the sleeping dreamer: some of the waking dreamer's strange sights, which his mind embraces in its foreign travels while his tongue runs rattling through his prayers as if they were mere sound without sense,[8] some of these strange sights are such filthy and abominable monstrosities that if they had been seen during sleep, certainly no one, no matter how shameless, would

8. Vergil, *Aeneid,* 10, 640.

have the nerve to recount such extravagant dreams after he woke up, not even in the company of stable-boys.

And undoubtedly that old saying is very true, that our looks are a mirror of our minds.[9] For certainly such a wild and deranged state of mind is distinctly reflected in the eyes, in the cheeks, eyelids, and eyebrows, in the hands, feet, and in short in the overall bearing of the entire body.[10] For just as our minds are inattentive when we set out to pray, so too we proceed to do so with an equally careless and sprawling deportment of our bodies.

True, we do pretend that the worship of God is our reason for wearing better than everyday clothes on feast days, but the negligence with which most of us pray makes it utterly clear that we have utterly failed to conceal the real motive, namely a haughty desire to show off in the eyes of the world. Thus in our negligence we sometimes stroll around, sometimes sit down on a stool. And even when we kneel down, we either place our weight on one knee, raising up the other and resting it on our foot, or we place a cushion under our knees, and sometimes (if we are especially spoiled) we even support our elbows on a cushion, looking for all the world like a propped up house that is threatening to tumble down.

And then our actions too, in how many ways do they betray that our minds are wandering miles away? We scratch our heads, clean our fingernails with a pocketknife, pick our noses with our fingers, meanwhile making the wrong responses. Having no idea what we have already said and what we have not said, we make a wild guess as to what remains to be said. Are we not ashamed to pray in such a deranged state of mind and body—to beseech God's favor in a matter so crucial for us, to beg His forgiveness for so many monstrous misdeeds, to ask Him to save us from eternal punishment?—so that even if we had not sinned before, we would still deserve tenfold eternal tor-

9. Cicero, *De oratore*, 3, 59, 221.   10. Cf. Cicero, *Pis.*, 1, 1.

ments for having approached the majesty of God in such a con-
temptuous fashion.

Imagine, if you will, that you have committed a crime of high
treason against some mortal prince or other who has your life in
his hands but who is so merciful that he is prepared to temper
his wrath because of your repentance and humble supplication,
and to commute the death sentence into a monetary fine or even
to suspend it completely if you give convincing signs of great
shame and sorrow. Now, when you have been brought into the
presence of the prince, go ahead and speak to him carelessly,
casually, without the least concern. While he stays in one place
and listens attentively, stroll around here and there as you run
through your plea. Then, when you have had enough of walking up and down, sit down on a chair, or if courtesy seems to
require that you condescend to kneel down, first command
someone to come and place a cushion beneath your knees, or,
better yet, to bring a prie-dieu with another cushion to lean your
elbows on. Then yawn, stretch, sneeze, spit without giving it a
thought, and belch up the fumes of your gluttony. In short, conduct yourself in such a way that he can clearly see from your
face, your voice, your gestures, and your whole bodily deportment that while you are addressing him you are thinking about
something else. Tell me now, what success could you hope for
from such a plea as this?

Certainly we would consider it quite mad to defend ourselves
in this way before a mortal prince against a charge that carries
the death penalty. And yet such a prince, once he had destroyed
our bodies, could do nothing further. And do we think it is reasonable, when we have been caught committing a whole series of
far more serious crimes, to beg pardon so contemptuously from
the king of all kings,[1] God Himself, who, when He has destroyed
our bodies, has the power to send both body and soul together
to hell?[2]

Still I would not wish anyone to construe what I have said as

1. Cf. 1 Tim. 6 : 15, Rev. 19 : 16.   2. Luke 12 : 4, Matt. 10 : 28.

meaning that I forbid anyone to pray while walking or sitting or even lying down. Indeed I wish that, whatever our bodies may be doing, we would at the same time constantly lift up our minds to God (which is the most acceptable form of prayer). For no matter where we may turn our steps, as long as our minds are directed to God, we clearly do not turn away from Him who is present everywhere.[3] But just as the prophet who says to God "I was mindful of you when I lay upon my bed"[4] did not rest content with that but also rose "in the middle of the night to pay homage to the Lord,"[5] so too I would require that, besides such prayers said while walking, we also occasionally say some prayers for which we prepare our minds more thoughtfully, for which we dispose our bodies more reverently, than we would if we were about to approach all the kings in the whole world sitting together in one place.

But of this much I can assure you: every time I think about this mental wandering, it vexes and plagues my mind.

Nevertheless, some ideas may be suggested to us during our prayers by an evil spirit or may creep into our imaginations through the normal functioning of our senses, and I would not assert that any one of these, not even if it is vile and quite horrible, must be immediately fatal, so long as we resist it and drive it away. But otherwise, if we accept it with pleasure or allow it through negligence to grow in intensity over a long period of time, I have not the slightest doubt that the force of it can become so aggravated as to be fatally destructive to the soul.

Certainly, when I consider the immeasurable glory of God's majesty, I am immediately compelled and forced to believe that if even these brief distractions of mind are not crimes punishable by death, it is only because God in His mercy and goodness deigns not to exact death for them, not because the wickedness inherent in their own nature does not deserve death—and for this reason: I simply cannot imagine how such thoughts can gain

3. Cf. Jer. 23 : 23–24.   4. Ps. 62 : 7 (AV, 63 : 6).
5. Ps. 118 : 62 (AV, 119 : 62).

entrance into the minds of men when they are praying (that is, when they are speaking to God) unless it be through weakness of faith. Otherwise, since our minds do not go wool-gathering while we are addressing a mortal prince about some important matter or even speaking to one of his ministers who might be in a position of some influence with his master, certainly it could never happen that our minds should stray even the least bit while we are praying to God, certainly not, that is, if we believed with a strong and active faith that we are in the presence of God, who not only listens to our words and looks upon our facial features and bodily deportment as outward signs and indications from which our interior state of mind can be gathered, but who also pierces into the most secret and inward recesses of our hearts with a vision more penetrating than the eyes of Lynceus[6] and who illuminates everything with the immeasurable brightness of His majesty—it could not happen, I say, if we believed that God is present, God in whose glorious presence all the princes of the world in all their glory[7] must confess (unless they are out of their minds) that they are the merest mites and earth-creeping worms.

Therefore, since our Savior Christ saw that nothing is more profitable than prayer, but since He was also aware that this means of salvation would very often be fruitless because of the negligence of men and the malice of demons—so much so that it would very frequently be perverted into an instrument of destruction—He decided to take this opportunity, on the way to His death, to reinforce His teaching by His words and example, and to put the finishing touches on this most necessary point just as He did on the other parts of His teaching.

He wished us to know that we ought to serve God not only in soul but also in body, since He created both, and He wanted us to learn that a reverent attitude of the body, though it takes its origin and character from the soul, increases by a kind of reflex

6. Cf. 2 Par. 6 : 30 and Jer. 17 : 9–10. Lynceus, one of the Argonauts, was famed for the sharpness of his sight.
7. Cf. Matt. 6 : 29, Luke 12 : 27.

the soul's own reverence and devotion toward God. Hence He presented the most humble mode of subjection and venerated His heavenly Father in a bodily posture which no earthly prince has dared to demand, or even to accept if freely offered, except that drunken and debauched Macedonian [Alexander] and some other barbarians puffed up with success, who thought they ought to be venerated as gods.

For when He prayed He did not sit back or stand up or merely kneel down, but rather He threw His whole body face-forward and lay prostrate on the ground. Then, in that pitiable posture, He implored His Father's mercy and twice called His Father by name, begging Him that, since all things are possible to Him, He might be moved by His prayers to take away the cup of His passion if this could be done, that is, if He had not imposed it on Him by an immutable decree. But He also asked that His own will, as expressed in this prayer, might not be granted, if something else seemed better to His Father's will, which is absolutely best.

This passage should not lead you to think that the Son was ignorant of the will of the Father. Rather, because He wanted to instruct men, He also wanted to express the feelings of men. By saying the word "Father" twice, He wanted to remind us that all fatherhood proceeds from Him, both in heaven and on earth.[8] Moreover, He also wanted to impress upon us that God the Father is His father in a double sense—namely by creation, which is a sort of fatherhood (for we come from God, who created us from nothing, more truly than we do from the human father who begot us, since, in fact, God created beforehand that begetter Himself and since He created and supplied beforehand all the matter out of which we were begotten); but when Christ acknowledged God as His Father in this sense, He did so as a man. On the other hand, as God, He knows Him as His natural and coeternal Father.

And yet another reason for His calling on His Father twice

8. Eph. 3 : 15.

may not be far from the truth: He intended not only to acknowledge that God the Father is His natural father in heaven, but
also to signify that He has no other father on earth, since He was
conceived by a virgin mother according to the flesh, without any
male seed, when the Holy Spirit came upon His mother—the
Spirit, I say, both of the Father and of Himself, whose works
coexist in identity and cannot be radically distinguished by any
human insight.[9]

Moreover, this forceful repetition of His Father's name, since
it expresses an intense desire to gain what He asked for, might
serve to teach us a very wholesome lesson: that when we pray for
something without receiving it we should not give up like King
Saul, who, because he did not immediately receive a prophecy
from God, resorted to witchcraft and went off to the woman
with a spirit, engaging in a practice forbidden by the law and
formerly suppressed by his own decree.[10]

Christ teaches us that we should persevere in our prayers
without murmuring at all if we do not obtain what we seek—and
for good reason, since we see that the Son of God our Savior did
not obtain the reprieve from death which He sought from His
Father with such urgency, but always with the condition (and
this is what we ought to imitate most of all) that His will was subject to the will of His Father.

"And He went to His disciples and found them sleeping."[11]

Notice here how much greater one love is than another. Notice how Christ's love for His own was much greater than the
love they gave Him in return, even those who loved Him most.
For even the sadness, fear, dread, and weariness which so
grievously assailed Him as His most cruel torment drew near,
could not keep Him from going to see them. But they, on the
other hand, however much they loved Him (and undoubtedly
they loved Him intensely), even at the very time when such an

9. Cf. John 5 : 16–19.
10. 1 Kings 28 : 5–25 and 1 Par. 10 : 13–14.
11. Matt. 26 : 40, Mark 14 : 37, Luke 22 : 45.

enormous danger was threatening their loving master, could still give in to sleep.

"And He said to Peter, 'Simon, are you sleeping? Could you not stay awake one hour with me? Stay awake and pray that you may not enter into temptation. For the spirit indeed is willing, but the flesh is weak.' " [12]

This short speech of Christ is remarkably forceful: the words are mild, but their point is sharp and piercing. For by addressing him as Simon and reproaching him under that name for his sleepiness, Christ tacitly lets it be known that the name Peter, which Christ had previously given him because of his firmness, would hardly be altogether appropriate now because of this infirmity and sleep. Moreover, not only was the failure to use the name Peter (or rather, Cephas) a barbed omission, but the actual use of the name Simon also carries a sting. For in Hebrew, the language in which Christ was speaking to him, "Simon" means "listening" and also "obedient." But in fact, he was neither listening nor obedient, since he went to sleep against Christ's express wishes.

Over and above these, our Savior's gentle words to Peter seem to carry certain other barbed implications, which if He were chiding him more severely, would be something like this: "Simon, no longer Cephas, are you sleeping? For how do you deserve to be called Cephas, that is, rock? I singled you out by that name because of your firmness,[1] but now you show yourself to be so infirm that you cannot hold out even for an hour against the inroads of sleep. As for that old name of yours, Simon, certainly you live up to that remarkably well: can you be called listening when you are sleeping this way? or can you be called obedient when in spite of my instructions to stay awake, I am no sooner gone than you relax and doze and fall asleep? I always made much of you Simon, and yet Simon are you sleeping? I paid you many high honors, and yet Simon are you sleep-

12. Matt. 26 : 40–41, Mark 14 : 37–38.   1. John 1 : 42.

ing? A few moment ago you boasted that you would die with me,[2] and now Simon are you sleeping? Now I am pursued to the death by the Jews and the gentiles and by one worse than either of them, Judas, and Simon are you sleeping? Indeed, Satan is busily seeking to sift all of you like wheat,[3] and Simon are you sleeping? What can I expect from the others, when, in such great and pressing danger, not only to me but also to all of you, I find that you Simon, even you are sleeping?

Then, lest this seem to be a matter which concerned Peter only, He turned and spoke to the others. "Stay awake and pray," He says, "that you may not enter into temptation. The spirit indeed is willing, but the flesh is weak."[4]

Here we are enjoined to be constant in prayer, and we are informed that prayer is not only useful but also extremely necessary—for this reason: without it, the weakness of the flesh holds us back, somewhat in the way a remora-fish retards a ship,[5] until our minds, no matter how willing to do good, are swept back into the evils of temptation. For whose spirit is more willing than Peter's was? And yet that he had great need of God's protection against the flesh is clear enough from this fact alone: when sleep kept him from praying and begging for God's help, he gave an opening to the devil, who not long afterwards used the weakness of Peter's flesh to blunt the eagerness of his spirit and impelled him to perjure himself by denying Christ.[6] Now if such things happened to the apostles, who were like flourishing green branches, that is, if they entered into temptation when they allowed sleep to interrupt their prayers, what will happen to us, who are like sapless sticks by comparison, if, when we are suddenly faced by danger (and when, I ask you, are we not in danger, since our enemy the devil constantly prowls like a roaring lion looking everywhere for someone who is ready to fall

2. Mark 14 : 31, Luke 22 : 33.   3. Luke 22 : 31.
4. Matt. 26 : 41.
5. The remora (suck-fish) was thought to be able to stop a large ship simply by attaching itself to the hull.
6. Matt. 26 : 69–74, Mark 14 : 71.

because of the weakness of the flesh, ready to pounce upon such a man and devour him[7]), in such great danger, I say, what will become of us if we do not follow Christ's advice by being steadfast in wakefulness and prayer?

Christ tells us to stay awake, but not for cards and dice, not for rowdy parties and drunken brawls, not for wine and women, but for prayer. He tells us to pray not occasionally, but constantly. "Pray," He says, "unceasingly."[8] He tells us to pray not only during the day (for it is hardly necessary to command anyone to stay awake during the day) but rather He exhorts us to devote to intense prayer a large part of that very time which most of us usually devote entirely to sleep. How much more, then, should we be ashamed of our miserable performance and recognize the enormous guilt we incur by saying no more than a short prayer or two, perhaps, during the day, and even those said as we doze and yawn. Finally our Savior tells us to pray, not that we may roll in wealth, not that we may live in a continuous round of pleasures, not that something awful may happen to our enemies, not that we may receive honor in this world, but rather that we may not enter into temptation. In fact, He wishes us to understand that all those worldly goods are either downright harmful, or else, by comparison with that one benefit, the merest trifles; and hence in His widsom He placed this one petition at the end of the prayer which He had previously taught His disciples, as if it were a summary, in a way, of all the rest: "And lead us not into temptation, but deliver us from evil."[9]

"And again He went away, for the second time, and said the same prayer over again, in these words: 'My Father, if this cup cannot pass away without my drinking it, let your will be done.' And He came again and found them sleeping, for their eyes were heavy. And they did not know what answer to make to Him. And leaving them, He went away again and kneeling down

7. 1 Pet. 5 : 8.   8. 1 Thess. 5 : 17. Cf. Luke 18 : 1.
9. Matt. 6 : 13.

said the same prayer, in these words: 'Father, if you are willing, take this cup from me. Yet not my will but yours be done.' "[10]

Thus, after He had given His disciples this warning, He went back to pray again, and He repeated the same prayer He had said before, but still in such a way as to commit the whole matter once more to the will of the Father. Thus He teaches us to make our petitions earnest without being absolutely definite, but rather to trust the whole outcome to God, who desires our welfare no less than we ourselves do[11] and who knows what is likely to produce it a thousand times better than we do.

"My Father," He says, "if this cup cannot pass away without my drinking it, let your will be done." That pronoun "my" has a twofold effect: for it expresses great affection, and it makes it clear that God the Father is the father of Christ in a singular way—that is, not only by creation (for in this way He is the father of all things), not by adoption (in this way He is the father of Christians), but rather by nature He is God the Father of God the Son. And then He teaches the rest of us to pray thus: "Our Father who art in heaven." By these words we acknowledge that we are all brothers who have one Father in common, whereas Christ Himself is the only one who can rightfully, because of His divinity, address the Father as He does here, "My Father." But if anyone is not content to be like other men[12] and is so proud as to imagine that he alone is governed by the secret Spirit of God and that he has a different status from other men, it certainly seems to me that such a person arrogates to himself the language of Christ and prays with the invocation "My Father" instead of "Our Father," since he claims for himself as a private individual the Spirit which God shares with all men. In fact, such a person is not much different from Lucifer, since he arrogates to himself God's language, just as Lucifer claimed God's place.[1]

Christ's language here—"If this cup cannot pass away without my drinking it, let your will be done"—also makes it perfectly

10. Mark 14 : 39–40, Matt. 26 : 42–44.   11. Cf. Matt. 6 : 26.
12. Cf. Luke 18 : 11.   1. Cf. Isa. 14 : 13–14.

clear on what basis He calls a thing possible or impossible, namely on no other basis than the certain, immutable, unconstrained decision of His Father concerning His death. For otherwise, if He had thought that He was ineluctably and necessarily destined to die, either because of the course of the heavenly bodies or because of some more abstract overall scheme of things such as fate, and if this had been the sense in which He said "If this cup cannot pass away without my drinking it," then it would have been completely pointless for Him to add the phrase "let your will be done." For how could He have left the matter to be decided by the Father if He believed that its outcome depended on something besides the Father, or if He thought that the Father had to make a certain choice necessarily, that is, willy-nilly?

But at the same time, while we examine the words with which Christ begged His Father to avert His death and humbly submitted everything to the will of His Father, we must also constantly bear in mind that, though He was both God and man, He said all these things not as God, but insofar as He was man. We ourselves provide a parallel: because we are composed of body and soul, we sometimes apply to our whole selves things which actually are true only of the soul and on the other hand we sometimes speak of ourselves when strict accuracy would require us to speak of our bodies alone. For we say that the martyrs go straight to heaven when they die, whereas actually only their souls are taken up to heaven. And, on the other hand, we say that men, however proud they may be, are still only dust and ashes and that when they have finished with this brief life they will rot in a common ordinary grave. We constantly talk this way, even though the soul does not enter into the grave or undergo death but rather outlives the body, either in miserable torment if it lived badly while in the body, or else in perpetual well-being if it lived well.

In a similar fashion, then, Christ speaks of what He did as God and what He did as man, not as if He were divided into two persons but as one and the same person, and that rightly, since

He was one person; for in the omnipotent person of Christ humanity and divinity were joined and made one no less closely than His immortal soul was united to a body which could die. Thus because of His divinity He did not hesitate to say "I and the Father are one"[2] and "Before Abraham came to be, I am."[3] Moreover, because of both His natures, He said, "I am with you all days even to the end of the world."[4] And, conversely, because of His humanity alone He said "The Father is greater than I"[5] and "A little while I am with you."[6] It is true, of course, that His glorious body is really present with us, and always will be till the end of the world, under the appearance of bread in the venerable sacrament of the eucharist; but that bodily form in which He once associated with His disciples (and this is the kind of presence He had in mind when He said "A little while I am with you") was taken away after Christ's ascension, unless He Himself chooses to show it so someone, as He sometimes does.

Therefore, in this passage about Christ's agony, whichever of these deeds, sufferings, or prayers of His are so lowly that they seem quite incompatible with the lofty height of divinity, let us remember that the same Christ performed them as a man. Indeed some of them had their origin only in the lower part of His humanity. I mean the part concerned with sensation; and these served to proclaim the genuineness of His human nature and to relieve the natural fears of other men in later times. Nothing, then, in these words or in any of all the other things that the sequence of His agony presented as signs of His afflicted humanity, was considered by Christ to be unworthy of His glory; indeed so little did He think so that He Himself took special care to see that they became widely known.

For, though everything written by all the apostles was dictated throughout by one and the same spirit of Christ, still I find it hard to recall any of His other deeds which He took such particular pains to preserve in the memories of men. To be sure, He

2. John 10 : 30.   3. John 8 : 58.   4. Matt. 28 : 20.
5. John 14 : 28.   6. John 13 : 33.

told His apostles about His intense sadness, so that they might be
able to hand it down from Him to posterity. But the words of
His prayer to His Father they could hardly have heard even if
they had been awake (since the nearest of them were a stone's
throw away), and even if they had been present when it happened, they still could not have heard because they were asleep.
Certainly they would have been even less able, at that time of
night, to make out when He knelt down or when He threw Himself face forward on the ground. As for those drops of blood
which flowed like sweat from His whole body,[7] even if they had
later clearly seen the stain left on the ground, I think they would
have drawn almost any number of conclusions without guessing
the right one, since it was an unprecedented phenomenon for
anyone to sweat blood.

Yet in the ensuing time before His death it seems unlikely that
He spoke of these things either to His mother or to the apostles,
unless one is willing to believe that He told the apostles the
whole story of His agony when He left off praying and came
back to them—that is, while they were either still sleeping or
barely awake and quite drowsy—or else that He told them at the
very time when the troops were at hand. The remaining alterna-
tive, then, and the one that seems most likely to be true, is that,
after He rose from the dead and there could no longer be any
doubt that He was God, His most loving mother and beloved
disciples heard from His own most holy lips this detailed account, point by point, of His human suffering, the knowledge of
which would benefit both them and (through them) others who
would come after them, and which no one could have recounted
except Christ Himself. Therefore, to those whose hearts are
troubled, meditation on this agony provides great consolation,
and rightly so, since it was for this very purpose, to console the
afflicted, that our Savior in His kindness made known His own
affliction, which no one else knew or could have known.

Some may be concerned about another point: when Christ

7. Luke 22 : 44.

came back from that prayer to see His apostles and found them sleeping and so startled by His arrival that they did not know what to say, He left them, so that it might seem He had come only for the purpose of finding out whether they were awake, whereas He could not have lacked this knowledge (insofar as He was God) even before He came.

The answer to such persons, if there are any, should be this: nothing that *He* did was done in vain. It is true that His coming into their presence did not rouse them to complete vigilance but only to such a startled, half-waking drowsiness that they hardly raised their eyes to look at Him, or else (what is worse yet) if His reproaches did wake them up completely, still they slipped back into sleep the moment He went away. Nevertheless, He Himself both demonstrated His anxious concern for His disciples and also by His example gave to the future pastors of His church a solemn injunction not to allow themselves the slightest wavering, out of sadness or weariness or fear, in their diligent care of their flock, but rather to conduct themselves so as to prove in actual fact that they are not so much concerned for themselves as for the welfare of their flock.

But perhaps some meticulous fussy dissector of the divine plan might say: "Either Christ wished the apostles to stay awake or He did not. If He did not, why did He give such an explicit command? If He did, what use was there in going back and forth so often? Since He was God, could He not at one and the same time speak the command and insure its execution?"

Doubtless He could have, my good man, since He was God, who carried out whatever He wished, who created all things with a word:[8] He spoke and it was done, He commanded and they were created.[9] He opened the eyes of a man blind from birth,[10] and could He not, then, find a way to open the eyes of a man who was asleep? Clearly, even someone who was not God could easily do that. For anyone can see that if you merely prick the eyes of sleepy men with a tiny pin they will stay awake and will certainly not go right back to sleep.

8. Cf. Sap. 9 : 1.   9. Ps. 32 : 9 (*AV*, 33 : 9).   10. John 9 : 32.

Doubtless Christ could have caused the apostles not to sleep at all but to stay awake, if that had been what He wished in an absolute and unqualified sense. But actually His wish was modified by a condition—namely that they themselves wish to do so, and wish it so effectually that each of them do his very best to comply with the outward command Christ Himself gave and to cooperate with the promptings of His inward assistance. In this way He also wishes for all men to be saved[1] and for no one to suffer eternal torment, that is, always provided that we conform to His most loving will and do not set ourselves against it through our own willful malice. If someone stubbornly insists on doing this, God does not wish to waft him off to heaven against his will, as if He were in need of our services there and could not continue His glorious reign without our support. Indeed, if He could not reign without us, He would immediately punish many offenses which now, out of consideration for us, He tolerates and overlooks for a long time to see if His kindness and patience will bring us to repent. But we meanwhile abuse this great mercy of His by adding sins to sins,[2] thus heaping up for ourselves (as the apostle says) a treasure of wrath on the day of wrath.[3]

Nevertheless, such is God's kindness that even when we are negligent and slumbering on the pillow of our sins, He disturbs us from time to time, shakes us, strikes us, and does His best to wake us up by means of tribulations. But still, even though He thus proves Himself to be most loving even in His anger, most of us, in our gross human stupidity, misinterpret His action and imagine that such a great benefit is an injury, whereas actually (if we have any sense) we should feel bound to pray frequently and fervently that whenever we wander away from Him He may use blows to drive us back to the right way, even though we are unwilling and struggle against Him.

Thus we must first pray that we may see the way and with the church we must say to God, "From blindness of heart, deliver us, O Lord."[4] And with the prophet we must say, "Teach me to do

1. 1 Tim. 2 : 4.   2. Cf. Ecclus. 5 : 5 and Isa. 30 : 1.
3. Rom. 2 : 5.
4. Part of the litany of the saints in the breviary of Salisbury.

your will"[5] and "Show me your ways and teach me your paths."[6]
Then we must intensely desire to run after you eagerly, O God,
in the odor of your ointments,[7] in the most sweet scent of your
Spirit. But if we grow weary along the way (as we almost always
do) and lag so far behind that we barely manage to follow at a
distance,[8] let us immediately say to God, "Take my right hand"[9]
and "Lead me along your path."[10]

Then if we are so overcome by weariness that we no longer
have the heart to go on, if we are so soft and lazy that we are
about to stop altogether, let us beg God to drag us along[1] even
as we struggle not to go. Finally, if we resist when He draws us
on gently, and are stiffnecked against the will of God, against
our own salvation, utterly irrational like horses and mules which
have no intellects,[2] we ought to beseech God humbly in the most
fitting words of the prophet, "Hold my jaws hard, O God, with a
bridle and bit when I do not draw near to you."[3]

But then, since fondness for prayer is the first of our virtues
to go when we are overtaken by sloth, and since we are reluctant
to pray for anything (however useful) that we are reluctant to receive, certainly if we have any sense at all we ought to take this
weakness into account well in advance, before we fall into such
sick and troubled states of mind—we ought, in other words, to
pour out to God unceasingly such prayers as I have mentioned,
and we should humbly implore Him that, if at some later time
we should ask for anything untoward—allured perhaps by the
enticements of the flesh or seduced by a longing for worldly
things or overthrown by the clever snares of the devils—He may
be deaf to such prayers and avert what we pray for, showering
upon us instead those things He knows will be good for us, however much we beg Him to take them away. In fact, this is the way

5. Ps. 142 : 10 (*AV*, 143 : 10).   6. Cf. Ps. 24 : 4 (*AV*, 25 : 4).
7. Cf. Cant. 1 : 3.   8. Matt. 26 : 58, Mark 14 : 54, Luke 23 : 54.
9. Cf. Ps. 72 : 24 (*AV*, 73 : 23), Isa. 42 : 6 and 45 : 1.
10. Cf. Ps. 5 : 9 (*AV*, 5 : 8), 26 : 11 (*AV*, 27 : 11), 138 : 24 (*AV*, 139 : 24).
1. Cf. Cant. 1 : 3, John 6 : 44, 12 : 32.
2. Tob. 6 : 17, Ps. 31 : 9 (*AV*, 32 : 9).   3. Ps. 31 : 9 (*AV*, 32 : 9).

we normally act (if we are wise) when we are expecting a fever: we give advance warning to those who are to take care of us in our sickness that, even if we beg them, they should not give us any of those things which our diseased condition makes us perversely long for, though they are harmful to our health and only make the disease worse.

And when we are so fast asleep in our vices that even the calls and stirrings of divine mercy do not make us willing to rouse ourselves and wake up to virtuous living, we ourselves sometimes supply the reason why God goes away and leaves us to our vices; some He leaves so as never to come back again, but others He lets sleep only until another time, according as He sees fit in His wondrous kindness and the inscrutable depths of His wisdom.

Christ's action provided a sort of paradigm of this fact: when He went back to check on the apostles, they were unwilling to stay awake but rather went right on sleeping, and so He went away and left them. For "leaving them He went away again and kneeling down said the same prayer, in these words: 'Father, if you are willing, take this cup from me. Yet not my will but yours be done.' "[4]

Notice how He again asks the same thing, again adds the same condition, again sets us an example to show that when we fall into great danger, even for God's sake, we should not think we are not allowed to beg God urgently to provide us a way out[5] of that crisis. For one thing, it is quite possible that He permits us to be brought into such difficulties precisely because fear of danger makes us grow fervent in prayer when prosperity has made us cold, especially when it is a question of bodily danger— for most of us are not very warmly concerned about danger to our souls. Now as for those who are concerned (as they ought to be) about their souls, unless someone is strengthened and inspired by God to undergo martyrdom—a condition which must be either directly experienced in an unexplainable way or else

4. Matt. 26 : 42, Mark 14 : 39.   5. Cf. 1 Cor. 10 : 13.

judged by appropriate indications—apart from such a case everyone has sufficient grounds to be afraid that he may grow weary under his burden and give in. Hence everyone, to avoid such overconfidence as Peter's,[6] ought to pray diligently that God in His goodness may deliver him from such a great danger to his soul. But it must be stressed again and again that no one should pray to escape danger so absolutely that he would not be willing to leave the whole matter up to God, ready in all obedience to endure what God has prepared for him.

These are some of the reasons, then, why Christ provided us with this salutary example of prayer, not that He Himself was in any need of such prayer—nothing could be further from the truth. For, insofar as He was God, He was not inferior to the Father. Insofar as He was God, not only His power but also His will was the same as the Father's.[7] Certainly insofar as He was man, His power was infinitely less,[8] but then all power, both in heaven and on earth, was finally given to Him by the Father.[9] And though His will, insofar as He was man, was not identical with the Father's, still it was in such complete conformity with the will of the Father that no disagreement was ever found between them.[10]

Thus the reasoning power of His soul, in obedience to the will of the Father, agrees to suffer that most bitter death, while at the same time, as a proof of His humanity, His bodily senses react to the prospect with revulsion and dread. His prayer expresses vividly both the fear and the obedience: "Father," He said, "if you are willing, take this cup from me. Yet not my will but yours be done."

His deeds, however, present this dual reaction even more clearly than His words. That His reasoning faculties never drew back from such horrible torture but rather remained obedient to the Father even to death, even to the death of the cross,[1] was demonstrated by the succeeding events of the passion. And that

6. Matt. 26 : 33–35.   7. John 5 : 17–18.   8. John 14 : 28.
9. Matt. 11 : 27, 28 : 18.   10. Cf. John 5 : 30.
1. Cf. Phil. 2 : 8.

His feelings were overwhelmed by an intense fear of His coming
passion is shown by the words which come next in the gospel.

"And there appeared to Him an angel from heaven to
strengthen Him."[2]

Do you realize how intense His mental anguish must have
been, that an angel should come from heaven to strengthen
Him?

But when I consider this passage, I cannot help wondering
what pernicious nonsense has gotten into the heads of those who
contend that it is futile for anyone to seek the intercession of any
angel or departed saint, namely on the grounds that we can confidently address our prayers to God Himself, not only because
He alone is more present to us than all the angels and all the
saints put together but also because He has the power to grant
us more, and a greater desire to do so, than any of the saints in
heaven, of whatever description.

With such trivial and groundless arguments as these, they
express their envious displeasure at the glory of the saints, who
are in turn equally displeased with such men; for they strive to
undermine the loving homage we pay to the saints and the saving assistance they render to us. Why should these shameless
men not follow the same line of reasoning here and argue that
the angel's effort to offer consolation to our Savior Christ was
utterly pointless and superfluous? For what angel of them all
was as powerful as He Himself or as near to Him as God, since
He Himself was God? But in fact, just as He wished to undergo
sadness and anxiety for our sake, so too for our sake He wished
to have an angel console Him, for a number of reasons: both to
refute the foolish arguments of such men, and to make it clear
that He was truly man (for just as angels ministered to Him as
God when He had triumphed over the temptations of the devil,
so too an angel came to console Him as man while He was making His lowly progress toward death) and moreover to give us

2. Luke 22 : 43.

hope that if we direct our prayers to God when we are in danger we cannot lack consolation, always provided we do not pray in a lazy and perfunctory way, but rather intimate Christ in this passage by sighing and praying from the bottom of our hearts.

"For in His agony He prayed more earnestly, and His sweat became like drops of blood running down to the ground."[3]

Most scholars affirm that what Christ suffered for us was more painful than the suffering of any of all the martyrs, of whatever time or place, who underwent martyrdom for the faith. But others disagree, because there are various other sorts of torture than those to which Christ was subjected and some torments have been extended over a period of several days, a longer time than those of Christ lasted. Then, too, they think that, since one drop of Christ's precious blood, because of His infinite divinity, would have been far more than enough to redeem all mankind, therefore His ordeal was not ordained by God according to the standards of anyone else's suffering, but according to the proper measure of His own unfathomable wisdom. And since no one can know this measure with certainty, they hold that it is not prejudicial to the faith to believe that Christ's pain was less than that of some of the martyrs. But as for me, apart from the widespread opinion of the church which fittingly applies to Christ Jeremiah's words about Jerusalem ("O all you who pass by the way, look and see if there is any sorrow like mine"[4]), certainly I find that this passage also provides very convincing reasons to believe that no martyr's torments could ever be compared with Christ's suffering, even on this point of the intensity of the pain.

Even if I should grant what I have good reasons to think need not be granted, namely that any of the martyrs was subjected to more kinds of torture, and greater ones, even (if you like) longer ones than Christ endured, still I find it not at all hard to believe that tortures which to all appearances may be considerably less

3. Luke 22 : 44.
4. Lam. 1 : 12. The text was recited at matins and lauds of Good Friday; there the words are imagined as spoken by Christ rather than by Jerusalem.

fierce actually caused Christ to suffer more excruciating pain
than someone might feel from tortures that seem much more
grievous, and for this reason: I see that Christ, as the thought of
His coming passion was borne in upon Him, was overwhelmed
by mental anguish more bitter than any other mortal has ever
experienced from the thought of coming torments. For who has
ever felt such bitter anguish that a bloody sweat broke out all
over his body and ran down in drops to the ground? The intensity of the actual pain itself, therefore, I estimate by this standard: I see that even the presentiment of it before it arrived was
more bitter to Christ than such anticipation has ever been to
anyone else.

Nor could this anguish of the mind ever have grown to sufficient intensity to cause the body to sweat blood if He had not,
of His own free will, exercised His divine omnipotence, not only
to refrain from alleviating this painful pressure, but even to add
to its force and strength. This He did in order to prefigure the
blood which future martyrs would be forced to pour forth on
the ground, and at the same time to offer this unheard of, this
marvelous example of profound anguish as a consolation to
those who would be so fearful and alarmed at the thought of
torture that they might otherwise interpret their fear as a sign of
their downfall and thus yield to despair.

At this point, if someone should again bring up those martyrs
who freely and eagerly exposed themselves to death because of
their faith in Christ, and if he should offer his opinion that they
are especially worthy of the laurels of triumph because with a joy
that left no room for sorrow they betrayed no trace of sadness,
no sign of fear, I am perfectly willing to go along with him on
that point, so long as he does not go so far as to deny the
triumph of those who do not rush forth of their own accord but
who nevertheless do not hang back or withdraw once they have
been seized, but rather go on in spite of their fearful anxiety and
face the terrible prospect out of love for Christ.

Now if anyone should argue that the eager martrys receive a
greater share of glory than the others, I have no objection—he
can have the argument all to himself. For I rest content with the

fact that in heaven neither sort of martyr will lack a glory so great that while they were alive their eyes never saw the like, nor did their ears ever hear it, nor did it ever enter into their hearts [to conceive of it].[5] And even if someone does have a higher place in heaven, no one else envies him for it—quite the opposite, everyone enjoys the glory of everyone else because of their mutual love.

Besides, just who outranks whom in the glory assigned by God in heaven is not, I think, quite crystal-clear to us, groping as we are in the darkness of our mortality.

For, though I grant that God loves a cheerful giver,[6] still I have no doubt that He loved Tobias, and holy Job, too. Now it is true that both of them bore their calamities bravely and patiently, but neither of them, so far as I know, was exactly jumping with joy or clapping his hands out of happiness.

To expose one's self to death for Christ's sake when the case clearly demands it or when God gives a secret prompting to do so, this, I do not deny, is a deed of preeminent virtue. But otherwise I do not think it very safe to do so, and among those who willingly suffered for Christ we find outstanding figures who were very much afraid, who were deeply distressed, who even withdrew from death more than once before they finally faced it bravely.

Certainly I do not mean to derogate from God's power to inspire martyrs; indeed I believe that He exercises it on occasion (either granting this favor to holy persons as a reward for the labors of their past lives or giving it purely and simply out of His own generosity) by filling the whole mind of a martyr with such joy that he not only wards off those grievous emotional disturbances but also keeps himself completely free from what the Stoics call "incipient emotions," freely admitting that even their factitious wisemen are susceptible to them.

Since we often see it happen that some men do not feel wounds inflicted in battle until their awareness, which had been

5. 1 Cor. 2 : 9.   6. 2 Cor. 9 : 7.

displaced by strong feeling, returns to them and they notice the injury,[7] certainly there is no reason why I should doubt that a mind exulting in the high hopes of approaching glory can be so rapt and transported beyond itself that it neither fears death nor feels torments.

But still, even if God did give someone this gift, I would certainly be inclined to call it an unearned felicity or the recompense of past virtue, but not the measure of future reward in heaven. Now I might have believed that this future reward corresponds to the pain suffered for Christ except that God in His generosity bestows it in such good measure—so full, so concentrated, so overflowing[8]—that the sufferings of this time are by no means worthy to be compared to that future glory which will be revealed in those[9] who loved God so dearly that they spent their very life's blood for His glory, with such mental agony and bodily torment. Besides is it not possible that God in His goodness removes fear from some persons not because He approves of or intends to reward their boldness, but rather because He is aware of their weakness and knows that they would not be equal to facing fear. For some have yielded to fear, even though they won out later when the actual tortures were inflicted.

Now as for the point that those who eagerly suffer death encourage others by their example, I would not deny that for many they provide a very useful pattern. But on the other hand, since almost all of us are fearful in the face of death, who can know how many have also been helped by those whom we see face death with fear and trembling but whom we also observe as they break bravely through the hindrances blocking their path, the obstacles barring their way with barriers harder than steel, that is, their own weariness, fear, and anguish, and by bursting these iron bars and triumphing over death take heaven by storm?[10] Seeing them, will not weaklings who are, like them, cowardly and afraid take heart so as not to yield under the stress

7. Cf. Cicero, *Tusculan Disputations,* 2, 24, 58–59.   8. Luke 6 : 38.
9. Rom. 8 : 18.   10. Cf. Matt. 11 : 12.

of persecution even though they feel great sadness welling up within them, and fear and weariness and horror at the prospect of a ghastly death?

Thus the wisdom of God, which penetrates all things irresistibly and disposes all things sweetly,[1] foreseeing and contemplating in His ever-present sight how the minds of men in different places would be affected, suits His examples to various times and places, choosing now one destiny, now another, according as He sees which will be most profitable. And so God proportions the temperaments of His martyrs according to His own providence in such a way that one rushes forth eagerly to his death, another creeps out hesitantly and fearfully, but for all that bears his death none the less bravely—unless someone perhaps imagines he ought to be thought less brave for having fought down not only his other enemies but also his own weariness, sadness, and fear—most strong feelings and mighty enemies indeed.

But the whole drift of the present discussion finally comes to this: we should admire both kinds of most holy martyrs, we should venerate both kinds, praise God for both, we should imitate both when the situation demands it, each according to his own capacity and according to the grace God gives to each.

But the person who is conscious of his own eagerness needs not so much encouragement to be daring as perhaps a reminder to be afraid lest his presumption, like Peter's,[2] lead to a sudden relapse and fall. But if a person feels anxious, heavy-hearted, fearful, certainly he ought to be comforted and encouraged to take heart. For both sorts of martyrs this anguish of Christ is most salutary: it keeps the one from being over-exultant and it makes the other be of good hope when his spirit is crestfallen and downcast. For if anyone feels his mind swelling with ungovernable enthusiasm, perhaps when he recalls this lowly and anguished bearing of his commander, he will have reason to fear lest our sly enemy is lifting him up on high for a while so

1. Sap. 8 : 1.   2. Matt. 26 : 33–35, 69–75.

that a little later he can dash him to the ground all the harder.[3] But whoever is utterly crushed by feelings of anxiety and fear and is tortured by the fear that he may yield to despair, let him consider this agony of Christ, let him meditate on it constantly and turn it over in his mind, let him drink deep and health-giving draughts of consolation from this spring. For here he will see the loving shepherd lifting the weak lamb on his shoulders,[4] playing the same role as he himself does, expressing his very own feelings, and for this reason: so that anyone who later feels himself disturbed by similar feelings might take courage and not think that he must despair.

Therefore let us give Him as many thanks as we can (for certainly we can never give Him enough); and in our agony remembering His (with which no other can ever be compared), let us beg Him with all our strength that He may deign to comfort us in our anguish by an insight into His; and when we urgently beseech Him, because of our mental distress, to free us from danger, let us nevertheless follow His own most wholesome example by concluding our prayer with His own addition: "Yet not as I will but as you will." If we do these things diligently, I have no doubt at all that, just as an angel brought Him consolation in answer to His prayer, so too each of our angels will bring us from His Spirit consolation that will give us the strength to persevere in those deeds that will lift us up to heaven. And in order to make us completely confident of this fact, Christ went there before us by the same method, by the same path. For after He had suffered this agony for a long time, His spirits were so restored that He arose, returned to His apostles, and freely went out to meet the traitor and the tormentors who were seeking Him to make Him suffer. Then, when He had suffered (as was necessary) He entered into His glory,[5] preparing there a place

3. Cf. Job 30 : 22 and Ps. 101 : 11 (*AV*, 102 : 10). Cf. Claudian, *In Rufinum,* I, 22.
4. Cf. Luke 15 : 5 and John 10 : 14.   5. Luke 24 : 26.

also for those of us who follow in His footsteps.[6] And lest we should be deprived of it by our own dullness, may He Himself because of His own agony deign to help us in ours.

"And when He had arisen from prayer and come to His disciples, He found them sleeping for sadness, and He said to them, 'Why are you sleeping?[7] Sleep on now and take your rest. That is enough. Get up and pray that you may not enter into temptation. Behold, the hour is coming when the Son of Man will be betrayed into the hands of sinners. Get up, let us go. Behold, the one who will betray me is near at hand.' "[8]

See now, when Christ comes back to His apostles for the third time, there they are, buried in sleep, though He commanded them to bear up with Him and to stay awake and pray because of the impending danger; but Judas the traitor at the same time was so wide awake and intent on betraying the Lord that the very idea of sleep never entered his mind.

Does not this contrast between the traitor and the apostles present to us a clear and sharp mirror image (as it were), a sad and terrible view of what has happened through the ages from those times even to our own? Why do not bishops contemplate in this scene their own somnolence? Since they have succeeded in the place of the apostles, would that they would reproduce their virtues just as eagerly as they embrace their authority and as faithfully as they display their sloth and sleepiness! For very many are sleepy and apathetic in sowing virtues among the people and maintaining the truth, while the enemies of Christ in order to sow vices[9] and uproot the faith (that is, insofar as they can, to seize Christ and cruelly crucify Him once again) are wide awake—so much wiser (as Christ says) are the sons of darkness in their generation that the sons of light.[10]

But although this comparison of the sleeping apostles applies very well to those bishops who sleep while virtue and the faith

6. John 14 : 2, 1 Pet. 2 : 21.   7. Luke 22 : 45–46.
8. Matt. 26 : 45–46, Mark 14 : 41–42.
9. Cf. Matt. 13 : 24–29, Luke 8 : 5–15.   10. Luke 16 : 8.

are placed in jeopardy, still it does not apply to all such prelates
at all points. For some of them—alas, far more than I could
wish—do not drift into sleep through sadness and grief as the
apostles did. Rather they are numbed and buried in destructive
desires; that is, drunk with the new wine[11] of the devil, the flesh,
and the world,[1] they sleep like pigs sprawling in the mire. Certainly the apostles' feeling of sadness because of the danger to
their master was praiseworthy, but for them to be so overcome
by sadness as to yield completely to sleep, that was certainly
wrong. Even to grieve because the world is perishing or to weep
because of the crimes of others bespeaks a reverent outlook, as
was felt by the writer who said "I sat by myself and groaned"[2]
and also by the one who said "I was sick at heart because of sinners abandoning your law."[3] Sadness of this sort I would place
in the category of which he says[4]   But I would
place it there only if the feeling, however good, is checked by the
rule and guidance of reason. For if this is not the case, if sorrow
so grips the mind that its strength is sapped and reason gives up
the reins,[5] if a bishop is so overcome by heavy-hearted sleep that
he neglects to do what the duty of his office requires for the salvation of his flock—like a cowardly ship's captain who is so dis-
heartened by the furious din of a storm that he deserts the helm,
hides away cowering in some cranny, and abandons the ship to
the waves—if a bishop does this, I would certainly not hesitate to
juxtapose and compare his sadness with the sadness that leads,
as[6]   says, to hell; indeed, I would consider it far worse, since
such sadness in religious matters seems to spring from a mind
which despairs of God's help.

The next category, but a far worse one, consists of those who

11. Cf. Acts 2 : 13.   1. Cf. 1 John 2 : 15–16.   2. Lam. 3 : 28.
3. Ps. 118 : 53 (AV, 119 : 53).
4. For the blank space after this word More may have intended to
quote 2 Cor. 7 : 10.
5. Plato, Phaedrus, 246, 254.
6. Left blank in the manuscript. More perhaps intended "Paul," refer-
ring to 2 Cor. 7 : 10.

are not depressed by sadness at the danger of others but rather
by a fear of injury to themselves, a fear which is so much the
worse as its cause is the more contemptible, that is, when it is not
a question of life or death but of money.[7]

And yet Christ commands us to contemn the loss of the body
itself for His sake. "Do not be afraid," He says, "of those who destroy the body and after that can do nothing further. But I will
show you the one you should fear, the one to fear: fear him
who, when He has destroyed the body, has the power to send the
soul also to hell. This, I tell you, is the one you must fear."[8]

And though He lays down this rule for everyone without ex-
ception when they have been seized and there is no way out, He
attaches a separate charge over and above this to the high office
of prelates: He does not allow them to be concerned only about
their own souls or merely to take refuge in silence until they are
dragged out and forced to choose between open profession or
lying dissimulation, but He also wished them to come forth if
they see that the flock entrusted to them is in danger and to face
the danger of their own accord for the good of their flock. "The
good shepherd," says Christ, "lays down his life for his sheep."[9]
But if every good shepherd lays down his life for his sheep, certainly one who saves his own life to the detriment of his sheep is
not fulfilling the role of a good shepherd.

Therefore, just as one who loses his life for Christ (and he
does this if he loses it for the flock of Christ entrusted to him)
saves it for life everlasting, so too one who denies Christ (and
this he does if he fails to profess the truth when his silence in-
jures his flock) by saving his life, he actually proceeds to lose it.[1]
Clearly, it is even worse if, driven by fear, he denies Christ
openly in words and forsakes Him publicly. Such prelates do not
sleep like Peter, they make his waking denial. But under the
kindly glance of Christ most of them through His grace will
eventually wipe out that failure and save themselves by weeping,

7. Cf. Terence, *Phormio,* 631.   8. Luke 12 : 4–5, Matt. 10 : 28.
9. John 10 : 11.   1. Matt. 10 : 33, 39; Mark 8 : 35; Luke 9 : 24.

if only they respond to His glance and friendly call to repentance with bitterness of heart[2] and a new way of life, remembering His words and contemplating His passion and leaving behind the shackles of evil which bound them in their sins.

But if anyone is so set in evil that he does not merely neglect to profess the truth out of fear but like Arius and his ilk preaches false doctrine, whether for sordid gain or out of a corrupt ambition, such a person does not sleep like Peter, does not make Peter's denial, but rather stays awake with wicked Judas and like Judas persecutes Christ. This man's condition is far more dangerous than that of the others, as is shown by the sad and horrible end Judas came to.[3] But since there is no limit to the kindness of a merciful God, even this sort of sinner ought not to despair of forgiveness. Even to Judas God gave many opportunities of coming to his senses. He did not deny him His companionship. He did not take away from him the dignity of his apostleship. He did not even take the purse-strings from him, even though he was a thief.[4] He admitted the traitor to the fellowship of His beloved disciples at the last supper. He deigned to stoop down at the feet of the betrayer and to wash with His innocent and most sacred hands Judas' dirty feet, a most fit symbol of his filthy mind.[5] Moreover, with incomparable generosity, He gave him to eat, in the form of bread, that very body of His which the betrayer had already sold; and under the appearance of wine, He gave him that very blood to drink which, even while he was drinking it, the traitor was wickedly scheming to broach and set flowing.[6] Finally when Judas, coming with his crew to seize Him, offered Him a kiss, a kiss that was in fact the terrible token of his treachery, Christ received him calmly and gently.[7] Who would not believe that any one of all these could have turned the traitor's mind, however hardened in crime, to better courses? Then too, even that beginning of repentance, when he admitted he had sinned, and gave back the

2. Cf. Luke 22 : 61–62.   3. Matt. 27 : 5, Acts 1 : 18.
4. John 12 : 6, 13 : 29.   5. John 13 : 4–11.   6. Luke 22 : 21.
7. Matt. 26 : 48–50, Luke 22 : 47–48.

pieces of silver, and threw them away when they were not accepted, crying out that he was a traitor and confessing that he had betrayed innocent blood[8]—I am inclined to believe that Christ prompted him thus far so that He might if possible (that is, if the traitor did not add despair to his treachery) save from ruin the very man who had so recently, so perfidiously betrayed Him to death.

Therefore, since God showed His great mercy in so many ways even toward Judas, an apostle turned traitor, since He invited him to forgiveness so often and did not allow him to perish except through despair alone, certainly there is no reason why, in this life, anyone should despair of any imitator of Judas. Rather, according to that holy advice of the apostle "Pray for each other that you may be saved,"[9] if we see anyone wandering wildly from the right road, let us hope that he will one day return to the path, and meanwhile let us pray humbly and incessantly that God will hold out to him chances to come to his senses, and likewise that with God's help he will eagerly seize them, and having seized them will hold fast and not throw them away out of malice or let them slip away from him through wretched sloth.

And so when Christ had found His apostles sleeping for the third time, He said to them "Why are you sleeping?"[10] as if to say: "Now is not the time to sleep. Now is the crucial time for you to stay awake and pray, as I myself have already warned you twice before, only a little while ago." And as for them, since they did not know what to reply to Him[11] when He found them sleeping for the second time, what suitable excuse could they possibly have devised now that they had been so quickly caught in the same fault for the third time? Could they use as an excuse what the evangelist mentions—that is, could they say they were sleeping because of their sadness? Certainly the fact is mentioned by Luke,[1] but it is also quite clear that he does not praise

8. Matt. 27 : 3–5.   9. James 5 : 16.   10. Luke 22 : 46.
11. Mark 14 : 40.   1. Luke 22 : 45.

it. It is true, he does suggest that their sadness itself was praiseworthy, as it certainly was. Still, the sleep that followed from it was
not free of moral blame. For the sort of sadness that is poten-
tially worthy of great reward sometimes tends toward great evil.
Certainly it does if we are so taken up by it that we render it
useless—that is, if we do not have recourse to God with our petitions and prayers and seek comfort from Him, but instead, in a
certain downcast and desperate frame of mind, try to escape our
awareness of sadness by looking for consolation in sleep. Nor
will we find what we are looking for: losing in sleep the consolation we might have obtained from God by staying awake and
praying, we feel the weary weight of a troubled mind even during sleep itself and also we stumble with our eyes closed into
temptations and the traps set by the devil.

And so Christ, as if He intended to preclude any excuse for
this sleepiness, said: " 'Why are you sleeping?[2] Sleep on now and
take your rest. That is enough. Get up and pray that you may
not enter into temptation. Behold, the hour has almost come
when the Son of Man will be betrayed into the hands of sinners.
Get up, let us go. Behold, the one who will betray me is near at
hand.' And while Jesus was still speaking, behold Judas Iscariot,
etc."[3]

Immediately after He had aroused the sleeping apostles for
the third time, He undercut them with irony, not indeed that
trivial and sportive variety with which idle men of wit are accustomed to amuse themselves, but rather a serious and weighty
kind of irony. " 'Sleep on now,' He said, 'and take your rest.
That is enough. Get up and pray that you may not enter into
temptation. Behold, the hour has almost come when the Son of
Man will be betrayed into the hands of sinners. Get up, let us go.
Behold, the one who will betray me is near at hand.' And while
He was still speaking, Judas, etc."

Notice how He grants permission to sleep in such a way as
clearly shows He means to take it away. For He had hardly said

2. Luke 22 : 46.   3. Matt. 26 : 45–47, Mark 14 : 41–43.

"Sleep" before He added "That is enough," as if to say: "Now there is no need for you to sleep any longer. It is enough that throughout the whole time you ought to have been staying awake, you have been sleeping—and that even against my direct orders. Now there is no time left to sleep, not even to sit down. You must get up immediately and pray that you may not enter into temptation, the temptation, perhaps, of deserting me and giving great scandal by doing so. Otherwise, so far as sleep is concerned, sleep on now and take your rest—you have my permission—that is, if you can. But you will certainly not be able to. For there are people coming—they are almost here—who will shake the yawning sleepiness out of you. For behold the hour has almost come when the son of man will be betrayed into the hands of sinners and behold the one who will betray me is near at hand." And He had hardly finished these few admonitions and was still speaking when, behold, Judas Iscariot, etc.

I am not unaware that some learned and holy men do not allow this interpretation, though they admit that others, equally learned and holy, have found it agreeable. Not that those who do not accept this interpretation are shocked by this sort of irony, as some others are—also pious men to be sure, but not sufficiently versed in the figures of speech which sacred scripture customarily takes over from common speech. For if they were, they would have found irony in so many other places that they could not have found it offensive here.

What could be more pungent or witty than the irony with which the blessed apostle gracefully polishes off the Corinthians?—I mean where he asks pardon because he never burdened any of them with charges and expenses: "For how have I done any less for you than for the other churches, except this, that I have never been a burden to you? Pardon me for this injustice."[4] What could be more forceful or biting than the irony with which God's prophet ridiculed the prophets of Baal as they called upon the deaf statue of their god: "Call louder," he said,

4. 2 Cor. 12 : 13.

"for your god is asleep or perhaps has gone somewhere on a trip."[5] I have taken this occasion to bring up these instances in passing, because some readers, out of a certain pious simplicity, refuse to accept in sacred scripture (or at least do not notice there) these universally used forms of speech, and by neglecting the figures of speech they very often also miss the real sense of scripture.

Now concerning this passage St. Augustine says that he finds the interpretation I have given to be not unacceptable but also not necessary. He claims that the plain meaning without any figure is adequate. He presents such an interpretation of this passage in the work he wrote entitled *The Harmony of the Gospels*. "It seems," he says, "that the language of Matthew here is self-contradictory. For how could He say 'Sleep on now and take your rest' and then immediately add 'Get up, let us go'? Disturbed by this seeming inconsistency some try to set the tone of the words 'Sleep on now and take your rest' as reproachful rather than permissive. And this would be the right thing to do if it were necessary. But Mark reports it in such a way that when Christ had said 'Sleep on now and take your rest,' He added 'That is enough' and then went on to say 'The hour has come when the Son of Man will be betrayed.' Therefore it is surely at least implied that after He had said 'Sleep and take your rest' the Lord was silent for a while so that they could do what He had allowed them to do, and that He then went on to say 'Behold, the hour has almost come.' That is the reason why Mark includes 'That is enough,' that is, 'You have rested long enough.' "[6]

Subtle indeed this reasoning of the most blessed Augustine, as he always is; but I imagine that those of the opposite persuasion do not find it at all likely that, after Christ had already reproached them twice for sleeping when His capture was imminent, and after He had just rebuked them sternly by saying "Why are you sleeping?" He should then have granted them

5. 3 Kings 18 : 27.
6. More quotes Augustine's *De consensu evangelistarum* (*Corpus Scriptorum Ecclesiasticorum Latinorum 43*, 282–83) from the *Catena aurea* of Aquinas.

time to sleep, especially at the very time when the danger which was the reason they ought not to have slept before, was now pounding on the door, as they say. But now that I have presented both interpretations, everyone is free to choose whichever he likes. My purpose has been merely to recount both of them; it is not for such a nobody as me to render a decision like an official arbitrator.

"Get up and pray that you may not enter into temptation."[7]

Before, He ordered them to watch and pray.[8] Now that they have twice learned by experience that the drowsy position of sitting lets sleep gradually slip up on them, He teaches an instant remedy for that sluggish disease of somnolence, namely to get up. Since this sort of remedy was handed down by our Savior Himself, I heartily wish that we would occasionally be willing to try it out at the dead of night. For here we would discover not only that well begun is half done (as Horace says),[9] but that once begun is all done.

For when we are fighting against sleep, the first encounter is always the sharpest. Therefore, we should not try to conquer sleep by a prolonged struggle, but rather we should break with one thrust the grip of the alluring arms with which it embraces us and pulls us down, and we should dash away from it all of a sudden. Then, once we have cast off idle sleep, the very image of death,[10] life with its eagerness will resume its sway. Then, if we devote ourselves to meditation and prayer, the mind, collected and composed in that dark silence of the night,[11] will find that it is much more receptive to divine consolation than it is during the daytime, when the noisy bustle of business on all sides distracts the eyes, the ears, and the mind, and dissipates our energy in manifold activities, no less pointless than they are divers. But Lord spare us, though thoughts about some trifling matter, some worldly matter at that, may sometimes interrupt

7. Luke 22 : 46.   8. Matt. 26 : 41, Mark 14 : 38.
9. Horace, *Epistulae*, 1, 2, 40.   10. Cf. Ovid, *Amores*, 2, 9, 41.
11. Cf. Virgil, *Aeneid*, 4, 123.

our sleep and keep us awake for a long time and hardly let us go back to sleep at all, prayer does not keep us awake: in spite of the immense loss of spiritual benefits, in spite of the many traps set for us by our deadly enemy, in spite of the danger of being utterly undone, we do not wake up to pray, but lie in a drugged sleep watching the dream-visions induced by mandragora.

But we must continually keep in mind that Christ did not command them simply to get up, but to get up in order to pray. For it is not enough to get up if we do not get up for a good purpose. If we do not, there would be far less sin in losing time through slothful drowsiness than in devoting waking time to the deliberate pursuit of malicious crimes.

Then, too, He does not merely order them to pray but shows them the need for it and teaches what they should have prayed for: "Pray," He says, "that you may not enter into temptation." Again and again He drove home this point to them,[12] that prayer is the only safeguard against temptation and that if someone refuses it entrance into the castle of his soul and shuts it out by yielding to sleep, through such negligence he permits the besieging troops of the devil (that is, temptations to evil) to break in.

Three times He admonished them verbally to pray. Then, to avoid the appearance of teaching merely by these words and in order to teach them by His example as well, He Himself prayed three times, suggesting in this way that we ought to pray to the Trinity, namely to the unbegotten Father, to the coequal Son begotten by Him, and to the Spirit equal to each and proceeding from each of them. From these three we should likewise pray for three things: forgiveness for the past, grace to manage the present, and a prudent concern for the future. But we should pray for these things not lazily and carelessly but incessantly and fervently. Just how far from this kind of prayer nearly all of us are nowadays, everyone can judge privately from his own con-

12. Matt. 6 : 13. Christ's command appears once in Matt. (26 : 41), once in Mark (14 : 38), and twice in Luke (22 : 40, 46).

science and we may all publicly learn (God forbid) by the de-
creasing fruits of prayer, falling off gradually from day to day.

Nevertheless, since a little earlier I bore down on this point as
vigorously as I could by attacking that sort of prayer in which
the mind is not attentive but wandering and distracted among
many ideas, it would be well at this point to propose an emollient
from Gerson[13] to alleviate this sore point, lest I seem to be like a
harsh surgeon touching this common sore too roughly, bringing
to many tender-souled mortals not a healing medicine but rather
pain, and taking away from them hope of attaining salvation. In
order to cure these troublesome inflammations of the soul, Gerson uses certain palliatives which are analogous to those medica-
tions which doctors use to relieve bodily pain and which they call
"anodynes."

And so this John Gerson, an outstanding scholar and a most
gentle handler of troubled consciences, saw (I imagine) some
people whom this distraction of mind made so terribly anxious
that they repeated the individual words of their prayers one
after the other with a belabored sort of babbling, and still got
nowhere and sometimes were even less pleased with their prayer
the third time than the first time. He saw that such people,
through sheer weariness, lost all sense of consolation from their
prayers and that some of them were ready to give up the habit
of prayer as useless (if they were to pray in this way) or even
harmful (as they feared). This kind man, then, in order to relieve them of their troublesome difficulty, pointed out three
aspects of prayer: the act, the virtue, and the habit.

But to make his meaning clearer, he explains it by the example of a person setting out from France on a pilgrimage to St.
James [of Compostella].[1] For such a person sometimes goes forward on his journey and at the same time meditates on the holy
saint and the purpose of the pilgrimage. And so this man

13. In what follows More paraphrases John Gerson's seventh "consideration" in *De oratione et ejus valore*.
1. Compostella is a city in northwest Spain traditionally supposed to be
the place of burial of St. James the Greater.

throughout this whole time continues his pilgrimage by a double act, namely (and I shall use Gerson's own words) by a "natural continuity" and a "moral continuity": natural, because he actually and in fact proceeds toward that place; moral, because his thoughts are occupied with the matter of his pilgrimage. By "moral" he refers to that moral intention by which the act of setting out, otherwise indifferent, is perfected by the pious reason for setting out.

Sometimes, however, the pilgrim goes his way considering other matters, without thinking anything about the saint or the place, thinking perhaps about something even holier, such as God Himself. In such a case he continues the act of his pilgrimage on a natural, but not a moral level. For though he actually moves his feet along, he does not actually think about the reason for setting out nor perhaps even about the way he is going. But though the moral act of his pilgrimage does not continue, its moral virtue does. For that whole natural act of walking is informed and imbued with a moral virtue because it is silently accompanied by the pious intention formed at the beginning, since all this motion follows from that first decision just as a stone continues in its course because of the original impetus, even though the hand which threw it has been withdrawn.

Sometimes, however, the moral act takes place when there is no natural act, as, for example, whenever the person thinks about his pilgrimage when he is perhaps sitting and not walking. Finally, it often happens that both kinds of act are missing, as, for example, when we are sleeping, for then the pilgrim neither performs the natural act of walking nor the moral act of thinking about the pilgrimage; but still in the meantime the moral virtue, so long as it is not deliberately renounced, remains and persists habitually.

And so this pilgrimage is never truly interrupted in such a way that its merit does not continue and persist at least habitually, unless an opposite decision is made, either to give up the pilgrimage completely or at least to put it off until another time. And so by means of this comparison he draws the same conclu-

sions about prayer, namely that once it has been begun attentively it can never afterwards be so interrupted that the virtue of
the first intention does not remain and persist continuously—that is, either actually or habitually—so long as it is not
relinquished by making a decision to stop nor cut off by turning
away to mortal sin.

Hence he says that those words of Christ "You should pray
always and not cease"[2] were not spoken figuratively but in a
simple and straightforward sense, and that in fact they are actually and literally fulfilled by good men. He supports his opinion
with that well-known adage of learned men "Whoever lives well
is always praying"—which is true, because whoever does everything according to the apostle's precept for the glory of God,[3]
once he has begun praying attentively, never afterwards inter-
rupts his prayer in such a way that its meritorious virtue does
not persist, if not actually then at least habitually.

This is the explanation given by that most learned and virtuous man John Gerson in his short treatise entitled *Prayer and its
Value*. But nevertheless he intends it as a consolation for those
who are troubled and saddened because their attention slips
away from them unawares during prayer, even though they are
earnestly trying to pay attention; he does not intend that it
should provide a flattering illusion of safety for those who out of
careless laziness make no effort to think about their prayers. For
when we perform such a grave duty negligently, we say prayers
indeed, but we do not pray, and we do not (as I said before)
render God favorable to us but drive Him far from us in His
wrath.

And why should anyone be surprised if God is angry when He
sees Himself addressed so contemptuously by a lowly human
creature? And how can we imagine that a person does not approach and address God contemptuously when he says to God
"O God, hear my prayer"[4] while his own mind all the time is

2. Luke 18 : 1.   3. 1 Cor. 10 : 31.
4. Ps. 54 : 2 (*AV*, 55 : 1) and 63 : 2 (*AV*, 64 : 1).

turned away to other matters—vain and foolish and, would that they were not, sometimes also wicked matters—so that he does not even hear his own voice but murmurs his way by rote through well-worn prayers, his mind a complete blank, emitting (as Virgil says) sounds without sense.[5] Thus when we have finished our prayers and gone our way, very often we are immediately in need of other prayers to beg forgiveness for our former carelessness.

And so when Christ had said to His apostles "Get up and pray that you may not enter into temptation," He immediately warned them how great the impending danger was, in order to show that no drowsy or lukewarm prayer would suffice: "Behold," He said, "the hour has almost come when the Son of Man will be betrayed into the hands of sinners,"[6] as if to include the following implications: "I predicted to you that I must be betrayed by one of you—you were shocked at the very words.[7] I foretold to you that Satan would seek you out to sift you like wheat—you heard this carelessly and made no response, as if his temptation were not much to be reckoned with.[8] So that you might know that temptation is not at all to be contemned, I predicted that you would all be scandalized because of me—you all denied it. To him who denied it most of all, I predicted that he would deny me three times before the cock crowed—he absolutely insisted it would not be so and that he would rather die with me than deny me, and so you all said.[9] Lest you should consider temptation a thing to be taken lightly, I again and again commanded you to watch and pray lest you enter into temptation—but you were always so far from recognizing the strength of temptation that you took no pains to pray against it or even to stay awake.

"Perhaps you were encouraged to scorn the power of the devil's temptation by the fact that before, when I sent you out two by two to preach the faith, you came back and reported to

5. Virgil, *Aeneid,* 10, 640.   6. Matt. 26 : 45, Mark 14 : 41.
7. Matt. 26 : 21–22.   8. Luke 22 : 31–34.
9. Matt. 26 : 31–35.

me that even the demons were subject to you. But I, to whom
the nature of demons, as well as your own nature, is more
deeply known than either is to you, since indeed I established
each of them, I immediately cautioned you not to glory in such
vanity, because it was not your power that subjected the demons
but rather I myself did it, and I did it not for your sakes but for
the sake of others who were to be converted to the faith; and I
admonished you rather to glory in a real source of joy, namely
that your names are written in the book of life.[10] This really and
truly belongs to you because once you have attained that joy you
can never lose it, though all the ranks of the demons should
struggle against you. But still the power you exerted against
them at that time gave you such high confidence that you seem
to scorn their temptations as matters of little moment.

"And so, though I foretold that there was danger impending
on this very night, up to now you have still viewed these temptations as it were from a distance. But now I warn you that not
only the very night but even the very hour is at hand. For behold, the hour has almost come when the Son of Man will be betrayed into the hands of sinners. Now, therefore, there is no
more chance to sit and sleep. Now you will be forced to stay
awake, and there is hardly a moment left to pray. Now, therefore, I no longer foretell future events, but I say to you right
now, at this present moment: Get up, let us go—behold, the one
who will betray me is at hand. If you are not willing to stay
awake so that you might be able to pray, at least get up and go
away quickly lest you be unable to escape. For, behold, the one
who will betray me is at hand"—unless perhaps He did not say
"Get up, let us go" as intending that they should run away in
fear, but rather that they should go forward with confidence.
For He himself did so: He did not turn back in another direction but even as He spoke He freely went on to encounter those
butchers who were making their way toward Him with murder
in their hearts: "While Jesus was still saying these things, behold,

10. Luke 10 : 17–20.

Judas Iscariot, one of the twelve, and with him a large crowd with swords and clubs, sent by the chief priests and the scribes and the elders of the people."[11]

Although nothing can contribute more effectively to salvation, and to the implanting of every sort of virtue in the Christian breast, than pious and fervent meditation on the successive events of Christ's passion, still it would certainly be not unprofitable to take the story of that time when the apostles were sleeping as the Son of Man was being betrayed, and to apply it as a mysterious image of future times. For Christ, to redeem man truly became a son of man—that is, although He was conceived without male seed, He was nevertheless really descended from the first men and therefore truly became a son of Adam, so that by His passion He might restore Adam's posterity, lost and cast off into wretchedness through the fault of our first parents, to a state of happiness even greater than their original one.[1]

This is the reason that, in spite of His divinity, He constantly called Himself the Son of Man (since He was also really a man), thus constantly suggesting, by mentioning that nature which alone was capable of death, the benefit we derive from His death. For, though God died, since He who was God died, nevertheless His divinity did not undergo death, but only His humanity, or actually only His body, if we consider the fact of nature more than the custom of language. For a man is said to die when the soul leaves the dead body, but the soul which departs is itself immortal. But since He did not merely delight in the phrase describing our nature but was also pleased to take upon Himself our nature for our salvation, and then finally to unite with Himself, in the structure of one body[2] (as it were), all of us whom He regenerated by His saving sacraments and by faith, granting us a share even of His names (since scripture calls all the faithful both gods[3] and Christs[4]), I think we would not be

11. Matt. 26 : 47, Mark 14 : 43.   1. Cf. Rom. 5 : 12–21.
2. Cf. Jer. 13 : 11.
3. E.g., John 10 : 34–35 (quoting Ps. 81 : 6, *AV*, 82 : 6), Exod. 22 : 8–9.
4. E.g., Mark 9 : 40, 1 Par. 16 : 22, Ps. 104 : 15 (*AV*, 105 : 15).

far wrong if we were to fear that the time approaches when the Son of Man, Christ, will be betrayed into the hands of sinners, as often as we see an imminent danger that the mystical body of Christ,[5] the church of Christ, namely the Christian people, will be brought to ruin at the hands of wicked men. And this, alas, for some centuries now we have not failed to see happening somewhere, now in one place, now in another, while the cruel Turks invade some parts of the Christian dominion and other parts are torn asunder by the internal strife of manifold heretical sects.

Whenever we see such things or hear that they are beginning to happen, however far away, let us think that this is no time for us to sit and sleep but rather to get up immediately and bring relief to the danger of others in whatever way we can, by our prayers at least if in no other way. Nor is such danger to be taken lightly because it happens at some distance from us. Certainly if that saying of the comic poet is so highly approved, "Since I am a man, I consider nothing human to be foreign to me,"[6] how could it be anything but disgraceful for Christians to snore while other Christians are in danger? In order to suggest this, Christ directed His warning to watch and pray not only to those He had placed nearby but also to those He had caused to remain at some distance. Then, too, if we are perhaps unmoved by the misfortunes of others because they are at some distance from us, let us at least be moved by our own danger. For we have reason to fear that the destructive force will make its way from them to us, taught as we are by many examples how rapid the rushing force of a blaze can be and how terrible the contagion of a spreading plague. Since, therefore, all human safeguards are useless without the help of God to ward off evils, let us always remember these words from the gospel and let us always imagine that Christ Himself is again addressing to us over and over those words of His: "Why are you sleeping? Get up and pray that you may not enter into temptation."

5. Cf. 1 Cor. 12 : 27. 6. Terence, *Heautontimorumenos*, 77.

At this juncture another point occurs to us: that Christ is also betrayed into the hands of sinners when His most holy body in the sacrament is consecrated and handled by unchaste, profligate, and sacrilegious priests. When we see such things happen (and they happen only too often, alas), let us imagine that Christ Himself again says to us "Why are you sleeping? Stay awake, get up, and pray that you may not enter into temptation, for the Son of Man is betrayed into the hands of sinners." From the example of bad priests the contamination of vice spreads easily among the people. And the less suitable for obtaining grace those persons are whose duty it is to watch and pray for the people, the more necessary it is for the people to stay awake, get up, and pray all the more earnestly for themselves—and not only for themselves but also for priests of this sort. For it will be much to the advantage of the people if bad priests improve.

Finally, Christ is betrayed into the hands of sinners in a special way among those of a certain sect: these people, though they receive the venerable sacrament of the eucharist more frequently and wish to give the impression of honoring it more piously by receiving it under both species (contrary to public custom, without any necessity, but not without a great affront to the Catholic Church), nevertheless these people blaspheme against what they have received under a show of honor, some of them by calling it true bread and true wine, some of them—and this is far worse—by calling it not only true but also mere bread and wine. For they altogether deny that the real body of Christ is contained in the sacrament, though they call it by that name [corpus Christi]. When at this late date they set out to do such a thing, against the most open passages of scripture, against the clearest interpretations of all the saints, against the most constant faith of the whole church for so many centuries, against the truth most amply witnessed to by so many thousands of miracles—this group that labors under the second kind of infidelity (by far the worse), how little difference is there, I ask you, between them and those who took Christ captive that night? How little difference between them and those troops of Pilate who in jest bent their knees before Christ as if they were honoring Him while they insulted Him and called Him the king of the Jews, just as these people kneel before the eucharist and call it the body of Christ—which according to their own profession they no more believe than the soldiers of Pilate believed Christ was a king.

Therefore, whenever we hear that such evils have befallen other peoples, no matter how distant, let us immediately imagine that Christ is urgently addressing us: "Why are you sleeping? Get up and pray that you may not enter into temptation." For the fact is that wherever this plague rages today most fiercely, everyone did not catch the disease in a single day. Rather the contagion spreads gradually and imperceptibly while those persons who despise it at first, afterwards can stand to hear it and respond to it with less than full scorn, then come to tolerate wicked discussions, and afterwards are carried away into error, until like a cancer (as the apostle says) the creeping disease finally takes over the whole country.[7] Therefore let us stay awake, get up, and pray continually that all those who have fallen into this miserable folly through the wiles of Satan may quickly come to their senses and that God may never suffer us to enter into this kind of temptation and may never allow the devil to roll the blasts of this storm of his to our shores. But so much for my digression into these mysteries; let us now return to the historical events.

"Judas, therefore, when he had received a cohort from the chief priests and servants from the pharisees, came there with lanterns and torches.[8] And while Jesus was still speaking, behold, Judas Iscariot, one of the twelve, and with him a large crowd with swords and clubs, sent by the chief priests and scribes and elders of the people. The traitor, however, had given them a sign, etc."[9]

I tend to believe that the cohort which, according to the ac-

---

7. 2 Tim. 2 : 17.   8. John 18 : 3.
9. Matt. 26 : 47–48, Mark 14 : 43–44.

counts of the evangelists, was handed over to the traitor by the high priests was a Roman cohort assigned to the high priests by Pilate. To it the pharisees, scribes, and elders of the people had added their own servants, either because they did not have enough confidence in the governor's soldiers or because they thought extra numbers would help prevent Christ from being rescued through some sudden confusion caused by the darkness, or perhaps for another reason, their desire to arrest at the same time all the apostles, without letting any of them escape in the dark. They were prevented from executing this part of their plan by the power of Christ Himself, who was Himself captured only because He, and He alone, wished to be taken.

They carry smoking torches and dim lanterns so that they might be able to discern through the darkness of sin the bright sun of justice,[10] not that they might be enlightened by the light of Him who enlightens every man that comes into this world,[11] but that they might put out that eternal light of His which can never be darkened. And like master like servant, for those who sent them strove to overthrow the law of God for the sake of their traditions. Even now some still follow in their footsteps and persecute Christ by striving mightily to overshadow the splendor of God's glory for the sake of their own glory. But in this passage it is worthwhile to pay close attention to the constant revolutions and vicissitudes of the human condition. For not six days before, even the gentiles had been eager to get a look at Christ, because of His remarkable miracles, together with the great holiness of His life.[1] But the Jews had welcomed Him with truly extraordinary reverence as He rode into Jerusalem. But now the Jews, joining forces with the gentiles, come to arrest Him like a thief; and not merely among them but at their head was a man worse than all the gentiles and Jews put together, Judas. Thus in His death Christ took care to provide this contrast as a notable warning to all men that no one should expect blind Fortune to stand still for him, and that no Christian especially, as one who

10. Mal. 4 : 2.   11. John 1 : 9.   1. John 12 : 20–22.

hopes for heaven, should pursue the contemptible glory of this world.

The persons responsible for sending the crowd after Christ were priests—and not merely that, but princes of the priests—pharisees, scribes and elders of the people. Here we see that whatever is best by nature turns out in the end to be the worst, once it begins to reverse its direction. Thus Lucifer, created by God as the most eminent among the angels in heaven, became the worst of the demons after he yielded to the pride which brought his downfall. So too, not the dregs of the crowd but the elders of the people, the scribes, pharisees, priests, and high priests, the princes of the priests, whose duty it was to see that justice was done and to promote the affairs of God, these were the very ringleaders in a conspiracy to extinguish the sun of justice[2] and to destroy the only begotten son of God—to such insane extremes of perversity were they driven by avarice, arrogance, and envy.

Another point should not be passed over lightly but should be given careful consideration: Judas, who in many other places is called by the infamous name "traitor," is here also disgraced by the lofty title "apostle." "Behold," he says, "Judas Iscariot, one of the twelve," Judas Iscariot—who was not one of the unbelieving pagans, not one of the Jewish enemies, not one of Christ's ordinary disciples (and even that would have been incredible enough), but (O the shame of it!) one of Christ's chosen apostles—can bear to hand over his Lord to be captured, and even to be the leader of the captors himself.

There is in this passage a lesson to be learned by all who exercise high public office: when they are addressed with solemn titles, they do not always have reason to be proud and congratulate themselves; rather, such titles are truly fitting only if those who bear them know in their hearts that they have in fact lived up to such honorific names by conscientiously performing their duties. For otherwise, they may very well be overcome with

2. Mal. 4 : 2.

shame (unless they find pleasure in the empty jingle of words), since wicked men in high office—whether they be great men, princes, great lords, emperors, priests, bishops, it makes no difference as long as they are wicked—certainly ought to realize that whenever men titillate their ears by crooning their splendid titles of office, they do not do so sincerely, in order to pay them true honor, but rather to reproach them freely by seeming to praise those honors which they bear in so unpraiseworthy a fashion. So too, in the gospel, when Judas is celebrated under his title of apostle in the phrase "Judas Iscariot, one of the twelve," the real intent is anything but praise, as is clear from the fact that in the next breath he is called a traitor. "For the traitor," according to the account, "had given them a signal, saying, 'Whomever I kiss, that is the one. Seize him.' "[3]

At this point the usual question is why it was necessary for the traitor to give the crowd a signal identifying Jesus. To this some answer that they agreed on a signal because more than once before Christ had suddenly escaped from the hands of those who were trying to apprehend Him. But since this usually happened in the daytime, when He was escaping from the hands of those who already recognized Him, and since He did it by employing His divine power, either to disappear from their sight or to pass from their midst while they were in a state of shock, against this sort of escape giving a signal to identify Him could not be of any use.

And so others say that one of the two James's looked very much like Christ—and for that reason, they think, he was called the brother of Christ[4]—so much so that unless you looked at them closely you could not tell them apart. But since they could have arrested both of them and taken both away with them to be identified later at their leisure by comparing them at close quarters, what need was there to worry about a signal?

The gospel makes it clear that the night was far advanced, and, although daybreak was drawing near, it was still nighttime

3. Matt. 26 : 48, Mark 14 : 44.   4. Gal. 1 : 19.

and quite dark, as is evident from the torches and lanterns they carried, which gave enough light to make them visible from some distance but hardly enough for them to discern anyone else from afar. And, although on that night they perhaps had the advantage of some faint light from the full moon, it could only have been enough to make out the shapes of bodies in the distance, not to get a good view of facial features and distinguish one person from another. Hence, if they went rushing in at random in the hope of capturing all of them at once, each man choosing his victim without knowing who he was, they were afraid, and rightly so, that out of so many some (by all odds) might perhaps get away and that one of the fugitives might well be the very man they had come for. For those who are in the greatest danger are likely to be the quickest to look out for themselves.

Thus, whether they thought of this or whether Judas himself suggested it, they set their trap by having the betrayer go on ahead to single out the Lord by embracing and kissing Him. In this way, when they had all fixed their eyes on Him alone, each and every one of them could try to get his hands on Him. After that, if any of the others got away, it would not be such a dangerous matter. "Therefore the traitor had given them a signal, saying, 'Whomever I kiss, that is the one. Seize him and take him away carefully.' "[5]

O the lengths to which greed will go! Couldn't you be satisfied, you treacherous scoundrel, with betraying your Lord (who had raised you to the lofty office of an apostle) into the hands of impious men by the signal of a kiss, without also being so concerned that He should be taken away carefully, lest He might escape from His captors? You were hired to betray Him; others were sent to take Him, to guard Him, to produce Him in court. But you, as if your role in the crime were not important enough, go on to meddle in the duties of the soldiers; and as if the villainous magistrates who sent them had not given them ade-

5. Mark 14 : 44.

quate instructions, there was a need for a circumspect man like you to add your own gratuitous cautions and commands, that they must lead Him away carefully once He is captured. Were you afraid that, even though you had fully performed your criminal task by betraying Christ to His assassins, still if the soldiers had somehow been so remiss that Christ escaped through their carelessness or was rescued by force against their will— were you afraid that then your thirty pieces of silver, that illustrious reward of your heinous crime, would not be paid? Have no fear, they will be paid. But believe me, you are no more eager and greedy to get them now than you will be impatient and anxious to throw them away once you have gotten them. Meanwhile you will go on to complete a deed that brings pain to your Lord and death to you, but salvation to many.

"He went ahead of them and came up to Jesus to kiss Him. And when he had come, he went right up to Him and said 'Rabbi, hail Rabbi' and he kissed Him. Jesus said to him, 'Friend, why have you come?[6] Judas, are you betraying the Son of Man with a kiss?' "[7]

Though Judas really did, as a matter of historical fact, precede the crowd, still this also means in a spiritual sense that among those who share in the same sinful act, the one who has most reason to abstain takes precedence in God's judgment of their guilt.

"And he came up to Him to kiss Him. And when he had come, he went right up to Him and said 'Rabbi, hail Rabbi.' And he kissed Him." In this same way Christ is approached, greeted, called "Rabbi," kissed, by those who pretend to be disciples of Christ, professing His teaching in name but striving in fact to undermine it by crafty tricks and stratagems. In just this way Christ is greeted as "Rabbi" by anyone who calls Him master and scorns His precepts. In just this way is He kissed by those priests who consecrate the most holy body of Christ and then put to

6. Matt. 26 : 49–50; cf. Mark 14 : 45.   7. Luke 22 : 48.

death Christ's members, Christian souls, by their false teaching
and wicked example. In just this way is Christ greeted and kissed
by those who demand to be considered good and pious because
at the persuasion of bad priests, they, though laymen, receive
the sacred body and blood of Christ under both species, without
any real need for it, but not without great contempt for the
whole Catholic Church and therefore not without grave sin. And
this these latter-day saints do against the long-standing practice
and custom of all Christians. And not only do they themselves
do it (that we could somehow manage to put up with) but they
condemn everyone who receives both substances under only one
of the two species—that is, apart from themselves, all Christians
everywhere for these many years. And still, though they hotly
insist that both species are necessary for the laity, most of
them—both laymen and priests—eliminate the reality, that is the
body and blood, from both species, keeping only the words
"body" and "blood." In this respect, indeed, they are not unlike
Pilate's guards, who mocked Christ by kneeling before Him and
saluting Him as the king of the Jews. For these men likewise
genuflect in veneration of the eucharist and call it the body and
blood of Christ though they no more believe it is the one or the
other than the soldiers of Pilate believed Christ was a king.

Now all these groups which I have enumerated certainly bring
to our minds the traitor Judas in that they combine a greeting
and a kiss with treachery. But just as they renew an action of the
past, so Joab (2 Kings 20) once provided a prophetic figure of
the future: for "when he had greeted Amasa thus, 'Greetings,
my brother,' and had caressed Amasa's chin with his right hand"
as if he were about to kiss him, he steathily unsheathed a hidden
sword and killed him with one stroke through his side,[8] and by a
similar trick he had formerly killed Abner,[9] but later (as was
only right) he justly paid with his life for his heinous deception.[10] Judas rightly calls to mind and represents Joab, whether

8. 2 Kings 20 : 8–10.   9. 2 Kings 3 : 26–30.
10. 3 Kings 2 : 28–35.

you consider the status of the persons involved or the deceitful treachery of the crime, or the vengeance of God and the bad end both came to—with this difference, that Judas surpassed Joab in every respect.

Joab enjoyed great favor and influence with his prince; Judas had even more with an even greater prince. Joab killed Amasa who was his friend; Judas killed Jesus who was an even closer friend, not to say also his Lord. Joab was motivated by envy and ambition because he had heard that the king would promote Amasa above him;[11] but Judas, enticed by greed for a miserable reward, for a few pieces of silver, betrayed the Lord of the world to His death. In the same degree, therefore, as Judas' crime was worse, the vengeance exacted from him was the more devastating. For Joab was killed by another, but the most wretched Judas hanged himself with his own hand.

But in the treacherous pattern of their deception, there is a nice equivalence between the crimes of Joab and Judas. For just as Joab kills Amasa in the very act of courteously greeting him and preparing to kiss him, so too Judas approaches Christ affably, greets Him reverently, kisses Him lovingly and all the time the villainous wretch has nothing else in mind than to betray his Lord to His death. But Joab was able to deceive Amasa by flattery; not so Judas with Christ. He receives his advances, listens to his greeting, does not refuse his kiss, and, though aware of his abominable treachery, He nevertheless acted for a while as if He were completely ignorant of everything. Why did He do this? Was it to teach us to feign and dissemble, and with polite cunning to turn the deception back upon the deceiver? Hardly, but rather to teach us to bear patiently and gently all injuries and snares treacherously set for us, not to smolder with anger, not to seek revenge, not to give vent to our feelings by hurling back insults, not to find an empty pleasure in tripping up an enemy through some clever trick, but rather to set ourselves against deceitful injury with genuine courage, to conquer evil with

11. 2 Kings 19 : 13.

good[12]—in fine, to make every effort by words both gentle and harsh, to insist both in season and out of season,[13] that the wicked may change their ways to good, so that if anyone should be suffering from a disease that does not respond to treatment, he may not blame the failure on our negligence but rather attribute it to the virulence of his own disease.

And so Christ as a most conscientious physician tries both ways of effecting a cure. Employing first of all gentle words, He says "Friend, why have you come?" When he heard himself called "friend," the traitor was left hanging in doubt. For, since he was aware of his own crime, he was afraid that Christ used the title "friend" as a severe rebuke for his hostile unfriendliness. On the other hand, since criminals always flatter themselves with the hope that their crimes are unknown, he was blind and mad enough to hope (even though he had often learned by personal experience that the thoughts of men lay open to Christ[14] and though his own treachery had been touched upon at the [last] supper),[1] nevertheless, I say, he was so demented and oblivious to everything as to hope that his villainous deed had escaped Christ's notice.

But because nothing could be more unwholesome for him than to be duped by such a futile hope (for nothing could work more strongly against his repentence than this), Christ in His goodness no longer allows him to be led on by a deceptive hope of deceiving but immediately adds in a grave tone, "Judas, do you betray the Son of Man with a kiss?" He addresses him by the name He had ordinarily used—and for this reason, so that the memory of their old friendship might soften the heart of the traitor and move him to repent. He openly rebukes his treachery lest he should believe it is hidden and be ashamed to confess it. Moreover, He reviles the impious hypocrisy of the traitor: "With a kiss," He says, "do you betray the Son of Man?"

Among all the circumstances of a wicked deed it is not easy to

12. Rom. 12 : 21.   13. Cf. 2 Tim. 4 : 2.
14. See, e.g., Matt. 9 : 4 and 12 : 25.   1. Matt. 26 : 21–25.

find one more hateful to God than the perversion of the real nature of good things to make them into the instruments of our malice. Thus lying is hateful to God because words, which are ordained to express the meaning of the mind, are twisted to other deceitful purposes. Within this category of evil, it is a serious offense against God if anyone abuses the law to inflict the very injuries it was designed to prevent. And so Christ reproaches Judas sharply for this detestable kind of sin: "Judas," He says, "do you betray the Son of Man with a kiss? Either be in fact as you wish to seem or else show yourself openly as you really are. For whoever commits such an unfriendly misdeed under the guise of a friend is a villain who compounds his villainy. Were you not satisfied, Judas, with betraying the Son of Man—indeed, I say, the son of that man through whom all men would have perished if this Son of Man, whom you imagine you are destroying, had not redeemed those who wish to be saved—was it not enough for you, I say, to betray this Son of Man without doing it with a kiss, thus turning the most sacred sign of charity into an instrument of betrayal? Certainly I am more favorably disposed toward this mob which attacks me with open force than toward you, Judas, who betray me to the attackers with a false kiss."

And so when Christ saw no sign of repentance in the traitor, wishing to show how much more willing He was to speak with open enemies than with a secret foe, having made it clear to the traitor that He cared not a whit for all his wicked stratagems, He immediately turned away from him and made His way, unarmed as He was, toward the armed crowd. For so the gospel says: "And then Jesus, knowing everything that was to happen to Him, went forward and said to them, 'Whom do you seek?' They replied to Him, 'Jesus of Nazareth.' Jesus said to them, 'I am He.' Now Judas, who betrayed Him, was also standing with them. When, therefore, He said to them, 'I am He,' they drew back and fell to the ground."[2]

2. John 18 : 4–6.

O saving Christ, only a little while ago, you were so fearful that you lay face down in a most pitiable attitude and sweat blood as you begged your Father to take away the chalice of your passion. How is that now, by a sudden reversal, you leap up and spring forth like a giant running his race[3] and come forward eagerly to meet those who seek to inflict that passion upon you? How is it that you freely identify yourself to those who openly admit they are seeking you but who do not know that you are the one they are seeking? Hither, hither let all hasten who are faint of heart. Here let them take firm hold of an unwavering hope when they feel themselves struck by a horror of death. For just as they share Christ's agony, His fear, grief, anxiety, sadness, and sweat (provided that they pray, and persist in prayer, and submit themselves wholeheartedly to the will of God), they will also share this consolation, undoubtedly they will feel themselves helped by such consolation as Christ felt; and they will be so refreshed by the spirit of Christ that they will feel their hearts renewed as the old face of the earth is renewed by the dew from heaven,[4] and by means of the wood of Christ's cross let down into the water of their sorrow, the thought of death, once so bitter, will grow sweet,[5] eagerness will take the place of grief, mental strength and courage will replace dread, and finally they will long for the death they had viewed with horror, considering life a sad thing and death a gain, desiring to be dissolved and to be with Christ.[6]

"And so Christ coming up close to the crowd asks, 'Whom do you seek?' They replied to Him 'Jesus of Nazareth.' Now Judas, who betrayed Him, was standing with them. And Jesus said to them, 'I am He.' When, therefore, Jesus said to them, 'I am He,' they drew back and fell to the ground." If Christ's previous fear and anxiety lessened His standing in anyone's mind, the balance must now be redressed by the manly courage with which He

3. Cf. Ps. 18 : 6 (*AV*, 19 : 5).
4. Ps. 103 : 30 (*AV*, 104 : 30). Cf. Exod. 16 : 13–14, Ps. 132 : 3 (*AV*, 133 : 3), Prov. 19 : 12, Mic. 5 : 7.
5. See Exod. 15 : 23–25.   6. Phil. 1 : 21–23.

fearlessly approaches that whole mass of armed men and, though He faces certain death ("for He knew everything which was to happen to Him"),[7] betrays Himself by His own act to those villains, who did not even know who He was, and thus offers Himself freely as a victim to be cruelly slaughtered.

Certainly this sudden and drastic change would rightly be considered marvelous viewed simply as occurring in His venerable human nature. But what sort of estimate of Him, how intense a reaction to Him must be produced in the hearts of all the faithful by the force of divine power flashing so wonderfully through the weak body of a man? For how was it that none of His pursuers recognized Him when He came up close to them? He had taught in the temple. He had overturned the tables of the moneychangers, He had driven out the moneychangers themselves,[8] He had carried out His activities in public, He had confuted the pharisees,[9] He had satisfied the sadducees,[10] He had refuted the scribes,[1] He eluded by a prudent answer the trick-question of the Herodian soldiers,[2] He had fed seven thousand men with five loaves,[3] He had healed the sick, raised the dead, made Himself available to all sorts of men, pharisees, tax-gatherers, the rich, the poor, just men, sinners, Jews, Samaritans, and gentiles, and now in this whole large crowd there was no one who recognized Him by His face or voice as He addressed them near at hand, as if those who sent them had taken special care not to send anyone along who had ever seen beforehand the person they were then seeking.

Had no one even singled out Christ from His meeting with Judas, from the embrace and the sign Judas gave with a kiss? Even more, the traitor himself, who was at that time standing together with them, did he suddenly forget how to recognize the

7. John 18 : 4.   8. Mark 11 : 15.   9. See, e.g., John 8 : 21–47.
10. Matt. 22 : 23–33.   1. E. g., Mark 2 : 6–12.
2. Matt. 22 : 15–22.
3. In all the gospel accounts the five loaves were distributed to 5000 men. See Matt. 14 : 16–21, Mark 6 : 38–44, Luke 9 : 13–17, John 6 : 8–13.

very person he had just betrayed by singling Him out with a kiss? What was the source of this strange happening? Indeed, no one was able to recognize Him for the very same reason that a little later Mary Magdalen, though she saw Him, did not recognize Him until He revealed Himself, and likewise neither one of the two disciples, though they were talking with Him, knew who He was until He let them know, but rather the two disciples thought that He was a traveller and she thought He was a gardener.[4] Finally, then, if you want to know how it was that no one could recognize Him when He came up to them, you should undoubtedly attribute it to the same cause you use to explain the fact that when He spoke no one could remain standing: "But when Jesus said, 'I am He,' they drew back and fell to the ground."

Here Christ proved that He truly is that word of God which pierces more sharply than any two-edged sword.[5] Thus a lightning bolt is said to be of such a nature that it liquefies a sword without damaging the sheath.[6] Certainly the mere voice of Christ, without damaging their bodies, so melted their souls that it deprived them of the strength to hold up their limbs.

Here the evangelist relates that Judas was standing together with them. For when he heard Jesus rebuke him openly as a traitor, whether overcome with shame or struck with fear (for he was acquainted with Peter's impulsiveness), he immediately withdrew and returned to his own kind. Thus the evangelist tells us he was standing together with them so that we may understand that like them he also fell down. And certainly the character of Judas was such that there was in that whole crowd no one worse or more worthy of being cast down. But the evangelist wished to impress upon everyone generally that they must be careful and cautious about the company they keep, for there is a danger that if they take their place with wicked men they will also fall together with them. It rarely happens that a person who is fool-

4. See John 20 : 14–16 and Luke 24 : 16–31.   5. Heb. 4 : 12.
6. Cf. Seneca, *Naturales Quaestiones*, 2, 31.

ish enough to cast his lot with those who are headed for ship-
wreck in an unseaworthy vessel gets back to land alive after the
others have drowned in the sea.

No one, I suppose, doubts that a person who could throw
them all down with one word could easily have dashed them all
down so forcibly that none of them could have gotten back up
again. But Christ, who struck them down to let them know that
they could inflict no suffering upon Him against His will, allowed them to get up again so that they could accomplish what
He wished to endure: "And so, when they had gotten up, He
asked them once more, 'Whom do you seek?' And they said to
Him, 'Jesus of Nazareth.' "[7]

Here, too, anyone can see that they were so daunted, stunned,
and stupefied by their meeting with Christ that they seem almost
to be out of their minds. For they might very well have known
that at that time of night and in that place they would not find
anyone who was not one of Christ's band of followers or else a
friend òf His and that the last thing in the world such a person
would do would be to lead them to Christ. And yet, suddenly
meeting a person whose identity was unknown to them as well as
the reason for His question, right away they foolishly blurt out
the heart of the whole affair, which they ought to have kept
carefully concealed until they had carried it out. For as soon as
He asked, "Whom do you seek?" they replied, "Jesus of Nazareth." Jesus answered, "I have told you I am He. If, therefore,
you seek me, let these men go their way"[8]—as if to say: If you
are looking for me, now that I have approached you and let you
know who I am by my own admission, why do you not arrest me
on the spot? Surely the reason is that you are so far from being
able to take me against my will that you cannot even remain
standing at my mere words, as you have just learned by falling
backwards. But now, if you have forgotten it so quickly, I again
remind you that I am Jesus of Nazareth. "If, therefore, you seek
me, let these men go their way."

7. John 18 : 7.   8. John 18 : 8.

By throwing them down, Christ made it very clear, I think, that His words, "Let these men go their way," did not constitute a request. But sometimes it happens that those who are planning some great piece of villainy are not content with the bare crime alone but with perverse wantonness make a practice of adding certain trimmings, as it were, beyond what is required by the scope of the crime itself. Moreover, there are some ministers of crime who are so preposterously faithful that, to avoid the risk of omitting any evil deed that has been entrusted to them, they will add something extra on their own for good measure. Christ implicitly refers to each of these two types: "If you seek me," He says, "let these go their way." If my blood is what the chief priests, the scribes, pharisees, and the elders of the people are longing to drain away with such an eager thirst, behold, when you were seeking me I came to meet you; when you did not know me, I betrayed myself to you; when you were prostrate, I stood nearby; now that you are arising, I stand ready to be taken captive; and finally I myself hand myself over to you (which the traitor was not able to do) to keep my followers and you from imagining (as if it were not crime enough to kill me) that their blood must be added over and above mine. Therefore, "if you seek me, let these men go their way."

He commanded them to let them go, but He also forced them to do so against their will, and by seeing to it that all were saved by flight He frustrated their efforts to capture them. An indication of this outcome was what He intended by this prophetic statement of His—"Let these men go their way"—so that those words He had spoken might be fulfilled: "Of those you have given me, I have not lost anyone."[9] The words of Christ which the evangelist is talking about here are those words He spoke to His Father that same night at supper: "Holy Father, preserve in your name those whom you have given to me."[10] And afterwards: "I have guarded those whom you gave to me, and none of them has perished except the son of perdition, that the

9. John 18 : 9.   10. John 17 : 11.

scripture might be fulfilled."[11] See how Christ here, as He foretells that the disciples will be saved when He is taken captive, declares that He is their guardian. Hence the evangelist recalls this to the minds of his readers, wishing them to understand that, in spite of His words to the crowd—"Let these men go their way"—He Himself by His hidden power had opened up a way for their escape.

The place in scripture which predicts that Judas would perish is in Psalm 108, where the psalmist prophesies in the form of a prayer: "May his days be few and may another take over his ministry."[12] Although these prophetic words were spoken about the traitor Judas such a long time before the event, nevertheless it would be hard to say whether anyone, apart from the psalmist himself, knew that they referred to Judas until Christ made this clear and the event itself bore out the words. Even the prophets themselves did not see everything foreseen by other prophets. For the spirit of prophecy is measured out individually.[13] Certainly it seems clear to me that no one understands the meaning of all scriptural passages so well that there are not many mysteries hidden there which are not yet understood, whether concerning the times of the Antichrist or the last judgment by Christ, and which will remain unknown until Elias returns to explain them.[1] Therefore it seems to me that I can justly apply the apostle's exclamation about God's wisdom to holy scripture (in which God has hidden and laid up the vast stores of His wisdom): "O the depth of the riches of the wisdom and knowledge of God! How incomprehensible are His judgments and how unsearchable His ways!"[2]

And nevertheless nowadays, first in one place, then in another, there are springing up from day to day, almost like swarms of wasps or hornets, people who boast that they are "autodidacts" (to use St. Hierome's word) and that, without the commentaries of the old doctors, they find clear, open, and easy all

11. John 17 : 12.   12. Ps. 108 : 8 (*AV*, 109 : 8).
13. Cf. Ephes. 4 : 7.   1. Mal. 4 : 5.   2. Rom. 11 : 33.

those things which all the ancient fathers confessed they found quite difficult—and the fathers were men of no less talent or training, of tireless energy, and as for that "spirit" which these moderns have as often on their lips as they do rarely in their hearts, here the fathers surpassed them no less than in holiness of life. But now these modern men, who have sprouted up overnight as theologians professing to know everything, not only disagree about the meaning of scripture with all those men who led such heavenly lives, but also fail to agree among themselves concerning great dogmas of the Christian faith. Rather, each of them, whoever he may be, insisting that he sees the truth, conquers the rest and is in turn conquered by them. But they all are alike in opposing the Catholic faith and all are alike in being conquered by it. He who dwells in the heavens laughs to scorn these wicked and vain attempts of theirs.[3] But I humbly pray that He may not so laugh them to scorn as to laugh also at their eternal ruination, but rather that He may inspire in them the health-giving grace of repentance, so that these prodigal sons[4] who have wandered so long, alas, in exile may retrace their steps to the bosom of mother church, and so that all of us together, united in the true faith of Christ and joined in mutual charity as true members of Christ, may attain to the glory of Christ our head,[5] which no one should ever be foolish enough to hope to arrive at outside the body of Christ and without the true faith.

But, to return to what I was saying, the fact that this prophetic utterance applies to Judas was suggested by Christ,[6] was made clear by Judas' suicide, was afterwards made quite explicit by Peter,[7] and was fulfilled by all the apostles when Matthias was chosen by lot[8] to take his place and thus another took over his ministry. And to make the matter even clearer, after Matthias took Judas' place, no replacement was ever taken into that group of twelve (although bishops succeed in the place of the apostles in an uninterrupted line), but rather, as the apostleship was

3. Ps. 2 : 4.   4. Cf. Luke 15 : 11–32.   5. Cf. Ephes. 4 : 1–16.
6. John 17 : 12.   7. Acts 1 : 20.   8. Acts 1 : 26.

transmitted gradually to more persons, that sacred number came to an end once the prophecy had been fulfilled.

Therefore, when Christ said "Let these men go their way," He was not begging for their permission, but rather declaring in veiled terms that He Himself granted His disciples the power to leave, that He might fulfill those words He had spoken: "Father, I have guarded those whom you gave to me, and none of them has perished except the son of perdition."[9] I think it worthwhile to consider here for a moment how strongly Christ foretold in these words the contrast between the end of Judas and the end of the rest, the ruination of the traitor Judas and the success of the others. For He asserts each future outcome with such certainty that He announces them not as future happenings but as events that have already definitely taken place. "I have guarded," He says, "those whom you gave to me." They were not defended by their own strength, nor were they preserved by the mercy of the Jews, nor did they escape through the carelessness of the cohort, but rather "I guarded them. And none of them perished except the son of perdition." For he, too, Father, was among those whom you gave to me. Chosen by me, he received me, and to him as well as to the rest who received me I had given the power to become a son of God.[1] But when in his insane greed he went over to Satan, leaving me, betraying me treacherously, refusing to be saved, then he became a son of destruction in the very act of pursuing my destruction, and perished like a wretch in his wretchedness.

Infallibly certain about the fate of the traitor, Christ expresses his future ruin with such certainty that He asserts it as if it had already come to pass. And for all that, as Christ is being arrested, the unhappy traitor stands there as the ferocious leader and standard-bearer of Christ's captors, rejoicing and exulting, I imagine, in the danger of his fellow-disciples and his master, for I am convinced he desired and hoped that all of them would be arrested and put to death. The raving madness and perversity of

9. John 17 : 12.   1. Cf. John 1 : 12.

ingratitude manifests itself in this peculiarity: the ingrate desires the death of the very victim he has unjustly injured. So too, the person whose conscience is full of guilty sores is so sensitive that he views even the face of his victim as a reproach and shrinks from it with dread. Thus as the traitor rejoiced in the hope that all of them would be captured together, he was so stupidly sure of himself that nothing was further from his mind than the thought that the death sentence passed on him by God was hanging over his head like a dreadful noose ready to fall around his neck at any moment.

In this connection I am struck by the lamentable obscurity of the miserable human condition: often we are distressed and fearful, ignorant all the while that we are quite safe; often, on the other hand, we act as if we had not a care in the world, unaware that the death-dealing sword hangs over our heads. The other apostles were afraid they would be seized together with Christ and put to death, whereas actually they were all to escape. Judas, who had no fears for himself and took pleasure in their fears, perished only a few hours later. Cruel is the appetite which feeds on the misery of others. Nor is there any reason why a person should rejoice and congratulate himself on his good fortune because he has it in his power to cause another man's death, as the traitor thought he had by means of the cohort that had been delivered to him. For though a man may send someone else to his death, he himself is sure to follow him there. Even more, since the hour of death is uncertain, he himself may precede the very person he arrogantly imagines he has sent to death ahead of him.

Thus the death of the wretched Judas preceded that of Christ, whom he had betrayed to His death—a sad and terrible example to the whole world that the wrongdoer, however he may flout his arrogant impenitence, ought not to think he is safe from retribution. For against the wicked all creatures work together in harmony with their creator.[2] The air longs to blow noxious

2. Cf. Sap. 5 : 21–24, 16 : 16–17; Cicero, *De Finibus*, 1, 16, 50–51; Ariosto, *Orlando Furioso*, 6, 1.

vapors against the wicked man, the sea longs to overwhelm him in its waves, the mountains to fall upon him, the valleys to rise up against him, the earth to split open beneath him, hell to swallow him up after his headlong fall, the demons to plunge him into gulfs of ever-burning flames. All the while the only one who preserves the wretch is the God whom he deserted.

But if anyone is such a persistent imitator of Judas that God finally decides not to offer any longer the grace which has been offered and refused so often, this man is really and truly wretched: however he may flatter himself in the delusion that he is floating high in the air on the wings of felicity, he is actually wallowing in the utter depths of misery and calamity. Therefore let each of us pray to the most merciful Christ, each praying not only for himself but also for others, that we may not imitate Judas in his stubbornness but rather may eagerly accept the grace God offers us and may be restored once more to glory through penance and mercy.

The severing of Malchus' ear, the flight of the apostles, and the capture of Christ

The severing of Malchus' ear

The apostles had previously heard Christ foretelling the very things they were now seeing happen.[3] On that occasion, though they were saddened and grieved, they treated the matter with much less concern than now when they see it happening before their very eyes. Now that they see the whole cohort standing there and openly admitting that they are seeking Jesus of Nazareth, there is no more room for doubt that they are seeking Him to take Him captive.

When the apostles saw what was about to happen, their minds were overwhelmed by a sudden welter of different feelings: anx-

3. Matt. 16 : 21. Cf. John 16 : 6, 22.

iety for their Lord whom they loved, fear for their own safety, and finally shame for that high-sounding promise[4] of theirs that they would all rather die than fail their master. Thus their impulses were divided between conflicting feelings. Their love of their master urged them not to flee; their fear for themselves, not to remain. Fear of death impelled them to run away; shame for their promise, to stand fast.

Moreover, they remembered what Christ had said to them that very night: He told them that, whereas before He had forbidden any of them to carry so much as a staff to defend himself with,[5] now whoever did not have a sword should even sell his tunic to buy one.[6] Now they were struck with great fear as they saw massed against them the Roman cohort and the crowd of Jews, all of them armed with weapons, whereas there were only eleven of them, and even of those none had any weapons (apart perhaps from table-knives) except two had swords. Nevertheless, they remembered that when they had said to Christ, "Look, here are two swords," He had replied, "That is enough."[7] Not understanding the great mystery contained in this reply, they suddenly and impulsively ask Him whether He wants them to defend Him with the sword, saying, "Lord, shall we strike with the sword?"[8]

But Peter's feelings boiled over so that he did not wait for a reply, but drew his sword, struck a blow at the servant of the high priest, and cut off his right ear—perhaps simply because this man happened to be standing near to Peter, perhaps because his fierce and haughty bearing made him conspicuous among the rest. At any rate he certainly seems to have been a notoriously wicked man, for the evangelists mention that he was the servant of the high priest, the chief and prince of all the priests. "The greater the house, the prouder the servants," as the satirist says,[9] and men know from experience that everywhere in he world the servants of great lords are more arrogant

4. Matt. 26 : 33–35.   5. Matt. 10 : 10.   6. Luke 22 : 35–36.
7. Luke 22 : 38.   8. Luke 22 : 49.   9. Juvenal, 5, 66.

and overbearing than their masters. That we might know that this man had some standing with the high priest and was for that reason all the more egregiously proud, John immediately adds his name. "The servant's name," he says, "was Malchus."[10] The evangelist does not ordinarily provide such information everywhere or without some special reason.

I imagine that this rascal, displaying such fierceness as he thrust himself forward, irked Peter, who chose this enemy to open the fight and who would have pressed the attack vigorously if Christ had not checked his course. For Christ immediately forbad the others to fight, declared Peter's zeal ineffectual, and restored the ear of this miserable creature. These things He did because He came to suffer death, not to escape it; and even if He had not come to die, He would not have needed such assistance. To make this more manifest, He first gave His reply to the question put by the other apostles: "Let them go this far."[11] Still give them leave for a while. For I cast them all down with a mere word, and yet even I, as you see, allowed them to get up so that for the present they may accomplish whatever they wish. Since, then, I allow them to go so far, you must do the same. The time will shortly come when I will no longer allow them any power against me. Even now, in the meantime, I do not need your help.

Thus to the others He answered only "Let them go this far." But turning to Peter separately, He said, "Put your sword away"[12]—as if to say: I do not wish to be defended with the sword, and I have chosen you for the mission of fighting not with such a sword but with the sword of the word of God.[13] Therefore return the sword of iron to the sheath where it belongs—that is, to the hands of worldly princes to be used against evildoers. You who are the apostles of my flock have yet another sword far more terrible than any sword of iron, a sword by which a wicked man is sometimes cut off from the church

10. John 18 : 10.   11. Luke 22 : 51.
12. Matt. 26 : 52, John 18 : 11.   13. Cf. Eph. 6 : 17.

(like a rotten limb[14] removed from my mystical body) and handed over to Satan for the destruction of the flesh to save the spirit[1] (provided only that the man is of a mind to be healed) and to enable him once more to be joined and grafted into my body—though it sometimes happens that a man suffering from a hopeless disease is also handed over to the invisible death of the soul, lest he should infect the healthy members with his disease. But I am so far from wishing you to make use of that sword of iron (whose proper sheath, you must recognize, is the secular magistrate) that I do not think even that spiritual sword, whose use properly pertains to you, should be unsheathed very often. Rather, wield with vigor that sword of the word,[2] whose stroke, like that of a scalpel, lets the pus out and heals by wounding. As for that other heavy and dangerous sword of excommunication, I desire that it be kept hidden in the sheath of mercy unless some urgent and fearful necessity requires that it be withdrawn.

In answering the other apostles Christ contented Himself with three words, because they were more temperate, or perhaps merely more tepid, than Peter; but Peter's fiery and wild assault He controlled and checked at greater length. He not only ordered him to put up his sword, but also added the reason why He did not approve of his zeal, however pious. "Do you not wish me," He said, "to drink the chalice my Father gave me?"[3] Some time ago Christ had predicted to the apostles that "it would be necessary for Him to go to Jerusalem and to suffer many things from the elders and scribes and princes of the priests, and to be killed and to rise on the third day. And taking Him aside, Peter began to chide Him, saying, 'Far be it from you, O Lord. This will not happen to you.' Christ turned and said to Peter, 'Get thee behind me, Satan, for you do not understand the things of God.' "[4] Notice how severely Christ here rebuked Peter.

Shortly before, when Peter had professed that Christ was the

14. Cf. Matt. 5 : 29–30.   1. 1 Cor. 5 : 5.   2. Eph. 6 : 17.
3. John 18 : 11.   4. Matt. 16 : 21–23.

son of God, Christ had said to him, "Blessed are you, Simon bar Jona, for flesh and blood have not revealed this to you, but rather my Father who is in heaven. And I say to you that you are Peter and upon this rock I will build my church, and the gates of hell shall not prevail against it. And to you I will give the keys of heaven, and whatever you bind on earth will also be bound in heaven, etc."[5] But here He almost rejects this same Peter and thrusts him behind Him and declares that he is a stumbling-block to Him and calls him Satan and asserts that he does not understand the things of God but rather those of men. And why does He do all this? Because Peter tried to persuade Him not to die. Then He showed that it was necessary for Him to follow through to His death, which was irrevocably decreed for Him by His own will; and hence not only did He not want them to hinder His death, He even wanted them to follow Him along the same road. "If anyone wishes to come after me," He said, "let him deny himself and take up his cross and follow me."[6] Not satisfied even with this, He went on to show that if anyone refuses to follow Him on the road to death when the case requires it, he does not avoid death, but incurs a much worse death; on the other hand, whoever gives up his life does not lose it but exchanges it for a more vital life.[7] "Whoever wishes to save his life," He says, "will lose it. But whoever loses his life for my sake will find it. For what does it profit a man if he gain the whole world but suffer the loss of his own soul? Or what will a man give in exchange for his soul? For the Son of Man is to come with His angels in the glory of His Father, and then He will render to everyone according to his deeds."[8]

Perhaps I have devoted more time to this passage than was necessary. But I ask you, who would not be led beyond the pale, as they say, by these words of Christ, so severe and threatening but also so effective in creating hope of eternal life? But the relevance of these words to the passage under discussion is this:

5. Matt. 16 : 17–19.   6. Matt. 16 : 24.
7. Cf. Cicero, *De amicitia*, 6, 22.   8. Matt. 16 : 25–27.

here we see Peter earnestly admonished not to be misled by his zeal into further hindering the death of Christ. And yet see now how Peter is again carried away by this same zeal to oppose Christ's death, except that this time he does not limit himself to verbal dissuasion but tries to ward it off by fierce fighting. Still, because Peter meant well when he did what he did, and also because Christ bore Himself with humility toward everyone as He drew near to His passion, Christ chose not to reprove Peter sharply. Rather, He first rebuked him by giving a reason, then He declared Peter's act to be sinful, and finally He announced that even if He wished to avoid death He would not need Peter's protection or any other mortal assistance, since if He wished help He had only to ask His Father, who would not fail to aid Him in His danger by sending a mighty and invincible array of angels against these puny mortals who were coming to take Him captive.

First of all, then, as I said, He checks Peter's zeal to strike out by presenting a rational argument. He says, "Do you not wish me to drink the chalice which my Father gave me?" My whole life up to this point has been a pattern of obedience and a model of humility. What lessons have I taught more frequently or more forcefully than that magistrates ought to be obeyed,[9] that parents should be honored,[10] that what is Caesar's should be rendered to Caesar, what is God's to God.[1] And now, when I ought to be applying the finishing touches to bring my work to full perfection, now can you wish that I should refuse the chalice extended to me by my Father, that the Son of Man should disobey God the Father, and thus unravel in a single moment all of that most beautiful fabric I have spent such a long time weaving?

Then He teaches Peter that he commited a sin by striking with the sword, and this He does by a parallel from the civil law. "For

9. In the gospels Christ does not have much to say about obeying magistrates, but More would assume that Paul (Rom. 13 : 4–7) and Peter (1 Pet. 2 : 17) were transmitting Christ's teaching.

10. Cf. Exod. 20 : 12, Eph. 6 : 1, and Col. 3 : 20.

1. Matt. 22 : 21, Mark 12 : 17, Luke 20 : 25.

everyone who takes up the sword," He says, "will perish by the sword."[2] According to the Roman law, which also applied to the Jews at that time, any person discovered wearing a sword without legitimate authority for the purpose of killing a man was placed in almost the same category as the man who had killed his victim.[3] Naturally, therefore, a person who not only wore a sword but also drew it and struck a blow was in even greater legal jeopardy. Nor do I think that Peter, in that moment of confusion and alarm, was so self-possessed that he deliberately avoided hitting Malchus' head and aimed only at his ear, so as merely to frighten him but not kill him.

But if someone should perhaps maintain that everyone has the right even to use force in order to protect an innocent person from criminal assault, this objection would require a longer discussion than I could conveniently introduce in this place. This much is certain: however much Peter's offense was mitigated by his loyal affection for Christ, nevertheless, his lack of any legitimate authority to fight is made quite clear by the fact that on a previous occasion Christ had sharply warned him not to try to prevent His passion and death, not even by verbal dissuasion, much less by actual fighting.

Next He checks Peter's attack by making another point: Peter's protection is quite unnecessary. "Do you not know," He says, "that I could ask my Father for help and He would immediately deliver to me more than twelve legions of angels?"[4]

About His own power He says nothing, but glories that He enjoys the favor of His Father. For as He drew near to His death, He wished to avoid lofty statements about Himself or any assertion that His own power was equal to that of the Father. Rather, wishing to make it clear that He had no need of help from Peter or any other mortal, He declares that the assistance of the heavenly angels (if He chose to ask for it) would immediately be at hand, sent by His omnipotent Father. "Do you not

2. Matt. 26 : 52.   3. *Corpus Juris Civilis, Digesta,* 48, 8, 1.
4. Matt. 26 : 53.

know," He says, "that I could ask my Father for help and He would immediately deliver to me more than twelve legions of angels?"—as if to say: You have just seen before your very eyes how I threw down, with a mere word, without even touching them, this whole crowd, such a large crowd that it would be sheer folly for you to think you are strong enough to defend me against them. If that could not convince you that I do not need your help, consider at least whose son you proclaimed me to be when I put the question "Who do you say I am?" and you immediately gave that heaven-inspired reply, "You are Christ, the son of the living God."[5] Therefore, since you know from God's own revelation that I am the son of God, and since you must know that mortal parents do not fail their children, do you imagine that, if I were not going to my death of my own free will, my heavenly Father would choose to fail me? Do you not know that, if I chose to ask Him, He would deliver to me more than twelve legions of angels, and that He would do so forthwith, without hesitation or delay? Against so many legions of angels, what resistance could be offered by this miserable cohort of puny mortals? Ten times twelve legions of creatures such as these would not dare even to look upon the angry frown of a single angel.

Then Christ returns to His first point, as the one closest to the central issue. "How, then," He says, "will the scriptures be fulfilled that say this is the way it must be?"[6]

The scriptures are full of prophecies concerning Christ's death, full of the mysteries of His passion and of mankind's redemption which would not have happened without that passion. Therefore, lest Peter or anyone else should mutter under his breath, "If you can obtain so many legions from your Father, Christ, why don't you ask for them?"—to counter this, Christ says, "How, then, will the scriptures be fulfilled that say this is the way it must be?" Since you understand from the scriptures that this is the only way chosen by the most just wisdom of God

5. Matt. 16 : 15–17.   6. Matt. 26 : 54.

to restore the human race to its lost glory, if I should now successfully implore my Father to save me from death, what would I
be doing but striving to undo the very thing I came to do? To
call down from heaven angels to defend me, what effect would
that have but precisely to exclude from heaven the whole human
race, which I come to redeem and restore to the glory of
heaven? With your sword, therefore, you are not fighting
against the wicked Jews but rather attacking the whole human
race, inasmuch as you are setting yourself against the fulfillment
of the scriptures and desiring me not to drink the chalice given
to me by my Father, that chalice by which I myself (unstained
and undefiled) will wipe away that defiling stain of fallen nature.

But now behold the most gentle heart of Christ, who did not
think it enough to check Peter's strokes but also touched the
severed ear of His persecutor and made it sound again, in order
to give us an example of rendering good for evil.

No one's body, I think, is so fully pervaded by his soul as the
letter of holy scripture is pervaded by spiritual mysteries. Indeed, just as one cannot touch any part of the body in which the
soul does not reside, providing life and sensation to even the
smallest part, so too no factual account in all of scripture is so
gross and corporeal (so to speak) that it does not have life and
breath from some spiritual mystery. Therefore, in considering
how Malchus' ear was cut off by Peter's sword and restored by
the hand of Christ, we should not feel bound to consider only
the facts of the account, though even these can teach us salutary
lessons, but let us look further for the saving mystery of the
spirit veiled beneath the letter of the story.

Thus Malchus, whose name is the Hebrew word for "king,"
can appropriately be taken as a figure of reason. For in man
reason ought to reign like a king, and it does truly reign when it
makes itself loyally subject to faith and serves God. For to serve
Him is to reign. The high priest, on the other hand, together
with his priests, with the pharisees, scribes, and elders of the
people, was given over to perverse superstitions, which he mixed
into the law of God, and he used piety as a pretext to oppose

piety and sought eagerly to eliminate the founder of true religion. Hence he together with his accomplices may rightly be
taken to represent wicked heresiarchs, the chief priests of pernicious superstition, together with their followers.

And so whenever the rational mind rebels against the truth
faith of Christ and devotes itself to heresies, it becomes a fugitive
from Christ and a servant of the heresiarch whom it follows, led
astray by the devil and wandering down the byways of error.
Keeping, therefore, its left ear, with which it listens to sinister
heresies, it loses its right ear, with which it ought to listen to the
true faith. But this does not always happen from the same mo-
tivation or with the same effect. For some minds turn to heresies
out of determined malice. Then the ear is not cut off by a swift
stroke but rots slowly and gradually as the devil infuses his
venom, until finally the purulent parts harden and block the
passages with a clot so that nothing good can penetrate within.
Such persons, alas, are hardly ever restored to health. For the
parts eaten away by the ravaging cancer are completely gone
and there is nothing left which can be put back in place.

But the ear cut off by a sudden stroke and sent whirling in
one piece to the ground because of imprudent zeal, stands for
those who turn from the truth to a false appearance of the truth
because they are overcome by a sudden impulse; or it also represents those who are deceived by a well-meaning zeal, concerning
whom Christ says, "The time will come when everyone who
etc.   performing a service for God."[7] Of this kind of person
the apostle Paul was a typical figure.[8] Some of these, because
their minds are confused by earthly feelings, allow the ear which
has been cut off from heavenly doctrine to remain lying on the
earth. But Christ often takes pity on the misery of such persons
and with His own hand picks up from the earth the ear which
has been cut off by a sudden impulse or by ill-considered zeal
and with His touch fastens it to the head again and makes it

7. John 16 : 2. The words More merely indicated by "etc." and a blank
space are "kills you will think he is."
8. Acts 9 : 1–2.

once more capable of listening to true doctrine. I know that the ancient fathers elicted various mysteries from this one passage, as each one, aided by the grace of the Holy Spirit, made his own particular discovery. But it is no part of my plan to review them all here because to do so would make too long an interruption in the account of the historical events.

"But Jesus said to those princes of the priests and magistrates of the temple and elders who had come, 'You have come out with swords and clubs to seize me as if I were a robber, though I was with you every day in the temple, and I sat teaching there and you did not detain me—you made no move to lay hands on me. But this is your hour and the power of darkness.' "[9]

Christ said this to those princes of the priests and magistrates of the temple and elders who had come. But here some readers are puzzled because the evangelist Luke reports that Jesus said these things to the princes of the priests and the magistrates of the temple and the elders of the people, while the other evangelists write in their accounts that these persons did not come themselves but sent the cohort and their servants.

Some solve the problem by saying that Jesus may indeed be said to have spoken to these persons because He spoke to those whom they had sent. In this sense princes ordinarily speak to one another through their ambassadors, and private persons everywhere speak to each other through messengers. Thus whatever we tell a servant who has been sent to us, we say to his master who sent him, for such servants will repeat to their master what they have been told.

Though I do not deny such a solution, I am certainly much more inclined to the opinion of those who think that Christ spoke face to face with the princes of the priests, magistrates of the temple, and elders of the people. For Luke does not say that Christ said these things to all the princes of the priests, or to all the magistrates of the temple, or to all the elders of the people,

9. Luke 23 : 52–53; cf. Matt. 26 : 55, Mark 14 : 48–49.

but only to those "who had come." These words seem to indicate rather clearly that, although the cohort and servants had been commissioned to seize Christ in the name of the whole assembly gathered together in council, still some members of each group—elders, pharisees, and princes—also went along with them. This opinion agrees exactly with Luke's words and does not contradict the accounts of the other evangelists.

Addressing, therefore, the princes of the priests, the pharisees, and the elders of the people, Christ implicitly reminds them that they should not attribute His capture to their own strength or adroitness and should not foolishly boast of it as a clever and ingenious achievement (according to that unfortunate tendency of those who are fortunate in evil). He lets them know that the foolish contrivances and maneuvers by which they labored to suppress the truth were powerless to accomplish anything against Him, but rather the profound wisdom of God had foreseen and set the time when the prince of this world[10] would be justly tricked into losing his ill-gotten prey, the human race, even as he strove by unjust means to keep it. If this were not the case, Christ explains to them, there would have been no need at all for them to pay for the services of the betrayer, to come at night with lanterns and torches, to make their approach surrounded by the dense ranks of the cohort and armed with swords and clubs, since they had previously had many opportunities to arrest Him as He sat teaching in the temple, and then they could have done it without expense, without any special effort, without spending a sleepless night, without any saberrattling at all.

But if they should take special credit for their prudent foresight and say that the arrest of Christ was no easy matter, as He claimed, but rather quite difficult because it necessarily brought with it the great danger of a popular uprising,[11] this difficulty, for the most part, had arisen only recently, after the resurrec-

10. John 12 : 31, 14 : 30, 16 : 11.
11. See, e.g., Matt. 21 : 46 and Luke 20 : 19.

tion of Lazarus.¹² Before that event, it had happened more than once that, in spite of the people's great love of His virtues and their profound respect for Him, He had had to use His own power to escape from their midst.¹³ On those occasions anyone attempting to capture and kill Him would not have been in the least danger from the crowd but would have found them to be willing accomplices in crime. So unfailingly unreliable is the common herd, always ready at a moment's notice to take the wrong side. Finally, what happened a little later showed how easy it is to brush aside the people's favor toward a person, and any fear that might arise from it; as soon as He was arrested, the people were no less furious at him as they cried out "Away with him! Crucify him!" than they had formerly been eager to honor Him when they cried "Blessed is He who comes in the name of the Lord!" and "Hosanna in the highest!"

And so up to that time God had caused the would-be captors of Christ to imagine purely fictitious grounds for fear and to tremble with dread where there was no reason to be afraid. But now that the proper time had come for all men (all, that is, who truly desire it) to be redeemed by the bitter death of one man¹⁴ and be restored to the sweetness of eternal life, these puny creatures stupidly imagined that they had achieved by clever planning what as a matter of fact God in His omnipotent providence (without which not a sparrow falls to earth)¹ had mercifully prescribed from all eternity. To show them how very wrong they were and to let them know that, without His own consent, the deceitfulness of the betrayer and their own cleverly laid snares and the power of the Romans would have been utterly ineffectual, Christ said, "But this is your hour and the power of darkness." These words of Christ are grounded firmly by what the evangelist says: "But all this was done so that the writings of the prophets might be fulfilled."²

Predictions of Christ's death are very frequent throughout the

12. John 11 : 45–48.   13. Luke 4 : 28–30.
14. Cf. Rom. 5 : 12–19.   1. Matt. 10 : 29.   2. Matt. 26 : 56.

prophets: "He was led like a lamb to the slaughter, and His cry was not heard in the streets,"[3] "They have pierced my hands and my feet,"[4] "I was struck with these blows in the home of those who loved me,"[5] "And He was reckoned among the wicked,"[6] "Truly He bore our infirmities,"[7] "By His bruises we have been healed,"[8] "He has been brought to His death by the wickedness of my people."[9] The prophets are full of very clear predictions of the death of Christ. In order that these might not remain unfulfilled, it was necessary that the matter depend not on human planning but rather on Him who foresaw and prearranged from all eternity what would happen (that is, on the Father of Christ, and likewise on Christ Himself, and on the Holy Spirit of both of them, for the actions of these three are always so harmoniously unified that there is no exterior act of any one of them that does not belong equally to all three). The most suitable times of fulfillment, then, were already foreseen and prescribed. Therefore, while the high priests and the princes of the priests, the scribes, pharisees and elders of the people, in short, all these accursed and wicked magistrates, were taking pride in their masterful plan for capturing Christ cleverly, they were nothing more than tools of God, eager in their ignorance, blind instruments of the most excellent and unchangeable will of almighty God, not only of the Father and the Holy Spirit, but also of Christ Himself; thus, foolish and blind with malice, they did great harm to themselves and great good to others, they inflicted a temporary death on Christ but contributed to a most happy life for the human race, and they enhanced the everlasting glory of Christ.

And so Christ said to them, "This is your hour and the power of darkness." In the past, although you hated me intensely, al-

3. More seems to have conflated Isa. 53 : 7 (cited also in Acts 8 : 32) and Ps. 143 : 14 (*AV*, 144 : 14).
4. Ps. 21 : 17 (*AV*, 22 : 16).   5. Zech. 13 : 6.
6. Luke 22 : 37, citing Isa. 53 : 12.   7. Isa. 53 : 4.
8. Isa. 53 : 5. Cf. 1 Pet. 2 : 24.
9. Apparently a conflation of Isa. 53 : 8 and 12.

though you longed to destroy me, although you could have done so at that time with less trouble (except that heavenly power prevented it), yet you did not detain me in the temple—you did not even make a single move to lay hands on me. Why was this? If was because the time and the hour had not yet come, the hour fixed not by the heavenly bodies, not by your cleverness, but rather by the unsearchable plan of my Father, to which I too had given my consent. Would you like to know when He did this? Not only as long ago as the times of Abraham, but from all eternity. For from all eternity, together with the Father, before Abraham came to be, I am.[1]

And so this is your hour and the power of darkness. This is the short hour allowed to you and the power granted to darkness, so that now in the dark you might do what you were not permitted to do in the daylight, flying in my face like winged creatures from the Stygian marsh, like harpies, like horned owls and screech-owls, like night-ravens and bats and night-owls, futilely swarming in a shrill uproar of beaks, talons, and teeth. You are in the dark when you ascribe my death to your strength. So too the governor Pilate will be in the dark when he takes pride in possessing the power to free me or to crucify me. For, even though my people and my high priests are about to hand me over to him, he would not have any power over me if it were not given to him from above. And for that very reason, those who will hand me over to him are the greater sinners.[2]

But this is the hour and the brief power of darkness. A man who walks in the dark does not know where he is going.[3] You also do not see or know what you are doing, and for that reason I myself will pray that you may be forgiven for what you are scheming to do to me.[4] But not everyone will be forgiven. Blindness will not be an excuse for everyone. For you yourselves create your own darkness, you put out the light, you blind your own eyes first and then the eyes of others so that you are the

1. John 8 : 58.   2. Cf. John 19 : 10–11.   3. John 12 : 35.
4. Cf. Luke 23 : 34.

blind leading the blind until both fall into a ditch.[5] This is your short hour. This is that mad and ungovernable power which brings you armed to take an unarmed man, which brings the fierce against the gentle, criminals against an innocent man, a traitor against his lord, puny mortals against God.

But this hour and this power of darkness are not only given to you now against me, but such an hour and such a brief power of darkness will also be given to other governors and other caesars against other disciples of mine. And this too will truly be the power of darkness. For whatever my disciples endure and whatever they say, they will not endure by their own strength or say of themselves, but conquering through my strength they will win their souls by their patience,[6] and it is my Father's spirit that will speak in them.[7] So too those who persecute and kill them will neither do nor speak anything of themselves. Rather, the prince of darkness who is already coming and who has no power over me[8] will instill his poison in the breasts of these tyrants and tormentors and will demonstrate and exercise his strength through them for the brief time allowed him. Hence my comrades-in-arms will be struggling not against flesh and blood but against princes and powers, against the rulers of the darkness of this world, against the spiritual forces of evil in high places.[9] Thus Nero is yet to be born, in whom the prince of darkness will kill Peter and to him will add Paul, who does not yet have that name and is still displaying his hatred of me. Through the prince of darkness other caesars and their governors will rise up against other disciples of my flock.

But although the nations have raged and the people devised vain things, although the kings of the earth have risen up and the princes gathered together against the Lord and against His Christ, striving to break their chains and to cast off that most sweet yoke which a loving God, through His pastors, places upon their stubborn necks, then He who dwells in the heavens

---

5. Matt. 15 : 14.   6. Luke 21 : 19.   7. Matt. 10 : 20.
8. John 14 : 30.   9. Eph. 6 : 12.

will laugh at them and the Lord will deride them. He sits not on a curule throne like earthly princes, raised up a few feet above the earth, but rather He rises above the setting of the sun,[10] He sits above the cherubim,[1] the heavens are His throne, the earth is the footstool beneath His feet,[2] His name is the Lord.[3] He is the king of kings and the lord of lords,[4] a terrible king who daunts the hearts of princes.[5] This king will speak to them in His anger, and in His rage He will throw them into confusion.[6] He will establish His Christ, the son whom He has today begotten, as king on His holy mountain of Sion,[7] a mountain which will not be shaken.[8] He will cast all His enemies down before Him like a footstool under His feet.[9] Those who tried to break His chains and cast off His yoke, He will rule against their will with a rod of iron, and He will shatter them like a potter's vessel.[1] Against them and their instigator, the prince of darkness, my disciples will be strengthened in the Lord.

And putting on the armor of God, their loins girt with truth, wearing the breastplate of justice, shod in preparation to preach the gospel of peace, taking up in all things the shield of faith and putting on the helmet of salvation and the sword of the spirit, which is the word of God,[2] they shall be clothed with power from on high.[3] And they will stand against the snares of the devil,[4] that is, against the soft speeches he will place on the lips of their persecutors to cajole them into leaving the way of truth. The open assaults of Satan they will also resist on the evil day:[5] compassed about by the shield of faith,[6] pouring forth

10. Ps. 67 : 5 (*AV*, 68 : 4).
1. Ps. 98 : 1 (*AV*, 99 : 1). Cf. Ps. 79 : 2 (*AV*, 80 : 1).   2. Isa. 66 : 1.
3. Ps. 67 : 5 (*AV*, 68 : 4).   4. 1 Tim. 6 : 15.
5. Ps. 75 : 12–13 (*AV*, 76 : 11–12).   6. Ps. 2 : 5.   7. Ps. 2 : 6–7.
8. Ps. 124 : 1 (*AV*, 125 : 1). Cf. Ps. 92 : 1 (*AV*, 93 : 1) and 95 : 10 (*AV*, 96 : 10).
9. Ps. 109 : 1 (*AV*, 110 : 1). Cf. 1 Cor. 15 : 25, Heb. 1 : 13 and 10 : 13.
1. Ps. 2 : 3, 9.   2. Eph. 6 : 10–17.   3. Luke 24 : 49.
4. Eph. 6 : 11.   5. Eph. 6 : 13.
6. Cf. Ps. 90 : 5 (*AV*, 91 : 4) and Eph. 6 : 16.

tears in their prayers and shedding their blood in the agony of their suffering, they shall extinguish all the fiery darts hurled against them by the underlings of that monster of evil, Satan.[7] Thus, when they have taken up their cross to follow me,[8] when they have conquered the prince of darkness, the devil, when they have trod under foot the earthly minions of Satan, then finally, riding aloft on a triumphal chariot, the martyrs will enter into heaven in a magnificent and marvelous procession.

But you who now give vent to your malice against me, and also that corrupt generation to come which will imitate your malice, that brood of vipers[9] which will assail my disciples with impenitent malice similar to yours, all of you, to your everlasting infamy, will be thrust down into the dark fires of hell. But in the meantime you are permitted to demonstrate and exercise your power. Still, lest you should take too much pride in it, remember that it must shortly come to an end. For the span of time allotted to your wanton arrogance is not endless but has been shortened to the span of a brief hour for the sake of the elect, that they might not be tried beyond their strength.[1]

And so this hour of yours and this power of darkness are not long-lasting and enduring but quite as brief as the present moment to which they are limited, an instant of time always caught between a past that is gone and a future that has not arrived. Therefore, lest you should lose any of this hour of yours which is so short, proceed immediately to use it for your own evil purposes. Since you seek to destroy me, be quick about it,[2] arrest me without delay, but let these men go their way.

The flight of the disciples

"Then all the disciples abandoned Him and fled."[3]

From this passage it is easy to see how difficult and arduous a

---

7. Eph. 6 : 16.   8. Matt. 10 : 38 and 16 : 24. Mark 8 : 34.
9. Cf. Matt. 3 : 7, 12 : 34, and 23 : 33; Luke 3 : 7.
1. Matt. 24 : 22, Mark 13 : 20, and 1 Cor. 10 : 13.   2. John 13 : 27.
3. Matt. 26 : 56 Mark 14 : 50.

virtue patience is. For many can bring themselves to face certain death bravely provided they can strike back at their assailants and give vent to their feelings by inflicting wounds on those who attack them. But to suffer without any comfort from revenge, to meet death with a patience that not only refrains from striking back but also takes blows without returning so much as an angry word, that, I assure you, is such a lofty peak of heroic virtue that even the apostles were not yet strong enough to scale it. Remembering that grand promise of theirs that they would die together with Him rather than desert Him,[4] even they held out at least to the point of professing themselves ready to die providing that they had the chance to die fighting. And in deed as well as word Peter gave concrete evidence of this willingness by striking Malchus. But when our Savior denied them permission to fight and withheld the power to defend themselves, "they all abandoned Him and fled."

I have sometimes asked myself this question: when Christ left off praying and returned to the apostles only to find them sleeping, did He go to both groups or only to those He had brought farther along and placed nearest to Him? But when I consider these words of the evangelist, "All of them abandoned Him and fled," I no longer have any doubt that it was all of them who fell asleep. While they should have been staying awake and praying that they might not enter into temptation (as Christ so often told them to do), instead they were sleeping and thus gave the tempter an opportunity to weaken their wills with thoughtless drowsiness and make them far more inclined to fight or flee than to bear all with patience. And this was the reason that they all abandoned Him and fled. And thus that saying of Christ was fulfilled, "This night you will all be scandalized because of me,"[5] and also that prediction of the prophet[6]

---

4. Matt. 26 : 35.   5. Matt. 26 : 31.
6. More almost surely intended the blank space he left after "prophet" to be filled with Christ's quotation (Matt. 26 : 31) of Zech. 13 : 7: "I will strike the shepherd and the sheep of the flock will be scattered."

"But a certain young man was following Him, having only a linen cloth wrapped about his naked body, and throwing it off, he fled from them naked."[7]

Just who this young man was has never been determined with certainty. Some think he was the James who was called the brother of the Lord and was distinguished by the epithet "the just." Others assert that he was the evangelist John, who always had a special place in our Lord's heart and who must have been still quite young, since he lived for so many years after Christ's death. For, according to Jerome, he died in the sixty-eighth year after our Lord's passion.[8] But there are also some ancient writers who say that this young man was not one of the apostles at all but one of the servants in the household where Christ had celebrated the Passover that night. And certainly I myself find this opinion easier to accept. Apart from the fact that I find it unlikely for an apostle to be wearing nothing but a linen cloth, and even that so loosely fastened that it could be quickly thrown off, I am inclined to this opinion first of all by the sequence of historical events and then by the very words of the account.

Now, among those who think the young man was one of the apostles, the preponderance of opinion is for John. But this seems to me unlikely because of John's own words: "But Simon Peter was following Jesus and so was another disciple. Now that disciple was known to the high priest, and he entered the courtyard of the high priest together with Jesus. But Peter was standing outside at the gate. So the other disciple, who was known to the high priest, went out and spoke to the portress, and brought Peter in."[9] Writers who assert that it was the blessed evangelist who followed Christ and fled when He was taken prisoner are faced with a slight hitch in their argument—namely, the fact that he threw off the linen cloth and fled naked. For this seems to conflict with what follows—namely, that John entered the court-

7. Mark 14 : 51.
8. *Adversus Jovinianum* 1, 26 (PL 23, 247) and *Liber de viris illustribus* 9 (PL 23, 625–26).
9. John 18 : 15–16.

yard of the high priest, that he brought Peter in (for everyone agrees that the disciple who did this was the evangelist), that he followed Christ all the way to the place of the crucifixion, and that he stood near the cross with Christ's most beloved mother (two pure virgins standing together), and that when Christ commended her to him he accepted her as his own mother from that day on.[10]

Now there can be no doubt that at all these times and in all these places John was wearing clothes. For he was a disciple of Christ, not of the cynic sect;[11] and therefore, though he had enough good sense not to avoid nakedness when circumstances required it or necessity demanded it, nevertheless I hardly think his virgin modesty would have allowed him to go out in public naked, for everyone to see, with no good reason at all. This difficulty they try to explain away by saying that he went somewhere else in the meantime and put on other clothes—a point I will not dispute, but it hardly seems likely to me, especially when I see in this passage that he continuously followed after Christ with Peter and that he entered the residence of Annas, the father-in-law of the high priest, together with Jesus.

Furthermore, another consideration that strongly persuades me to side with those who think that the young man was not one of the apostles but one of the servants of the inn is the sort of connection Mark makes between the apostles who ran away and the young man who stayed behind. "Then the disciples abandoned Him and all of them ran away. But a certain young man was following Him." Notice, he says not that some ran away but "all of them" and that the person who (unlike them) stayed behind and followed Christ was not any one of the apostles (for all of them had already run away) but rather a "certain" young man, that is, it would seem, an unknown young man, whose name Mark either did not know or thought it not worthwhile to report.

10. John 19 : 25–27.
11. Shamelessness, including public indecency, was recommended and practised by some cynic philosophers.

Here, then, is how I would imagine it. This young man, who
had previously been excited by Christ's fame and who now saw
Him in person as he was bringing in food to Christ and His disciples reclining at table, was touched by a secret breath of the
Spirit and felt the moving force of charity. Then, impelled to
pursue a life of true devotion, he followed Christ when He left
after dinner and continued to follow Him, at a little distance,
perhaps, from the apostles but still with them. And he sat down
and got up again together with them until finally, when the mob
came, he lost himself in the crowd. Furthermore, when all the
apostles had escaped in terror from the hands of the sluggish
soldiers, this young man dared to remain behind, with all the
more confidence because he knew that no one as yet was aware
of the love he felt for Christ. But how hard it is to disguise the
love we feel for someone! Although this young man had mingled with that crowd of people who hated Christ, still he betrayed himself by his gait and his bearing, making it clear to everyone that he pursued Christ (now deserted by the others) not
as a persecutor but as a devoted follower. And so, when they finally noticed that the rest of Christ's band had fled and saw that
this one had stayed behind and still dared to follow Christ, they
quickly seized him.

This act of theirs convinces me that they also intended to seize
all the apostles but were so taken by surprise that they lost their
chance, and thus that prophetic command of Christ, "Let these
men go their way," was indeed fulfilled. Christ did not intend
this command to be limited to the apostles, whom He had chosen (though it was meant to apply principally to them), but He
also wished to extend the riches of His kindness even more
abundantly by making the command apply also to this young
man, who, without being summoned, had followed Him of his
own accord and had slipped into the holy band of His apostles.
And in this way Christ displayed His own secret power more
clearly and at the same time exposed the weakness of the crowd
more fully, because not only did they lose through negligence
the eleven apostles, whose escape distressed them very much,

but also they could not even detain this one young man whom they had already seized and who was (one may conjecture) completely walled in by their ranks: for "they seized him and he threw off the linen cloth and fled from them naked." Moreover, I have not the slightest doubt that this young man, who followed Christ that night and could not be torn away from Him until the last possible moment, after all the apostles had fled—and even then it took manhandling and rough force—later took the first opportunity to return to Christ's flock and that even now he lives with Christ in everlasting glory in heaven, where I hope and pray that we will one day live with him. Then he himself will tell us who he was, and we will get a most pleasant and full account of many other details of what happened that night which are not contained in scripture.

In the meantime, in order to make our heavenward journey safer and easier, it will be of no small use for us to gather wholesome spiritual counsels from the flight of the disciples before they were captured and from the escape of this young man after he was captured: these counsels will be the provisions, as it were, for us to carry with us on the journey. The ancient fathers of the church warn us not to be so sure of our strength as to place ourselves willingly and needlessly in danger of falling into sin. But if someone should happen to find himself in a situation where he recognizes an imminent danger that he will be driven by force to offend God, he ought to do what the apostles did—avoid capture by fleeing. I do not say this to suggest that the apostles' flight was praiseworthy, on the grounds that Christ, in His mercy (though He is indeed merciful) had permitted them to do so because of their weakness. Far from praising it, He had foretold it that very night as occasion of sin for them. But if we feel that our character is not strong enough, let us all imitate this flight of theirs insofar as we can, without sinning, flee the danger of falling into sin. For otherwise, if a person runs away when God commands him to stand and face the danger confidently, either for his own salvation or for that of those whom he sees have been entrusted to his care, then he is acting foolishly indeed, unless he does it out of concern for this present life—no, even then he acts foolishly. For what could be more stupid than to choose a brief time of misery over an eternity of happiness?

But if he does it because of the future life, with the idea that if he does not run away he may be forced to offend God, he compounds not only his folly but also his crime. For to desert one's post is itself a very serious crime, and if one adds to it the enormous gravity of despair, it is quite as serious as going over to the enemy's side. What worse offense could be imagined than to despair of God's help and by running away to hand over to the enemy the battle-station which God had assigned you to guard? Furthermore, what greater madness could be conceived than to seek to avoid the possible sin that may happen if you stay, by committing the certain sin of running away? But when flight entails no offense against God, certainly the safer plan is to make haste to escape rather than to delay so long as to be captured and thus fall into the danger of committing a terrible sin. For it is easy and (where allowable) safe to run away in time, but it is difficult and dangerous to fight.

On the other hand, the example of this young man shows us what sort of person can afford to hold his ground longer with less danger and can easily escape from the hands of his captors if he should happen to be taken. For, although this young man stayed behind after all the others and followed Christ so long that they laid hands on him and held him, nevertheless, because he was not dressed in various garments but wore only a simple linen cloth—and even that not sewn together or buttoned on, but thrown carelessly over his naked body in such a way that he could easily shake it off—this young man suddenly threw off the cloth, leaving it there in the hands of his captors, and fled from them naked—taking the kernel, as it were, and leaving them holding the shell.[12] What is the figurative meaning of this? What else but this: just as a potbellied man, slowed down by his fat

12. Plautus, *Captivi*, 655.

paunch,[13] or a man who goes around wearing a heavy load of clothes, is hardly in a condition to run fast, so too the man who is hemmed in by a belt full of money-bags is hardly able to escape when troubles suddenly descend on him and put him in a bind. Neither will a man run very fast or very far if his clothing, however light it may be, is so tightly laced and knotted that he cannot breathe freely. For a man who is wearing a lot of clothing but can get rid of it quickly will find it easier to escape than a man who is wearing only a little but has it tied around his neck so tightly that he has to carry it with him wherever he runs. One sees rich men—less often, it is true, than I would like—but still, thank God, one sometimes sees exceedingly rich men who would rather lose everything they have than keep anything at all by offending God through sin. These men have many clothes, but they are not tightly confined by them, so that when they need to run away from danger, they escape easily by throwing off their clothes. On the other hand we see people—and far more of them than I would wish—who happen to have only light garments and quite skimpy outfits and yet have so welded their affections to those poor riches[1] of theirs that you could sooner strip skin from flesh than separate them from their goods. Such a person had better get going while there is still time. For once someone gets hold of his clothes, he will sooner die than leave his linen cloth behind. In summary, then, we learn from the example of this young man that we should always be prepared for troubles that arise suddenly, dangers that strike without warning and might make it necessary for us to run away; to be prepared, we ought not to be so loaded with various garments, or so buttoned up in even one, that in an emergency we are unable to throw away our linen cloth and escape naked.

Now anyone who is willing to devote a little more attention to this deed of the young man can see that it offers us another teaching, even more forceful than the first. For the body is, as it

13. Cf. Juvenal, 3, 107.
1. Cf. Horace, *Odes*, 3, 16, 28 and Ovid, *Metamorphoses*, 3, 466.

were, the garment of the soul. The soul puts on the body when it comes into the world and takes off the body when it leaves the world at death. Hence, just as the clothes are worth much less than the body, so too the body is far less precious than the soul. Thus, to give away the soul to buy the body is the same kind of raving lunacy as to prefer the loss of the body to the loss of a cloak. Concerning the body, Christ did indeed say, "Is not the body worth more than its clothing?"[2] But concerning the soul He was far more emphatic: "What does it profit you if you gain the whole world but suffer the loss of your soul? or what will a man give in exchange for his soul?[3] But I say to you, my friends, do not be afraid of those who kill the body, and after that have nothing more that they can do. But I will show you the one to be afraid of. Fear Him who, after He has killed, has the power to cast into hell. Yes, I say to you, fear Him."[4] Thus, the example of this young man warns us about what sort of clothing for our souls our bodies ought to be when we are faced with such trials: they should not be obese from debauchery and flabby from dissolute living but thin like the linen cloth, with the fat worked off by fasting; and then we should not be so strongly attached to them that we cannot willingly cast them off when God's cause demands it. This is the lesson which that young man teaches us; when he was in the clutches of wicked men, he preferred to leave his linen cloth behind and flee from them naked rather than be forced to do or say anything which might impugn the honor of Christ.

In a similar way, another young man who lived long before this one, the holy and innocent patriarch Joseph, left to posterity a notable example, teaching that one should flee from the danger of unchaste defilement no less than if it were an attempted murder. Because he had a handsome face and was a fine figure of a man, the wife of Potiphar, in whose house he was the chief servent, cast her eyes on him and fell passionately in love with him. She was so carried away by the raving madness of her desire that she not only offered herself freely and shame-

2. Matt. 6 : 25.   3. Matt. 16 : 26.   4. Luke 12 : 4–5.

lessly to the young man by her glances and words, enticing him to overcome his aversion, but also, when he refused, she went so far as to clutch his garment in her hands and presented the shameful spectacle of a woman wooing a man by force. But Joseph, who would rather have died than commit such a horrible sin and who also knew how dangerous it is to engage the embattled forces of Venus at close quarters and that against them the surest victory is flight, Joseph, I say, left his cloak in the hands of the adulteress and escaped by dashing out of doors.[5]

But, as I was saying, to avoid falling into grave sin we must throw off not merely a cloak or gown or shirt or any other such garment of the body but even the garment of the soul, the body itself. For if we strive to save the body by sin, we destroy it and we also lose the soul. But if we patiently endure the loss of the body for the love of God, then, just as the snake sloughs off its old skin (called, I think, its "senecta") by rubbing it against thorns and thistles, and, leaving it behind in the thick hedges, comes forth young and shining, so too those of us who follow Christ's advice and become wise as serpents[6] will leave behind on earth our old bodies, rubbed off like a snake's old skin among the thorns of tribulation suffered for the love of God, and will quickly be carried up to heaven, shining and young and never more to feel the effects of old age.

The capture of Christ

"Then they came up and laid hands on Jesus. The cohort and the tribune and the servants of the Jews seized Jesus and holding Him fast they bound Him and took Him first to Annas. For he was the father-in-law of Caiaphas. But it was Caiaphas who had advised the Jews that it is expedient that one man die for the people.[7] And all the priests, scribes, pharisees, and elders gathered together."[8]

Exactly when they first laid hands on Jesus is a point on which

5. Gen. 39 : 6–12.   6. Matt. 10 : 16.   7. John 18 : 12–14.
8. Matt. 26 : 57, Mark 14 : 53.

the experts disagree. Among the interpreters of the gospel accounts, which agree on the fact but vary in their way of presenting it (for one anticipates, another goes back to pick up a detail omitted earlier), some commentators follow one opinion, others another, though none of them impugn the historical truth of the accounts or deny that an opinion differing from their own may be the correct one. For Matthew and Mark relate the events in such an order as to allow the conjecture that they laid hands on Jesus immediately after Judas' kiss. And this is the opinion adopted not only by many celebrated doctors of the church but also approved by that remarkable man John Gerson, who follows it in presenting the sequence of events in his work entitled *Monotessaron* (the work which I have generally followed in enumerating the events of the passion in this discussion).

But in this one place I have departed from him and followed those interpreters (and they, too, are celebrated authorities) who are persuaded by very probable inferences from the accounts of Luke and John to adopt the opinion that only after Judas had given his kiss and returned to the cohort and the Jews, after Christ had thrown down the cohort merely by speaking to them, after the ear of the high priest's servant had been cut off and restored, after the other apostles had been forbidden to fight and Peter (who had already begun to fight) had been rebuked, after Christ had once more addressed the Jewish magistrates who were present at that time and had announced that they now had permission to do what they had not been able to do before—to take Him captive—after all the apostles had escaped by running away, after the young man who had been seized but could not be held had saved himself by his active and eager acceptance of nakedness, only then, after all these events, did they lay hands on Jesus.[9]

9. In the Valencia manuscript, this phrase is followed by seven entirely blank leaves, after which appears an independent composition by More, a catena of scriptural passages interspersed with some reflections on martyrdom (see *CW 14,* 627–91 and notes).

INSTRUCTIONS AND PRAYERS

A godly instruction,[10] written by Sir Thomas More Knight, within a while after he was prisoner in the Tower of London in the year of our Lord 1534.

Bear no malice nor evil will to no man living. For either the man is good or nought.[11] If he be good, and I hate him, then am I nought.

If he be nought, either he shall amend and die good, and go to God, or abide[12] nought, and die nought, and go the devil. And then let me remember that if he shall be saved, he shall not fail (if I be saved too, as I trust to be) to love me very heartily, and I shall then in likewise love him.

And why should I now then hate one for this while[13] which shall hereafter love me for evermore, and why should I be now, then, enemy to him with whom I shall in time coming be coupled in eternal friendship? And on the other side, if he shall continue nought and be damned, then is there so outrageous eternal sorrow towards[14] him that I may well think myself a deadly cruel wretch if I would not now rather pity his pain than malign his person. If one would say that we may well with good conscience wish an evil man harm, lest he should do harm to such other folk as are innocent and good, I will not now dispute upon that point, for that root hath mo[1] branches to be well weighed and considered than I can now conveniently write (having none other pen than a coal). But verily thus will I say, that I will give counsel to every good friend of mine, but if[2] he be put in such a room[3] as to punish an evil man lieth in his charge by reason of his office, else leave the desire of punishing unto God and unto such other folk as are so grounded in charity, and so fast cleave

---

10. lesson.   11. wicked.   12. remain.   13. period of time.
14. facing.   1. more.   2. *but if:* unless.   3. position.

to God, that no secret, shrewd,[4] cruel affection,[5] under the cloak of a just and a virtuous zeal, can creep in and undermine them. But let us that are no better than men of a mean[6] sort ever pray for such merciful amendment in other folk as our own conscience showeth us that we have need in ourself.

4. malicious.   5. inclination.   6. inferior.

A godly meditation, written by Sir Thomas More Knight while he was prisoner in the Tower of London in the year of our Lord 1534.[7]

Give me Thy grace, good Lord,
To set the world at nought;[8]

To set my mind fast[9] upon Thee,
And not to hang upon the blast[10]
   of men's mouths;

To be content to be solitary;
Not to long for worldly company;

Little and little utterly to cast off the world,
And rid my mind of all the business[11] thereof;

Not to long to hear of any worldly things,
But that the hearing of worldly fantasies[12] may
   be to me displeasant;[13]

Gladly to be thinking of God,
Pituously to call for His help;

To lean unto the comfort of God,
Busily to labor to love Him;

To know mine own vility[1] and wretchedness,
To humble and meeken myself under the
   mighty hand of God;

---

7. This heading is from the 1557 *English Works,* but the text of the prayer given here is taken directly from More's handwritten version in the margins of a book of hours he had with him in the Tower (*Thomas More's Prayer Book,* ed. Louis Martz and Richard Sylvester, London and New Haven, 1969, pp. xxxvii–xxxviii, 3–21).
8. *set . . . nought:* have no esteem for the world.   9. firmly.
10. utterance.   11. activity.   12. delusions.
13. disagreeable.   1. baseness.

To bewail my sins passed;
For the purging of them patiently to
   suffer adversity;

Gladly to bear my purgatory here;
To be joyful of tribulations;

To walk the narrow way that leadeth to life,
To bear the cross with Christ;

To have the last thing[2] in remembrance,
To have ever afore[3] mine eye my death that is
   ever at hand;

To make death no stranger to me,
To foresee and consider the everlasing fire of hell;

To pray for pardon before the judge come,
To have continually in mind the passion that Christ
   suffered for me;

For His benefits uncessantly[4] to give Him thanks,
To buy[5] the time again that I before have lost;

To abstain from vain confabulations,[6]
To eschew light[7] foolish mirth and gladness;

Recreations[8] not necessary—to cut off;
Of worldly substance, friends, liberty, life and all,
   to set the loss at right nought[9] for the
      winning[1] of Christ:

To think my most[2] enemies my best friends;
For the brethren of Joseph could never have done
   him so much good with their love and favor as
      they did him with their malice and
         hatred.

2. *last thing:* last judgment.   3. before.   4. continually.
5. redeem.   6. conversations.   7. frivolous.
8. pleasurable employments.   9. *right nought:* absolutely nothing.
1. gaining.   2. greatest.

These minds[3] are more to be desired of every man
than all the treasure of all the princes and kings,
Christian and heathen, were it gathered and
laid together all upon one heap.

3. attitudes.

A devout prayer, made by Sir Thomas More Knight after he was condemned to die, and before he was put to death, who was condemned the Thursday, the first day of July, in the year of our Lord God 1535, and in the twenty-seventh year of the reign of King Henry the Eight, and was beheaded at the Tower Hill at London the Tuesday following.[4]

Pater noster, Ave maria, Credo.[5]

O holy Trinity, the Father, the Son, and the Holy Ghost—three egal[6] and coeternal persons, and one almighty God—have mercy on me, vile, abject, abominable, sinful wretch, meekly knowledging[7] before Thine high majesty my long-continued sinful life, even from my very childhead[8] hitherto.

In my childhead in this point and that point, etc.[9]

After my childhead in this point and that point, etc., and so forth by every age.

Now, good gracious Lord, as Thou givest me Thy grace to knowledge them, so give me Thy grace, not in only word but in heart also, with very sorrowful contrition to repent them and utterly to forsake them. And forgive me those sins also in which by mine own default,[10] through evil affections[11] and evil custom, my reason is with sensuality so blinded that I cannot discern them for sin. And illumine, good Lord, mine heart, and give me

---

4. The prayer is both More's personal expression and a devotion intended for use by others.
5. This rubric indicates one should say the Our Father, Hail Mary, and the Creed.
6. equal.   7. confessing.   8. childhood.
9. Here and in the next sentence, one should think of one's own sins.
10. misdeed.   11. feelings.

Thy grace to know them and to knowledge them, and forgive me my sins negligently forgotten, and bring them to my mind with grace to be purely confessed of them.

Glorious God, give me from henceforth the grace, with little respect unto the world, so to set and fix firmly mine heart upon Thee that I may say with Thy blessed apostle Saint Paul, *Mundus mihi crucifixus est, et ego mundo. Mihi vivere Christus est et mori lucrum. Cupio dissolvi et esse cum Christo.*[12]

Give me the grace to amend my life and to have an eye to mine end without grudge of death,[1] which to them that die in Thee (good Lord) is the gate of a wealthy[2] life.

Almighty God, *Doce me facere voluntatem tuam. Fac me currere in odore unguentorum tuorum. Apprehende manum meam dexteram, et deduc me in via recta propter inimicos meos. Trahe me post te. In chamo et freno maxillas meas constringe, cum non approximo ad te.*[3]

O glorious God, all sinful fear, all sinful sorrow and pensiveness, all sinful hope, all sinful mirth and gladness take from me. And on the tother[4] side, concerning such fear, such sorrow, such heaviness,[5] such comfort, consolation, and gladness as shall be profitable for my soul, *Fac mecum secundum magnam bonitatem tuam Domine.*[6]

Good Lord, give me the grace in all my fear and agony to have recourse to that great fear and wonderful agony that Thou

---

12. Gal. 6 : 14 and Phil. 1 : 21–23. "The world is crucified to me, and I to the world. For to me to live is Christ and to die is gain. I wish to be dissolved and be with Christ."

1. *grudge of death:* reluctance to die.   2. possessing well-being.

3. Ps. 142 : 10 (*AV*, 143 : 10), Cant. 1 : 3, Ps. 72 : 24 (*AV*, 73 : 23), Ps. 26 : 11 (*AV*, 27 : 11), Ps. 31 : 9 (*AV*, 32 : 9). "Teach me to do your will. Make me run in the scent of your unguents. Take my right hand, and lead me in the right path because of my enemies. Draw me after you. With a muzzle and bridle restrain my jaws when I do not draw near to you."

4. other.   5. grief.

6. Cf. Ps. 118 : 124 (*AV*, 119 : 124). "Deal with me according to your great goodness, O Lord."

my sweet Savior hadst at the Mount of Olivet before Thy most bitter passion, and in the meditation thereof to conceive ghostly [7] comfort and consolation profitable for my soul.

Almighty God, take from me all vainglorious minds,[8] all appetites of mine own praise, all envy, covetise,[1] gluttony, sloth and lechery, all wrathful affections, all appetite of revenging, all desire or delight of other folks' harm, all pleasure in provoking any person to wrath and anger, all delight of exprobration[2] or insultation[3] against any person in their affliction and calamity.

And give me, good Lord, an humble, lowly, quiet, peaceable, patient, charitable, kind, tender, and pitiful mind, with all my works, and all my words, and all my thoughts to have a taste of Thy holy blessed Spirit.

Give me, good Lord, a full faith, a firm hope, and a fervent charity, a love to Thee, good Lord, incomparable[4] above the love to myself, and that I love nothing to Thy displeasure, but everything in an order to[5] Thee.

Give me, good Lord, a longing to be with Thee, not for the avoiding of the calamities of this wretched world, nor so much for the avoiding of the pains of purgatory, nor of the pains of hell neither, nor so much for the attaining of the joys of heaven, in respect of mine own commodity,[6] as even for a very[7] love to Thee.

And bear me, good Lord, Thy love and favor, which thing my love to Thee-ward[8] (were it never so great) could not but of Thy great goodness deserve.

And pardon me, good Lord, that I am so bold to ask so high petitions, being so vile a sinful wretch and so unworthy to attain the lowest. But yet, good Lord, such they be as I am bounden[9] to wish, and should be nearer the effectual desire of them if my manifold sins were not the let.[1] From which, O glorious Trinity,

7. spiritual. 8. attitudes.   1. covetousness.
2. reproaching.   3. insult.   4. incomparably.
5. *in . . . to:* for the sake of.   6. benefit.   7. genuine.
8. *to Thee-ward:* toward Thee.   9. obliged.   1. hindrance.

vouchsafe of Thy goodness to wash me with that blessed blood that issued out of Thy tender body (O sweet Savior Christ) in the divers torments of Thy most bitter passion.

Take from me, good Lord, this lukewarm fashion, or rather key-cold[2] manner, of meditation, and this dullness in praying unto Thee. And give me warmth, delight, and quickness[3] in thinking upon Thee, and give me Thy grace to long for Thine holy sacraments, and specially to rejoice in the presence of Thy very blessed body, sweet Savior Christ, in the holy sacrament of the altar, and duly to thank Thee for Thy gracious visitation therewith, and at that high memorial, with tender compassion to remember and consider Thy most bitter passion.

Make us all, good Lord, virtually[4] participant of that holy sacrament this day, and every day make us all lively[5] members, sweet Savior Christ, of Thine holy mystical body, Thy Catholic Church.

Dignare Domine die isto sine peccato nos custodire.[6]
Miserere nostri Domine, miserere nostri.[7]
*Fiat misericordia tua Domine super nos, quemadmodum speravimus
    in te.*[8]
In te Domine speravi, non confundar in aeternum.[9]
*Ora pro nobis, sancta Dei genetrix, ut digni efficiamur
    promissionibus Christi.*[1]

2. apathetic.   3. vitality.   4. with spiritual effect.
5. living.
6. "Deign, O Lord, on that day to preserve us without sin."
7. Ps. 122 : 3 (*AV*, 123 : 3). "Have mercy upon us, O Lord, have mercy upon us."
8. Ps. 32 : 22 (*AV*, 33 : 22). "Let your mercy, O Lord, be upon us, just as we have hoped in you."
9. Ps. 30 : 2 (*AV*, 31 : 1). "In you, O Lord, have I hoped, let me not be confounded forever."
1. "Pray for us, holy mother of God, that we may be made worthy of the promises of Christ" (from the prayer *Salve regina*).

Pro amicis.[2]

Almighty God, have mercy on N.[3] and N., etc., with special meditation and consideration of every friend, as godly affection and occasion requireth.

Pro inimicis.[4]

Almighty God, have mercy on N. and N., etc., and on all that bear me evil will, and would me harm; and their faults and mine together, by such easy tender merciful means as Thine infinite wisdom best can devise, vouchsafe to amend and redress, and make us saved souls in heaven together, where we may ever live and love together with Thee and Thy blessed saints. O glorious Trinity, for the bitter passion of our sweet Savior Christ, Amen.

Lord, give me patience in tribulation, and grace in everything to conform my will to Thine, that I may truly say: *Fiat voluntas tua, sicut in caelo, et in terra.*[5]

The things, good Lord, that I pray for, give me the grace to labor for. Amen.

2. "For friends."
3. The liturgical abbreviation for the Latin *nomen* ("name"), providing for one to add names appropriate to one's own prayer.
4. "For enemies."
5. Matt. 6 : 10. "Thy will be done on earth, as it is in heaven."

GLOSSARY

GLOSSARY

This glossary contains only archaic words that occur frequently in the texts. Other archaic words and difficult constructions are glossed as they appear.

afeard *adj.* afraid
affection *n.* feeling, inclination
afore *prep.* before
after *adv.* afterward
after *prep.* according to, in accordance with
again *adv.* against, in reply
allow *v.* approve, sanction
alway *adv.* always
ancients *n. pl.* elders
and *conj.* if
arbitror *n.* arbitrator
Austin *n.* Augustine
await *n.* watch, ambush

bare *v. pt.* held, bore
be *pp.* been
board *n.* table
bode *v. pt.* commanded, instructed
bounden *pp.* obliged; bound
brake *v. pt.* broke
business *n.* duty; commotion; concern
but *conj. but if* unless; *but that* that
buy *v.* redeem; *pt.* **bought**
by and by *adv.* immediately

clerk *n.* scholar
comen *pp.* come

commodity *n.* benefit, advantage
competent *adj.* suitable, proper
conster *v.* construe
convenient *adj.* suitable
conveniently *adv.* suitably
Corinthies *n. pl.* Corinthians
corps *n.* body
covetise *n.* covetousness
cunning *adj.* learned

danger *n.* power
declare *v.* explain
delivered *pp.* handed over (to destruction)
demand *v.* ask
desert *n.* wilderness
diligence *n.* utmost
doctors *n. pl.* early church fathers

eath *adj.* easy
egal *adj.* equal
ensample *n.* example
estate *n.* condition, status
expoun *v.* expound
eyen *n. pl.* eyes

fain *adv.* gladly
falsehead *n.* falsehood

fear *v. refl. I fear me* I am afraid
feastful *adj.* festal
fette *v. pt.* fetched
figure *n.* type
for *prep.* because of
fro *prep.* from
frowardness *n.* perversity

generation *n.* fruit
graciously *adv.* by means of divine grace
groat *n.* coin worth fourpence

hance *n.* lintel
hap *v.* chance, happen, occur
heaviness *n.* grief
heng *v. pt.* hung
his *pron.* its
housel *n.* eucharist
houseled *pp.* given communion

impassible *adj.* incapable of suffering
innocency *n.* innocence
insinuate *v.* impart to the mind subtly

lay *v.* present, allege
leese *v.* lose
let *v.* forbear, hesitate; prevent; *pt.* **letted**
letter *n.* text
lively *adj.* living

manhead *n.* human nature
manner *n.* kind(s) of
maundy *n.* last supper
mean *n.* method, means
meat *n.* food
mids *n.* midst
mo *comp. adj.* more
more *comp. adj.* greater; *superl.*

most greatest
motion *n.* prompting

new *adv.* anew
nothing *adv.* in no way
nought *adj.* wicked

of *prep.* by; out of
only *adj.* mere, single, sole
only *adv.* merely, solely, alone
other *pron. pl.* others
ought *v. pt.* owed
over *prep.* besides

part *n. have no part with* have nothing to do with
pascha *n.* Passover
paschal *n.* Passover
pass *v.* surpass
paynims *n. pl.* pagans
perfit *adj.* perfect

quick *adj.* living

refrain *v.* restrain
rehearse *v.* mention, recount
remember *v.* mention
remnant *n.* others

sabbot *n.* sabbath
sample *n.* example
scant *adv.* scarcely
sentence *n.* meaning
set *v. set by* esteem
sith *conj.* since
sore *adv.* grievously, severely
stablish *v.* establish
suggestions *n. pl.* temptations

taken *pp.* given
temper *v.* mix, mingle
testament *n.* covenant
think *v. me think(eth)* it seems to me

thorough *prep.* through
tone *pron.* one
tother *pron.* other
train *n.* snare, deceit

understand(en) *pp.* understood,
   interpreted
undiscreet *adj.* imprudent
unied *pp.* united
unkindly *adv.* ungratefully
unsensible *adj.* not endowed with
   sensation; imperceptible to the
   senses

unworthily *adv.* without proper
   regard
upon *prep.* on the basis of

use *v.* practice, follow; *v. refl.* behave, conduct oneself

valure *n.* value
very *adj.* actual, true, genuine
virtually *adv.* with spiritual effect
virtue *n.* efficacy

wealth *n.* well-being
ween *v.* suppose, think
went *v. pt. went about* undertook
which *pron.* who
winning *vbl. n.* gain
wise *n.* way, manner
wit *v.* know; *pt.* **wist**
worthily *adv.* with a fitting disposition
wot *v.* know

INDEX